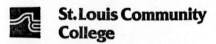

Television's Impact on Children and Adolescents

Television's Impact on Children and Adolescents

A Special Interest Resource Guide in Education

Compiled by Sara Lake,
San Mateo Educational Resources Center

ORYX PRESS
1981

The rare Arabian Oryx is believed to have inspired the myth of the unicorn. This desert antelope became virtually extinct in the early 1960s. At that time several groups of international conservationists arranged to have 9 animals sent to the Phoenix Zoo to be the nucleus of a captive breeding herd. Today the Oryx population is nearing 300 and herds have been returned to reserves in Israel, Jordan, and Oman.

Copyright © 1981 by The Oryx Press
2214 N. Central at Encanto
Phoenix, AZ 85004

Published simultaneously in Canada

Printed and Bound in the United States of America

The abstracts indicated throughout this Resource Guide by an asterisk after the title are published with permission of University Microfilms International, publishers of *Dissertation Abstracts International* (copyright © 1981 by University Microfilms International), and may not be reproduced without their prior permission.

The abstracts indicated throughout this Resource Guide by a dagger after the title are reprinted from the database of the National Technical Information Service.

Library of Congress Cataloging in Publication Data

Lake, Sara.
  Television's impact on children and adolescents.

  (A Special interest resource guide in education)
  Includes index.
    1. Television and children—Abstracts. 2. Television and youth—Abstracts. 3. Television in education—United States—Abstracts. 4. Television and children—Bibliography. 5. Television and youth—Bibliography.
6. Television in education—United States—Bibliography.
I. Title. II. Series: Special interest resource guide in education.
HQ784.T4L34   016.79145'01'3   81-1411
ISBN 0-912700-87-4   AACR2

Contents

Introduction

Television has become a tremendous force in American life over the past 30 years, raising special concern about its effect on young people. Does viewing television provide them with new vistas which broaden their experience or does it turn them into zombies incapable of reading and thinking, demanding only instant gratification? Both views are expressed in recent literature on the topic. It is the purpose of this Resource Guide to present a selection of current (1976 through September 1980) research and opinion which may help you form your own conclusions and, if desired, guidelines for promoting change.

The Guide is addressed to parents, educators, and all others concerned with the development of children and adolescents. It deals mainly with commercial television's impact on American youth at the preschool, elementary, and secondary levels but, when appropriate, also notes foreign studies, analyses of public and instructional television programing, and discussions of television's effects on society in general. To help you examine specific areas of interest, a subject index is provided.

The first chapter, "Television Viewing Habits of Children and Adolescents" cites studies of viewing habits: how much TV young people watch; why they watch it; and the types of programs they prefer. "How Children Perceive Television" presents research on how children watch television: how well they are able to comprehend what they see on the screen; how they attend; how much reality they credit to television; and how they are affected by the formal features of the medium, such as pacing, auditory cues, and program production techniques.

The third chapter, "The Impact of Television on Children and Adolescents," along with its six subsections, deals with television as a force shaping children's attitudes, behavior, and thought. While major attention is directed toward televised violence and advertising, other studies are cited which examine the effect of television relative to other socializing agents such as parents and peers on the learning of sex roles, interpersonal skills, consumer behavior, and social and political competencies. Television has also been assigned blame for the decline in school achievement and test scores. Both the amount of time spent viewing, which can curtail reading and other leisure activities, and the impact of the medium itself on the thought processes, creativity, and attention span of its viewers are questioned in the subsection on reading and school achievement.

"Television as a Teaching Tool," the fourth chapter, examines the potential of television as a positive force in teaching social and academic skills. Citations are presented both on the use of commercial TV in the classroom, such as television reading programs designed to motivate the reading of books and scripts related to broadcast programs, and the educational effectiveness of such public television shows as "Sesame Street" and made-for-the-classroom instructional television programs.

The three subsections of the final chapter, "Improving the Situation," cite methods for controlling television and/or mediating its negative effects. Teaching young people to be more sophisticated viewers of TV programs and commercials is an obvious first step, and learning strategies are presented to help teachers do that. Articles cited in the subsection concerning parental monitoring of TV offer advice on home use of television and techniques for getting parents involved in their children's viewing. Finally, literature is provided on the television industry itself: how programing and advertising are being regulated and what government, citizens' groups, and broadcasters themselves are doing to promote change.

Citations in this Resource Guide are selected from computer searches of eight databases: ERIC; Comprehensive Dissertation Index; National Technical Information Service (NTIS); Exceptional Child Educational Resources; Psychological Abstracts; Sociological Abstracts; Social SciSearch; and Magazine Index; as well as from manual searches of *Education Index* and the extensive library and information files of the San Mateo Educational Resources Center (SMERC).

Within each chapter or subsection, citations are arranged by document format: journal articles, microfiche documents, and books. Citations known to be available for purchase from a standard source are noted. On selected journal articles, an order number prefaced with the letters ''EJ'' plus the notation ''Reprint: UMI'' indicates that a photocopy of the article may be purchased from:

> Article Copy Service-CIJE
> University Microfilms International
> 300 North Zeeb Road
> Ann Arbor, Michigan 48106
> (800) 521-3042

All cited microfiche documents have order codes and source acronyms, indicating their availability from one of three ordering sources, as listed below:

DC*   University Microfilms
      Dissertation Copies
      P.O. Box 1764
      Ann Arbor, Michigan 48106
      (800) 521-3042

EDRS   ERIC Document Reproduction Service
      P.O. Box 190
      Arlington, Virginia 22210
      (703) 841-1212

NTIS†   National Technical Information Service
      5285 Port Royal Road
      Springfield, Virginia 22161
      (703) 557-4650

* An asterisk after the title of an abstract indicates it is published in this resource guide with permission of University Microfilms International, publishers of *Dissertation Abstracts International*.

† A dagger after the title of an abstract indicates it is reprinted in this resource guide from the database of the National Technical Information Service.

Television's Impact on Children and Adolescents

TELEVISION VIEWING HABITS OF CHILDREN AND ADOLESCENTS

Television Viewing Habits of Children and Adolescents

JOURNAL ARTICLES

1. Adolescents and Television. Hendry, Leo B.; Patrick, Helen. *Journal of Youth and Adolescence.* v6, n4, p325–36, Dec 1977.

Over 2,000 15–16 year old adolescents from central Scotland were surveyed to determine characteristics of high- v low- frequency television viewers. Personality characteristics, intelligence, attitudes toward school and sports, and socio-economic status were related to viewing habits. Sex of the viewer was found to be related to choice of programs.

2. Adolescents' Use of the Mass Media. Avery, Robert K. *American Behavioral Scientist.* v23, n1, p53-70, Sep-Oct 1979 (EJ 208 543; Reprint: UMI).

The article summarizes the developmental processes of adolescents (age 12–18) and reviews literature concerning the adolescent's use of television, newspapers, periodicals, records, and radio.

3. Children's Social Behavior in Three Towns with Differing Television Experience. Murray, John P.; Kippax, Susan. *Journal of Communication.* v28, n1, p19–29, Win 1978 (EJ 184 676; Reprint: UMI).

Discusses an Australian study designed to explore children's television viewing patterns and their perceptions of the media, and offers an evaluation of television's impact on the young child's lifestyle and leisure behavior.

4. Constant Television: A Background to Daily Life. Medrich, Elliott A. *Journal of Communication.* v29, n3, p171–76, Sum 1979 (EJ 217 490; Reprint: UMI).

Explores the conditions existing within constant television households—homes in which television is turned on for most of the day, whether or not anyone is watching. The number of constant television households tends to decrease as parents' educational and income levels increase.

5. Continuities and Discontinuities in Media Usage and Taste: A Longitudinal Study. Himmelweit, Hilde; Swift, Betty. *Journal of Social Issues.* v32, n4, p133–56, Fall 1976 (EJ 166 964; Reprint: UMI).

The role of social, personality, and outlook factors in accounting for media (television and reading) usage and taste was examined at several developmental stages across a 20 year time span in a sample of British males. This encompassed the period during which TV was introduced and absorbed into the leisure time of those sampled.

6. The Ecology of Adolescent Activity and Experience. Csikszentmihalyi, Mihaly et al. *Journal of Youth and Adolescence.* v6, n3, p281–94, Sep 1977.

Twenty-five adolescents reported 753 random daily activities and the quality of their experiences during a normal week, in response to an electronic paging device. These adolescents spent most of their time either conversing with peers or watching television. Television viewing was associated with deviant behavior and antisocial personality.

7. Ethnicity and Children's TV Preferences. Eastman, Harvey A.; Liss, Marsha B. *Journalism Quarterly.* v57, n2, p277–80, Sum 1980.

A sample of 658 Black, Hispanic, and Anglo elementary students were queried about their favorite types of television shows and favorite TV characters. Ethnic group patterns emerged for these preferences, and sex differences within these groups.

8. Families without Television. Edgar, Patricia. *Journal of Communication.* v27, n3, p73–78, Sum 1977 (EJ 165 670; Reprint: UMI).

Discusses lifestyles, attitudes, and beliefs of Australian families who have chosen not to own a television set.

9. The Family and Child Television Viewing. Abel, John D. *Journal of Marriage and the Family.* v38, n2, p331–35, May 1976.

Do the patterns of family interpersonal communication influence children's television viewing? In this study, the results indicate that in families where the pattern of communication emphasized parent-child relations, as opposed to child-idea relations, the children's viewing preferences are influenced by what they perceive their parents would prefer them to watch.

10. Interpersonal Factors in Adolescent Television Use. Chaffee, Steven H.; Tims, Albert R. *Journal of Social Issues.* v32, n4, p98–115, Fall 1976 (EJ 166 963; Reprint: UMI).

An examination of some interpersonal factors related to adolescents' television viewing is presented, with particular emphasis on dimensions of communication in the family and with peers.

11. The Mass Media Environment of Children. Wartella, Ellen et al. *American Behavioral Scientist.* v23, n1, p33–52, Sep-Oct 1979 (EJ 208 544; Reprint: UMI).

A review of research findings examines how children up to age 12 use media, especially television, and presents theoretical accounts of the functions media serve during childhood.

12. A Nation of Vidkids. Siegel, Alberta E. *National Elementary Principal.* v56, n3, p54–59, Jan-Feb 1977.

On the average, it is not until the age of eight or nine that children begin to develop a realistic understanding of commercials. By that time, they have been TV watchers for five or six years.

13. The Nonviewers: Who Are They? Jackson-Beeck, Marilyn. *Journal of Communication.* v27, n3, p65–72, Sum 1977 (EJ 165 669; Reprint: UMI).

Examines the television nonviewing audience in an effort to characterize them as a meaningful population subgroup that concludes that as a group they are socially insignificant.

14. Programming Strategies and the Popularity of Television Programs for Children. Wakshlag, Jacob J.; Greenberg, Bradley S. *Human Communication Research.* v6, n1, p58–68, Fall 1979.

Investigates the effects of various programing strategies, commonly employed by the television networks, on program popularity for children. Strategies include counterprograming by type, block programing by type, inheritance effects, starting time, program familiarity, and character familiarity. Confirms the effects of starting time and program familiarity on popularity.

15. Public Television: Whose Alternative? Lindsay, Carl A. et al. *Public Telecommunications Review.* v6, n2, p18–23, Mar-Apr 1978 (EJ 189 180; Reprint: UMI).

Findings of a survey to compare the viewing patterns of commercial and public TV audiences are presented for a sample of 208 households in Pennsylvania. Education and income characteristics are compared, as well as weekly viewing by age and type of household (those who watch PTV and those who do not).

16. Reading Profile of a Small Midwestern School. Heerman, Charles E.; Callison, Patricia R. *Reading Improvement.* v15, n2, p101–04, Sum 1978 (EJ 192 191; Reprint: UMI).

Surveys the reading and television viewing habits of K–12 children and the perceptions of K–8 students' parents about their children's use of time. Finds discrepancies between middle-grade students' reported reading times and parents' faith in their children's reading ability, suggesting the need to educate parents and to make changes in the reading curriculum.

17. The Relative Appeal to Children of Adult versus Children's Television Programming. Webster, James G.; Coscarelli, William C. *Journal of Broadcasting.* v23, n4, p437–51, Fall 1979 (EJ 216 473; Reprint: UMI).

Describes research undertaken to determine third- and fifth-grade children's television viewing preferences in a choice of adult or children's television shows. Two studies were carried out: (1) distribution of a forced choice questionnaire, and (2) showing of an edited videotape introduction to shows listed in the questionnaire.

18. Television: The Uncommon Common Medium. Lyle, Jack; Middleton, John. *National Elementary Principal.* v56, n3, p8–15, Jan-Feb 1977.

Presents information on children's viewing patterns, including seasonal variations, of commercial television. The expansion of instructional television is also considered.

19. Television Use by Children and Adolescents. Rubin, Alan M. *Human Communication Research.* v5, n2, p109–20, Win 1979.

Examines the relationships between child and adolescent television use motivations and various sociodemographic characteristics, television viewing levels, program preference, and television attitudes. Viewing motivations include learning, passing time, companionship, escape, arousal, and relaxation. Correlates motivations to demographic variables; extent of TV use; types of preferred programs; and perceived reality of television. Discusses implications within the conceptual rubric of the uses of gratifications research perspective.

20. Television—Viewing Habits and Parent-observed Behaviors of Third-grade Children. Woodrick, Charles et al. *Psychological Reports.* v40, n3, pt 1, p830, Jun 1977.

Summarizes a survey of the parents or guardians of 63 third-graders on the extent to which they monitor their childrens' television viewing; the categories of programs the children watched; behaviors children exhibited while viewing; parental satisfaction/dissatisfaction with current TV offerings; and changes parents would like to see in television programing.

21. Television Viewing Habits of Mentally Retarded Children. Ahrens, Michael G. *Australian Journal of Mental Retardation.* v4, n7, p1–3, Sep 1977 (EJ 175 782; Reprint: UMI).

The television viewing habits of 250 mentally retarded children (6 to 18 years old) from an institution; from a hostel for the intellectually handicapped; and from home were explored. The results indicate that these children do watch TV for extended periods, especially during the evening meal preparation period. They do not appear either to remember what they have seen for any length of time or to learn much from such activity. The shortcomings of commercially produced programs in relation to the retarded are discussed.

MICROFICHE

22. Canadian Public Television and Pre-Schoolers: Predictors of Users and Non-Users. Cohen, Mitchell E. et al. Aug 1979, 40p. Paper presented at the Annual Meeting of the Association for Education in Journalism (62nd, Houston, TX, August 5–8, 1979). Sponsoring agency: Ontario Educational Communications Authority, Toronto (ED 177 566; Reprint: EDRS).

A study of the preschool television audience in Ontario, Canada, investigated the types of programs children aged two-through six-years-old watch; in what kinds of households preschool children view TV Ontario (TVO), the Canadian public television network; and the kind of strategies that might best capture the potential preschool market. Information was obtained through interviews with parents in 634 households with preschool children, in which half of the children viewed TVO, and in which half of them did not view TVO. Among the results suggested by analyses of the data were that: TVO viewing correlated with a richer family media environment; higher socioeconomic status, and parental awareness of TVO; awareness of and attention to children's television viewing; and positive attitudes toward television. Only the attitudinal variables significantly predicted levels of TVO viewing among TVO households. The data also suggested that strategies designed to increase the TVO viewing of preschool children should focus on increasing TVO availability; on increasing knowledge and awareness about TVO; on appealing to concerns about the educational value of television programming; and on developing positive attitudes about TVO and television in general.

23. The Effect of Exposure to Two Hours per Day of Instructional Television in School upon the Length of Time Fourth Grade Children Devote to Viewing Television at Home.* Schneyer, Lois Jacqueline, Columbia University Teachers College, 1977, 271p (77–14,754; Reprint: DC).

This study introduced an instructional television program into a fourth-grade classroom two hours a day for four weeks. An experimental situation was set up to compare the amount of home viewing engaged in by the experimental subjects with the amount of home viewing engaged in by the control subjects. A

second phase of the study compared fourth and sixth grade viewing in the same town. The third and final phase of the study compared the role television plays in the lives of the fourth- and sixth-grade subjects with the role it has been found to play in the lives of other American children of elementary school age.

One hundred sixteen fourth-grade students and 127 sixth-grade students were involved in the study, undertaken during the late spring of 1975 in a semi-rural community located in the upper Hudson River valley of New York State.

The findings of all the statistical procedures detailed in the study indicated that there is no observable evidence at the .05 level to support the hypothesis that the viewing of two hours a day of ITV in school has a discernable effect upon the length of time fourth-grade students voluntarily watch television at home.

A comparison of the fourth- and sixth-grade subjects' home viewing habits indicated that boys and girls did not share the same preferences in television fare. Boys were attracted to programing involving sports, and girls were drawn to programs featuring adult themes. TV tastes changed with maturity. In general, programs dealing with adult news, religion or that were primarily educational in content, were rarely or never watched. The sixth-grade subjects watched more television than the fourth-grade subjects. The most popular types of programing for both age groups in order of percentage of reported viewers were programs designed for family viewing, adult shows and action/adventure programs. Viewing on both the fourth- and sixth-grade levels was hardly restricted to programs either specifically designed for young viewers or ending at 9 PM, the conclusion of the "family hour" presently observed by network affiliated stations.

Findings indicated that the viewing patterns of the subjects in grades four and six in "Surveytown," New York, are very similar to the viewing patterns of American children of elementary school age in general, during the current decade. The amount of time devoted to television watching and the content viewed correspond with the published findings of other researchers. Youngsters seem to have become more sophisticated about TV at an earlier age. Obvious differences based upon viewers' age and sex still exist. It was of interest to note that professed program popularity did not correlate with actual viewing data gathered.

24. Interest Patterns and Media Preferences of Middle-Grade Children Revisited. Feeley, Joan T. et al. 1979, 126p. Research prepared at the William Paterson College of New Jersey; Tables 3, 5 and Appendix B may not reproduce well due to light type (ED 172 167; Reprint: EDRS).

To update the findings of a 1971 study, a study seeking to identify the interest patterns and media preferences of fourth- and fifth-grade children was undertaken in 1978. The responses of 731 children to an interest inventory were subjected to separate factor analytic and analysis of variance procedures. The former were used to cluster degree-of-interest responses, and the latter were used to compare cluster scores of the subgroups to determine whether they varied according to geographic location or race. Sex as a factor was determined by an examination of the children's rank-order patterns. The results revealed the following: boys' responses clustered into six groupings (presented in rank order)—sports, media, historical/adventure, informational, fun and fantasy, and social empathy/arts; girls' responses clustered into eight groupings—media, animals, fun and fantasy, social empathy, sports, arts, historical, and informational; geographical location accounted for some differences while race accounted for very few differences; and separate, across-clusters analyses of variance of the "read" and "watch" scores revealed that the girls had significantly higher read scores and, to a lesser degree, higher watch scores than did the boys. The urban sample had a significantly higher watch score than did the suburban sample, and race did not account for any significant differences; an overall preference for viewing over reading for all categories was evident.

25. An Investigation of the Television Viewing Habits of Students in Grades Three through Eight in Vermillion, South Dakota. Wood, Robert W.; Eicher, Charles E., South Dakota University, Vermillion, Educational Research and Service Center, Apr 1976, 65p. Sponsoring agency: South Dakota University, Vermillion, School of Education (ED 141 858; Reprint: EDRS).

A sample of 422 students from grades three through eight in Vermillion, South Dakota schools completed a questionnaire about their television-viewing habits, including a day-by-day record of the amount of television viewed over a two-week period. Analysis of results indicated that the school population had an average of two television sets per household; that a majority of the respondents did not have a television set in their own rooms; that students watched television mainly for entertainment; that "Starsky and Hutch" received the highest mean rank of the favorite television programs for grades three through eight; that the majority watched television commercials; and that respondents viewed more television on weekend days than on weekdays. Extensive tables of data are included in the report; the questionnaire is included as an appendix.

26. 1979 Nielsen Report on Television. Nielsen (A.C.) Co., Chicago, IL, 1979, 40p. Parts may not reproduce clearly (ED 179 231; Reprint: EDRS; also available from A.C. Nielsen Company, Nielsen Plaza, Northbrook, IL 60062).

The Nielsen data on commercial television viewing and programing contained in this report are estimates of the audiences and other characteristics of television usage as derived from Nielsen Television Index and Nielsen Station Index measurements. Data and brief discussions are provided on the number of commercial and public stations; number of households owning television sets; television audience characteristics; percent of households using television; average hours of household TV usage per day; hours of TV usage per week by household characteristics; weekly viewing activity for women, men, and children of various age groups; prime time viewing; audience composition of selected prime time program types; TV specials by program type; most popular programs; cable television; and Nielsen television services.

27. Parental Control of Children's Television Viewing Behavior: Support for the Reverse Modeling Principle. Surlin, Stuart H. et al. Apr 1978, 16p. Paper presented at the Annual Meeting of the International Communication Association (Chicago, IL April 25–29, 1978) (ED 157 122; Reprint: EDRS).

A study was conducted to document the existence of the "reverse modeling" principle of television viewing behavior whereby children, rather than parents, determine the television viewing choices for family members. Through telephone interviews, 284 adult respondents were questioned regarding their knowledge of the television advisory warning system, its influence on their own or their children's viewing, their method of program selection, their definition of offensive content, and their estimated daily viewing time. In addition, each was asked how long the television remained turned on each day in their household. The sample was analyzed according to level of education (high or low), and presence or absence of children in the household. Although educational differences did not affect control over children's viewing, it was determined that in low-education households there was a relative lack of concern among parents about television violence; children tended to select programs by changing channels, rather than by consulting printed advertisements; the television set remained on for extended time periods; and parents watched television indiscriminately.

28. Patterns in the Life Cycle: Adolescents' Use of Mass Media. Avery, Robert K. Nov 1978, 16p. Paper presented at the Annual Meeting of the Speech Communication Association (64th, Minneapolis, MN, November 2–5, 1978) (ED 163 549; Reprint: EDRS).

Based on data from eight studies that have contributed the bulk of research on adolescents' use of and gratification from the medium of television, the following conclusions emerge: the time spent watching television peaks at age 12 and declines by 10 percent by age 18; television provides a means of escape, relaxation, entertainment, and relief from loneliness; senior high adolescents are more likely to attend to politically-oriented information than junior high adolescents; there is an increased tolerance by teenagers for the portrayal of sex and violence on television; teenagers make their own program choices or influence their parents' choices; lower income and working class adolescents watch more television than those from higher socioeconomic levels; television viewing is frequently done in conjunction with school work, reading, and interacting with others; and although television viewing declines in adolescence, there is a general increase in the use of other media such as magazines, radio, newspapers, movies, and phonograph records. Shortcomings in these data stem from the fact that researchers are not able to measure audience needs adequately, to identify behaviors in response to those needs, or to determine the success of those behaviors in resolving audience needs.

29. Primary School Panel: Some Descriptive Data. Report No. 2. Hedinsson, Elias; Johnsson-Smaragdi, Ulla, Lund University, Sweden, Jul 1978, 39p. Not available in hard copy due to print quality of original (ED 172 781; Reprint: EDRS—HC not available).

This report describes the first wave of a research project investigating both the mass media behavior of adolescents in size and character of consumption, and their relations with the TV content consumed. This longitudinal study examines 11- to 15-year-olds through the use of specially developed scales and other traditional measures. Included are descriptions of adolescents' TV viewing and program preferences and comparisons with those of their parents. Parental control over adolescents' TV use as described by the adolescents and their parents is also examined. Only data directly related to manifest mass media behavior are presented. Analyses of the scales measuring deeper relations to mass media content consumed are forthcoming in future reports. A list of references and 12 data tables are attached.

30. **The Relationship between Parental TV Viewing Patterns, Parental Influence, and Children's TV Viewing Patterns.** Rojas, Carlos Jorge, University of Oregon, 1978, 163p (7912584; Reprint: DC).

As an initial step in understanding how parents mediate television effects, this study investigated the relationship between (1) parental TV viewing patterns, (2) parental techniques for controlling children's TV viewing, and (3) children's TV viewing patterns. The following TV viewing patterns were studied: total weekly TV viewing; viewing frequency for particular programs; perception of violence in TV programs; and perception of TV's educational value.

The results revealed a moderate-positive relationship between parents and their children in total amount of viewing and viewing frequency of specific TV programs. Low-positive correlations between parents and their children were found for perception of violence and of educational value. These findings suggest that parents have a slight influence on sons' and daughters' TV viewing patterns.

Several findings emerged from the analysis of correlations between the Parental Control Index and children's TV viewing patterns. Slight negative relationships were found between amount of children's TV viewing and level of parental control. Also, it was found that, the more controlling the parents, the more likely it was that their sons: (1) perceived low educational value in TV programs; (2) did not watch sexually explicit programs; and (3) did watch family-oriented programs. No relationships between parental control and daughters' TV viewing patterns were observed. These results indicate that parents are more likely to control sons' TV viewing than they are to control daughters' TV viewing.

Analysis of variance revealed that the different members of the family unit (father, mother, son, daughter) tend to perceive similar levels of violence and educational value in TV. However, children spent significantly more time watching television than did their parents. Also, they perceived their parents as being less controlling than their parents perceived themselves to be.

The findings taken together suggest that parents have a slight to moderate influence on children's TV viewing patterns. Thus, if one were to make a systematic effort to improve children's TV viewing, it might not be advisable to train only the parents, since their training might not be sufficient to make an impact on their children's TV viewing. The training of both parents and children is probably the most appropriate method for making children more aware and critical of the TV message and of their own TV viewing habits.

31. **The Relationship between Television-Viewing Behavior and Social Development in Early Childhood.** Goldsmith, Allys Elaine, Oklahoma State University, 1977, 132p (7801257; Reprint: DC).

The children who participated in this study were 16 boys and 18 girls, ranging in age from three years, no months to four years, eight months. All were from middle-class homes, and all were in attendance at the University of Arkansas Nursery School. A Television-Viewing Inventory, developed as a part of this study provided children's viewing behavior: (1) each program the child watched, (2) the intensity with which the child watched each program, (3) the child's companion while he watched each program, (4) the parent's attitude toward each program watched. The Starkweather Social Conformity Test was used for measuring social conformity by providing the young child with opportunities to make choices in a situation in which he could follow a model or respond freely according to his own preferences. The Starkweather Social Relations Test, an instrument designed to measure a young child's reciprocal social value within his peer group, was used for measuring social relations. The attention span score was the total number of activity shifts of the child during three five-minute time samples while the child was engaged in free play. The data were analyzed for age and sex differences in social conformity, in social relations; for relationships between television-viewing behavior and social conformity, social relations, and attention span; and for relationships between social conformity and social relations.

Findings and conclusions included: (1) The actual amounts of television viewing of the children in this study ranged from 5.5 hours to 38.5 hours per child for the first recorded week and 9.5 to 49.5 hours per child for the second recorded week. (2) The degree of intensity most often indicated for the children's viewing was constant viewing with a median of 18 hours per child during the two weeks. (3) The types of programs watched by the largest number of children were situation comedies, cartoons, children's educational programs, adult variety programs, and movies. (4) The television programs with more than ten children viewing them at any one showing time were "World of Disney"; "Pink Panther"; "Sesame Street"; the movie "Chitty Chitty, Bang Bang"; "Donny and Marie"; "Six Million Dollar Man"; "Captain Kangaroo"; "Uncle Zeb's Cartoon Camp"; "Scooby Doo"; and "Happy Days." (5) The most frequent companion during television viewing was an adult. (6) Out of the 1613 programs viewed at some time during the two weeks by the 32 viewing children, the majority were approved by parents. Only 29 programs were designated as disapproved by parents as their children watched them. (7) There were no significant differences in total viewing time or in intensity of viewing according to age or sex.

32. **A Study of Preschool Children's Television Viewing Behavior and Circumstances.** Epstein, Robert H.; Bozler, Dianne A., International Association of Cybernetics, Namur, Belgium; University of Southern California, Los Angeles, Annenberg School of Communications, 1976, 22p. (ED 134 329; Reprint: EDRS). For related documents see citations 408, 417.

Presented are the findings of a telephone survey of randomly selected middle class families with preschool children. The survey, conducted as part of the Project in Television and Early Childhood Education at the University of Southern California, was initiated to provide a description of preschool children's viewing behavior and circumstances. The following information was elicited: (1) What were the attitudes of the parents? (2) Did the parents have any television rules, and if so, what were they based upon? (3) What were the circumstances under which the preschool child viewed television, and in what ways did she act upon the television experience? (4) What was the availability of television in the home and could the child physically operate the set on her own? and (5) What was the extent of the child's viewing from the first exposure to the present, the favorite shows and the time spent viewing? Background information on adult respondents includes age, sex, and educational level-role in household employment; family income and ethnic background. Child characteristics include age, sex, nursery school attendance, and other siblings under six.

33. A Survey of the Use of The Electric Company for Classroom Instruction, 1976–1977. Final Report.
Research Triangle Institute, Durham, NC, Aug 1977, 44p. Tabulations of tables are not provided because of minimal reproducibility of the original document. Sponsoring agency: Children's Television Workshop, New York NY (ED 153 620; Reprint: EDRS).

Information contained in this report concerns the sample survey design, survey operation, and estimation procedures applied to assess the use of the educational television series, "The Electric Company," in classroom instruction in 1976–77. The survey was national in scope, with schools being selected from sample schools appearing in a similar survey conducted in 1972–73. Survey results summarized include: (1) reliability and validity of the findings; (2) school adoption levels; (3) school adoption by grade levels by pupils; and (4) television viewing in schools, 1976–77. Extensive data tables are provided, as well as the school questionnaire.

34. A Survey of Viewership of Television Series Sponsored by ESAA Legislation. Final Report.
Hebbeler, Kathleen; Cosgrove, Michael, Applied Management Sciences, Inc., Silver Spring, MD, Jun 1978, 438p. Parts are marginally legible due to print quality. Sponsoring agency: Office of Education (DHEW), Washington, DC, Office of Planning, Budgeting, and Evaluation (ED 168 550; Reprint: EDRS). Executive Summary available as ED 165 551, 22p.

Results are presented of a national survey of in-school students, teachers, and principals to determine the viewership and availability of 11 television series which have been produced and distributed through funding provided by the Emergency School Aid Act (ESAA) to reduce cultural isolation among minority group members. In-home surveys were also conducted with many of the same students, their parents, and preschool siblings. Findings suggest that only a small number of children are aware of the ESAA-TV series. Although viewership is one measure of the success of the programs, comparisons across series must be interpreted cautiously, because of the differences among the ESAA-TV series. Similarly, viewership should be seen as one aspect of the funding-production-distribution system, and not as the sole measure of the worth of any individual series or the entire set of ESAA-TV projects. Appendices include technical methodology, survey instruments, construction of site-specific questionnaires, television program classification listing, cable coverage, ESAA-TV carriage information, and additional tables of survey data. TV series included in the survey were "La Bonne Aventure," "Que Pasa USA?" "La Esquina," "Mundo Real," "Gettin' Over," "South by Northwest," "Vegetable Soup," "Carrascolendas," "Villa Alegre," "Infinity Factory," and "Rebop."

35. Television and Our Children. A Report of the Activities of the Alternatives in Children's Broadcasting Project.
Mainse, David. May 1976, 245p (ED 146 915; Reprint: EDRS).

Two major objectives of the Alternatives in Children's Broadcasting Project were to determine the extent of the influence of violence in children's television and to determine if children's interest in prosocial programing makes it a viable alternative to violence programing. Both adults and eight to ten year old children were surveyed about their viewing habits and preferences, and the effects of television on their families. Included are a content analysis of television programs and a literature review. The establishment of a Canadian Communications Center is recommended to facilitate the flow of ideas about children's programing, and to serve evaluative and public awareness functions. Appended are summaries of television programs, and responses to the adult's and children's questionnaires.

36. Television and the Children of Ethnic Minorities.
Comstock, George; Cobbey, Robin E. Aug 1978, 30p. Paper presented at the Annual Meeting of the Association for Education in Journalism (61st, Seattle, WA. August 13–16, 1978) (ED 168 002; Reprint: EDRS).

The children of ethnic minorities appear to have a distinctive pattern in regard to television. The pattern is exemplified by a different orientation toward the medium, by differences in tastes and preferences, by atypical behavioral effects, and by different information needs. Minority children, however, may be presumed to share much about television with other children, including the common pattern of parental concern, limited parental control over viewing, and considerable potential for the exertion of parental influence over impact on attitudes and behavior. Prior findings lead to a research agenda emphasizing television's influence relative to that of other socializing agents, the feasibility and techniques for intervention by parents and schools in the communication flowing from television to the child, the bases of minority taste and preference, and the factors responsible for atypical behavioral effects. One hypothesis suggested by prior research is that television, by its portrayals, establishes the status hierarchy ascribed to characters portrayed on television independently of real world experience.

37. Television as a Dependent Variable, for a Change.
Banks, Seymour; Gupta, Rajinder. Sep 1979, 21p. Paper presented at the Annual Meeting of the American Psychological Association (87th, New York, NY, September 1–5, 1979) (ED 182 029; Reprint: EDRS).

This statistical analysis of questionnaire data from a study of 673 third-, fifth- and seventh-grade children and their parents was made to identify individual independent variables associated with children's total amount of television viewing. The data were analyzed by the stepwise linear regression method. The theoretical model guiding the analysis consisted of four broad elements: parents' and children's value systems, parent-child interaction, parents' TV viewing behavior and child's demographics. The variables in the data particularized the broad constructs. Findings indicated that all four components of the pre-specified model derived from socialization theory contributed to the children's television viewing behavior. The components and their share of the explained variances are: the child's own value systems (31 percent); child's own demographics (29 percent); parent-child interactions (20 percent); and parent's own TV behavior (20 percent). In terms of the individual variables studied, there is a positive relationship between a child's concern for her health and well being and her volume of television viewings. Analysis of the data within and across age groups argues against a simple hypothesis of the cumulative effects of television exposure upon children's anxiety, although hostility or detachment towards the parent is associated with heavy viewing behavior. Both TV volume and illness anxiety decrease with age. However, children's anxiety contributes most heavily to the "explained variance" of television viewing among the seventh grade children.

38. Television, Children, and Parents. A Report of the Viewing Habits, Program Preferences, and Parental Guidance of School Children in the Fourth through the Ninth Grades in Sedgwick County, Kansas (November, 1976). Mohr, Phillip J., Wichita State University, KS, Jun 1977, 483p. Sponsoring agency: American Broadcasting Co., New York, NY (ED 158 730; Reprint: EDRS—HC not available).

Television viewing habits, program preferences, and parental guidance at 5,167 randomly selected urban/rural Kansas children in grades four through nine were studied. Data collected by the administration of structured questionnaires to the children in 254 classrooms and separate questionnaires completed by 4,882 of the childrens' parents indicated that: (1) the children devoted approximately 3½ hours daily to television; (2) parental limitations on viewing times were more strict on nights before school days; 70 percent and 90 percent of the children and parents, respectively, reported that viewing must cease at or before 10:00 p.m., but on nights before nonschool days, no parental limitations on viewing times were reported by 60 percent to 70 percent of the respondents; (3) parents and children frequently differed in program preferences, suggesting difficulties for broadcasters in providing "common denominator" programs appropriate for family viewing; and (4) 80 percent to 90 percent of parents and children reported no parental guidance on 68 evening and 24 Saturday morning programs listed on the questionnaires. Demographic analyses of the data are also reported.

39. Television Viewing of Selected Sixth, Seventh, and Eighth Grade Students. Lehrer, Sandra G.; Cissna, Kenneth N. Leone. Apr 1978, 27p. Paper to be presented at the Annual Meeting of the International Communication Association (Chicago, IL, April 1978) (ED 144 120; Reprint: EDRS).

In this study of children's television viewing, 105 junior high school students reported the television programs they watched, the amount of time they spent each day watching television, and their reasons for watching television. The following results are reported: sixth graders watch more television than do seventh or eighth graders; sixth-grade females watch more television than sixth-grade males; more television viewing occurs on Saturday than on any other day of the week; situation comedies are the programs most often viewed, followed by a group of program categories that include adventure, cartoon/fantasy, and game shows; and the reasons for watching television vary by sex and grade but do not indicate a maturing pattern of program selection. The report concludes by comparing its findings with other studies of children's television viewing and by suggesting topics for further research.

40. A Trend Report on the Role and Penetration of Sesame Street in Ghetto Communities (Bedford Stuyvesant, East Harlem, Chicago and Washington, DC). Yankelovich, Skelly and White, Inc., New York, NY, Oct 1978, 128p. Sponsoring agency: Children's Television Workshop, New York, NY (ED 164 007; Reprint: EDRS).

The primary objectives of this study were: (1) to determine the extent to which "Sesame Street" is continuing to reach underprivileged preschool children and to compare its current performance with data established in the previous studies conducted in 1970, 71, and 73; (2) to examine the relationship of "Sesame Street" to school age children by determining how many watch the program, and how that influences their younger siblings; and (3) to explore the attitudes and values of parents/caretakers to determine the factors which lead them to encourage their children to watch the program. Bedford Stuyvesant, East Harlem, Chicago's Black ghetto area, and the inner city of Washington D.C. were the areas used for the distribution of the questionnaire designed to yield factual data about viewing habits, and attitudinal data based on verbatim opinions. A summary of the major findings and their implications, and the most significant findings with their supporting tables are reported in the first two sections. Verbatim quotes are included in the third, and the appendix describes characteristics of the respondents in each of the four areas studied.

41. Why College Students Watch Soap Operas. Breen, Myles P.; Powell, Jon T. Apr 1980, 16p. Paper presented at the Annual Meeting of the Broadcast Education Association (Las Vegas, NV, April 12, 1980) (ED 185 627; Reprint: EDRS).

A survey of 549 college students investigated the size and motivation of the campus audience for soap operas. About half the student population (40 percent of the women and 10 percent of the men) claimed to watch daytime serials. Most of the women viewing soap operas watched two or three serials per week, with 83.3 percent following at least two regularly, and 46.1 percent following at least three regularly. The serial-viewing males watched less; 41.4 percent watched only one serial, with percentages declining sharply and directly as the number of serials watched increased. "Intriguing plots" and "topics of conversation" were the reasons most often chosen for watching daytime serials. Despite the consensus of the critics, both male and female respondents thought that the female characters were more likely to be the troublemakers in the soaps, an apparent change from past conceptions of the long-suffering female being put upon by men.

BOOKS

42. Pre-School Children and Television: Two Studies Carried Out in Three Countries. Homberg, Erentraud, ed. New York: K. G. Saur Publishing, Inc., 1978, 78p.

This brochure presents the summaries of two major studies carried out in three European countries concerning the role of television in the life of preschool children. The first study involved participant observation and interviews of 90 families from England and 50 families from Ireland over a six-month period. The children studied were between the ages of three years and four years eight months. A major objective of the study was to obtain a comprehensive survey of the children's activities and not just of their viewing habits. Data are reported on the following: daily routines of the children; relations between the children's television consumption and family variables; the children's attentiveness to television programs; the relative popularity of different children's programs; the mothers' attitudes towards television commercials; parental appraisal of television; and the television producers' educational aims. The second study also involved observation and interviews, this time with 50 families from a large town and a small town in Sweden. Conclusions are stated regarding the relation between child's level of TV viewing and parents' level of education, child's age and sex; parents' attitudes and behavior towards and influence on children's viewing habits; indirect and direct, long-term effects of television on children; and the role of other mass media in the life of preschool children. Comments are also made on the role of television as an intellectual, social, emotional, and creative stimulus in children's development.

HOW CHILDREN PERCEIVE TELEVISION

How Children Perceive Television

JOURNAL ARTICLES

43. Black, White, White Gifted, and Emotionally Disturbed Children's Perceptions of the Reality in Television Programming. Donohue, William A.; Donohue, Thomas R. *Human Relations*. v30, n7, p609–21, Jul 1977.

Given the general and somewhat contradictory nature of previous research examining children's perceptions of the reality in television programming, this paper attempted (1) to separate the different levels of television content, (2) to determine the extent to which personal experience with specific role and situational stereotypes influence judgments of television's presentations, and (3) to examine a wide range of socio-economic status (SES) characteristics within the context of the same study to facilitate direct comparisons. The results of the study indicate that lower SES Blacks and emotionally distrubed children, pages 11–16, view specific role stereotypes and general situations as significantly more real than do Whites and gifted children. The implications of these findings relevant to the child's maturation process were explored.

44. Childhood Socialization and Television. Klapper, Hope Lunin. *Public Opinion Quarterly*. v42, n3, p426-30, Fall 1978.

This article summarizes a study, in which second and fifth graders were asked if televised fiction was like or unlike real life. The author stresses two points: (1) television should be kept in perspective as only one of the many factors in childhood socialization; and (2) the consequences of television for a particular child are, in parts, a consequence of the child itself; that is, the child is an active agent in his/her own socialization process.

45. Children's Comprehension of Family Role Portrayals in Televised Dramas: Effects of Socio-economic Status, Ethnicity, and Age. Newcomb, Andrew F.; Collins, W. Andrew. *Developmental Psychology*. v15, n4, p417-23, Jul 1979.

Middle and lower socioeconomic status (SES), White and Black children in grades two, five and eight participated in two fully-crossed replications of the same design. They viewed one of two edited television dramas that portrayed either a White middle-class family (Study 1) or a Black working-class family (Study 2) in similar conflict resolution situations. Participants' comprehension of central (plot-essential) and peripheral content and their inferences about actors' emotions and causes of action were assessed. Memory for content was age-related in both studies. However, in Study 1, middle-SES second graders viewing the middle-class family show scored higher than lower-SES second graders. In Study 2 lower-SES second graders who viewed the working-class family show achieved higher scores than their middle-class counterparts. There were no SES effects among fifth- and eighth-grade participants and no consistent effects of ethnicity at any age. Additional analyses indicated that congruence between televised characters and settings and viewers' own experiences, as indicated by SES, eased second graders' processing of program content. Implications of age-related processing skills for social effects of television were discussed.

46. Children's Literate Television Viewing: Surprises and Possible Explanations. Cohen, Akiba A.; Salomon, Gavriel. *Journal of Communication*. v29, n3, p156–63, Sum 1979 (EJ 217 488; Reprint: UMI).

Compares American middle-class children, as representatives of heavy television viewers, and Israeli middle-class children, as representatives of lighter television viewers, to determine the extent to which accumulated television viewing enhances the development of particular mental skills, particularly depth of processing.

47. Children's Perceptions of Television Characters. Reeves, Byron; Greenberg, Bradley S. *Human Communication Research*. v3, n2, p113–27, Win 1977.

This study explores the cognitive dimensions used by children in grades three, five and seven in differentiating among television characters. By linking content-free judgments of the differences among television characters with content attributes suggested by prior research, a four-dimensional mapping is identified. This cognitive mapping is virtually identical for children at three different ages. Further, dimensions identified are strong predictors of the children's desires to model the social behaviors of the TV characters. The dimensions identified and discussed include those of humor, attractiveness, strength, and activity. The findings also indicate that young boys and girls use the same dimensions in markedly different ways.

48. Children's Understanding of the Nature of Television Characters. Quarfoth, Joanne M. *Journal of Communication*. v29, n3, p210–18, Sum 1979 (EJ 217 494; Reprint: UMI).

Explores children's understanding of the nature of television characters by assessing their abilities to differentiate between human, animated, and puppet characters. Not until second grade were a majority of children able to make this distinction. A substantial number of second, third, and even fourth graders demonstrated an incomplete understanding of the functioning of cartoon and puppet characters.

49. Cognitive Development and Television Comprehension. Desmond. Roger Jon. *Communication Research—An International Quarterly*. v5, n2, p202–20, Apr 1978.

Reports a study conducted to determine whether several key concepts related to child development could be extended to existing theory and research concerning comprehension of television by kindergartners and early primary school children. Results indicate that children's individual differences partially explain amount and the kind of social learning, while chronological age is the most accurate index of content learning.

50. The Dimensional Structure of Children's Perceptions of Television Reality. Hawkins, Robert Parker. *Communication Research—An International Quarterly*. v4, n3, p299–320, Jul 1977.

Bases an explication of perceived reality on a proposed division into a variety of subdivisions and examines the distinction between the degree to which children believe they are viewing either ongoing life or drama, and the degree to which they believe television characters and events do or do not match their expectations about the world.

51. Impact of "All in the Family" on Children. Meyer, Timothy P. *Journal of Broadcasting*. v20, n1, p23–33, Win 1976.

A study of the impact of "All in the Family" on children concentrates on why they watch, how well they understand the plot, most and least admired characters, and information conveyed about standards of adult and family behavior.

52. The Reassuring Role of TV's Continuing Characters. Piltch, Charles N. *USA Today*. V107, n2406, p54–56, Mar 1979 (EJ 209 076; Reprint: UMI).

The author analyzes the series form of television program, particularly the qualities and functions of the continuing characters and their relationship to the plot. He discusses the reassuring psychological effects of a TV series on the audience and the implications of a decline in this type of programing.

53. The Relationship of Visual Attention to Children's Comprehension of Television. Lorch, Elizabeth Pugzles et al. *Child Development*. v50, n3, p722–27, Sep 1979 (EJ 212 951; Reprint: UMI).

Seventy-two five-year-olds viewed a 40-minute version of "Sesame Street." Half of the children viewed in the presence of toys and half viewed without toys. The children were then tested for their comprehension of the program. Although visual attention to the TV was nearly twice as high in the no-toys group, there was no difference between the groups in comprehension. Results suggested that variations in the comprehensibility of the program may determine variations in children's attention to television.

54. The Role of Fantasy in the Response to Television. Feshbach, Seymour. *Journal of Social Issues*. v32, n4, p71–85, Fall 1976 (EJ 166 961; Reprint: UMI).

The principle thesis of this paper is that an understanding of the functions of fantasy activities is critical to an understanding of the influence of television and other media upon behavior, particularly aggressive behavior.

55. Sesame Street Around the World: The Development of Attention. Levin, Stephen R.; Anderson, Daniel R. *Journal of Communication*. v26, n2, p126–35, Spr 1976.

Describes a continuing research program concerned with what U.S. preschoolers look at on television and how often they attend; and notes implications for the production of television material for young children.

56. Through a Glass Darkly: Television and the Perception of Reality. Cohen, Dorothy H. *National Elementary Principal*. v56, n3, p22–29, Jan-Feb 1977.

Presents several studies that indicate the ways in which television has a harmful effect on children's perception of reality, including one study that indicated a children's program induced sensory overload in some of its viewers.

57. Young Children's Perception of the Reality of Television. Brown, Mac H. et al. *Contemporary Education*. v50, n3, p129-33, Spr 1979 (EJ 208 685; Reprint: UMI).

This study of six- and seven-year-olds in rural Georgia sought to investigate the relationship between cognitive development and the children's perception of the reality of cartoon and human fantasy television episodes of "Star Trek." Results indicated that there is a relationship between children's perception of reality and their cognitive development; more specifically, conservers had a significantly higher degree of perceived reality than did nonconservers. However, this relationship was found to be independent of age. As in other studies, the children had a better perception of the reality of cartoons than of human-fantasy drama.

MICROFICHE

58. Active and Passive Processes in Children's Television Viewing. Anderson, Daniel R. Sep 1979, 24p. Paper presented at the Annual Meeting of the American Psychological Association (87th, New York, NY, September 1–5, 1979). Sponsoring agency: Children's Television Workshop, New York, NY: Grant Foundation, New York, NY; National Science Foundation, Washington, DC (ED 182 008; Reprint: EDRS).

The TV viewing situation involves an active transaction between the child, the TV, and the TV viewing environment. The TV viewing transaction is a blend of passive and active cognitive activities. Children begin to watch TV systematically at around 2½ years of age because at that time they have the cognitive ability to appreciate the meaning of the dynamic flow of images and sounds it presents. Evidence exists that preschool children look at the parts of a television program that are understandable, and that they engage in alternative activities such as toy play when the program momentarily is not understood. Preschoolers also use their peers' behaviors as cues for directing their visual attention in the TV viewing environment. One passive aspect of TV viewing may be called "attentional inertia": the longer a TV viewer continuously maintains visual attention to the television, the more probable it is that he or she will continue to do so. Although in general the young child stops attending to incomprehensible program material, attentional inertia may occasionally lead the child to new cognitive discoveries. TV viewing in young children is not simply the mesmerizing passively receptive activity it is represented to be in popular books. Directions for further research are suggested.

59. Active vs Passive Television Viewing: A Model of the Development of Television Information Processing by Children. Wright, John C. et al. Aug 1978, 20p. Paper presented at the Annual Meeting of the American Psychological Association (Toronto, Canada, August, 1978) (ED 184 521; Reprint: EDRS).

A conceptual model of how children process televised information was developed with the goal of identifying those parameters of the process that are both measurable and manipulable in research settings. The model presented accommodates the nature of information processing both by the child and by the presentation of the medium. Presentation is classified into two categories: simultaneous, where all stimuli or items of information are available at the same time; and successive, where the rapid stream of events is organized in its own sequence and does not repeat itself. Two modes are discussed: exploration and search processing. In the exploration mode, the child becomes familiar with the material by devoting attention to whatever is most physically salient or inherently attention-getting. In search behavior, the child tries to comprehend the message by actively imposing an order of processing on simultaneous arrays. Similarity of age and viewing experience, and effects of the viewing environment are also discussed. Twenty-one references are cited.

60. Adolescent Involvement with Television Characters and Differential Attribution Strategies.* Durall, Jean A., The University of Wisconsin-Madison, 1978, 242p (7822250; Reprint: DC).

This was an exploratory study focusing on adolescent involvement with television characters, attributions about the causes of television character's behavior, and their relationship. Involvement was conceptualized as two mutually exclusive levels: recognition, or feeling that you know the character; and, identification, or wanting to be like the character. Attributions were considered as ascribing causation to either factors in the person (dispositional) or to factors in the situation. It was predicted that recognition should lead to more situational attributions while identification would produce more dispositional attributions. Other variables were grade of subject (sixth or tenth), sex of subject, sex of television character, and, either adult or adolescent status of the TV characters.

Data were collected in personal interviews with 82 sixth graders and 68 tenth graders drawn from a probability sample of students attending two area middle and high schools. Questioning focused on three specific situation comedy programs: "Happy Days," "One Day at a Time," and "Welcome Back Kotter."

The general findings indicate that involvement, at least with situation comedy characters, is not very extensive. The recognition aspect of involvement, or feeling that you know the character, is more generalized than is identification, or wanting to be like the character. The most striking finding was the strong indication that these two aspects of involvement are not independent, as theorized, but that recognition is a necessary condition for identification. There was some support for grade and sex differences in both identification and recognition but these were not substantial except in the case of same-sex and cross-sex identification.

Considering the attribution measures alone, the evidence which emerged was more speculative. There was no indiciation of any relationship between measures of attribution across different television shows although there was some tendency for similarity between characters from the same show. A second finding was that, in general, attributions about television characters refer more to situational factors than to personal qualities. Much of the analysis and discussion surrounding the attribution measured involved different attempts to establish the reliability and validity of those measures and the associated findings.

61. Children and Television: Effects of Stimulus Repetition on Eye Activity.* Flagg, Barbara Nord, Harvard University, 1977, 112p (7730681; Reprint: DC).

Using eye movement recording, this study examines whether or not four-year-olds and six-year-olds view a television presentation differently in an undirected viewing situation. In addition, the study explores changes in the eye activity of each age group in response to repeated presentations of the experimental television segments.

Seventeen four-year-olds and 22 six-year-olds of both sexes participated. Each child viewed two 10-minute color videotapes comprised of calibration and "Sesame Street" materials. The videotapes included three short "Sesame Street" segments which on their initial presentation were unfamiliar to all subjects. Each of the three experimental segments was repeated in exact form over the two tapes; Segment A was repeated five times, Segment B four times and Segment C two times.

Eye activity data were recorded using a Whittaker Corporation Eye View Monitor which employs a pupil-center/corneal-reflection measurement technique. The data were reduced into the following eye activity measures: mean and variance of fixation duration, mean and variance of interfixation distance, fixation frequency, percent of television screen covered by fixations, and cumulative additive indices. The latter measure indicates how much new display area a child scanned with each successive repetition.

No differences were found between the eye activity patterns of four-year-olds and six-year-olds during the viewing of the initially unfamiliar "Sesame Street" segments and subsequent repetitions. The similarity in viewing patterns on the initial presentation may be a function of the fact that the television display structurally organizes the visual information for the viewer to such a degree that the younger child's attention patterns do not differ from the six year olds.

The cumulative additive indices revealed that the children looked at less new information with each repeated presentation. Moreover, eye activity showed gradual signs of habituation over the four or five repetitions of the same stimulus presentation; mean fixation duration increased, mean interfixation distance decreased, and mean percent of television area fixated decreased. It appears that most of the work in comprehending and exploring the segments is completed by the first or second presentations. The fact that no age differences occurred and a limited amount of exploratory activity was noted over repetitions yields the impression that the segments did not impose a significant load on the children's processing capacities.

62. Children and Television: The Development of the Child's Understanding of the Medium. Wartella, Ellen. 1979, 67p. Legibility of the bibliography varies. Sponsoring agency: Federal Communications Commission, Washington, DC (ED 184 515; Reprint: EDRS).

This review of the current state of research on how children make sense of television and its content examines age-related differences in children's interpretations of television entertainment content in general, and advertising content in particular. A brief analysis and description of the fundamental principles of cognitive development theory are offered in section one, including a brief review of crucial terms, assumptions, and characterization of the changing cognitive skills available to children, as well as a critique of cognitive development theory with emphasis on the work of Piaget. Section two reviews the growing literature on children's information processing of television dramatic program content. The discussion in the next section focuses on several pragmatic questions regarding children's understanding of the purpose of television and their information processing of advertising content. The paper concludes with an explanation of some of the possible policy options which seem unwarranted by the preceding review.

63. Children's Attention to the Television Screen: A Time Series Analysis. Krull, Robert; Husson, William G. Aug 1977, 47p. Paper presented at the Annual Meeting of the Association for Education in Journalism (60th, Madison, WI, August 21–24, (ED 147 842; Reprint: EDRS).

The relationship between television program variables and children's attention was examined using sample shows from two nationally distributed educational programs, "Sesame Street" and "The Electric Company." Shows were coded at 30-second intervals on four measures of program complexity and two measures of the relationship between verbal and visual content. Children's visual-attention levels were measured individually and averaged over the sample. Single time series analysis indicated the predictability of children's attention levels to be no more than 30 seconds. Younger children's attention in adjacent program segments was found to be more highly interdependent than was older children's attention. Multiple time series analysis indicated the attention of older children could be explained very well, based on the program variables measured. Older children also appeared to be affected more by variations in program complexity and, in particular, by visual complexity. Younger children were more affected by verbal variables, and attention levels were found to be more due to children's consistently attending than to program variables. Forty-four percent to 58 percent of the variance in attention was explained by these models.

64. Children's Processing of Motive Information in a Televised Portrayal. Purdie, Sharon I. et al. Apr 1979, 10p. Paper presented at the National Conference of the Association for Childhood Education International (St. Louis, MO, April 8–13, 1979). Sponsoring agency: Minnesota University, Minneapolis. Institute of Child Development (ED 172 955; Reprint: EDRS).

Second and fifth graders viewed one of two edited versions of a commercial action-adventure television program portraying an aggressive action associated with antisocial motives and punishing consequences. The versions differed only in the amount of time elapsing between the focal action and the motives for that action. Children's comprehension of explicit events in the program and inferences about relations among them (e.g., causality) were assessed using a recognition-memory measure. When motive information was portrayed in close proximity to the aggressive action (proximal-motive version), both second and fifth graders understood the explicit motive and action details and implicit relations between them better than they did when the motives and aggression occurred in different scenes (distal-motive version). Even when children understood the explicit motive and action information, those in the distal-motive version were less likely than those in the proximal version to evaluate the aggressor negatively. Fifth graders comprehended better than second graders in both versions and were also more likely to infer implicit relations. Additional data indicated that the younger viewers' difficulties were not due to forgetting or interference effects in the course of viewing. Results are discussed in terms of characteristics of children's processing of audiovisual narratives and implications for social-learning and behavioral effects of televised dramatic content.

65. The Development of Preschoolers' Apprehension of a Televised Narrative. Wilder, Paula Gillen, Harvard University, Cambridge, MA Harvard Project Zero, Oct 1979, 22p. Sponsoring agency: John and Mary R. Markle Foundation, New York, NY: National Institute of Education (DHEW), Washington, DC (ED 184 118; Reprint: EDRS).

Nine preschool children viewed a videotaped story at regular intervals in a longitudinal study of their understanding of a televised narrative. Observations focused on children's attention to the story, their reactions during viewing, and their postviewing story reconstructions. It was found that the children sensed certain interpersonal conflicts from an early age, and that they became increasingly sensitive to conflicts embedded in the story. That a child's prior knowledge and experience with a character appeared to influence narrative comprehension was consistent with the impression that television encourages the development and perpetuation of stereotypes. Although children's knowledge from other sources was apparent, their repeated exposures to a single narrative on television did not assure a competent grasp of that narrative. The difficulties that many of the children had in reconstructing the narrative raised the issue of how television affects children's symbolic play. Specific television features that affected the children's narrative recall were the appearance of characters in closeup shots, increased volume, decreased pace of the dialogue, and repetition of statements throughout the narrative.

66. Developmental Aspects of Children's Impression Formations of Television Characters.* Hong, Kisun, University of Minnesota, 1978, 216p (7912023; Reprint: DC).

Guided by Piaget's theoretical framework, this study analyzed differences in children's impression formation at the concrete and formal operational stages. Children's free descriptions of their favorite TV characters were discussed in terms of differences in their organization, accuracy, and abstraction levels.

In order to operationalize the developmental constructs of interest, particularly those which deal with differences between the concrete and formal operational stages, three age groups of children—second, fifth, and eighth graders—were sampled.

The level of abstraction contained in each child's description was determined by examining the number of assertions the child made about physical/social identity, general behavior, and personal traits of characters.

The data suggested a developmental shift toward increased use of personal trait assertions. This shift was most apparent between the fifth (concrete operational stage) and eighth (formal operational stage) grades, especially among girls.

According to the data, with age, children make increasingly abstract and organized character impressions. This change is especially pronounced between the fifth and eighth grades, supporting our hypotheses based on Piagetian cognitive developmental theory.

With regard to sex differences, this study suggests that girls experience relatively clear developmental changes in their verbal descriptions of TV characters between the fifth and eighth grades. These sex differences may be due to the different social expectations which are placed on boys and girls and their subsequent adjustment to these.

The accuracy of descriptions was determined by assessing how accurately each child estimated the ratio between characters' pro-social and aggressive behaviors. The level of accuracy was defined as the difference between the children's estimates and pro-social/aggressive ratio values which were computed by means of program content analyses. With the exception of the second grade boys, all of the children shared similar accuracy levels.

With age, however, children (especially girls) tended to evaluate TV characters as being more aggressive. Also, with age, perceptual biases due to liking of characters decreased: this shift was most apparent between the fifth and eighth grades. This implies that stage-like developmental changes also occurred in the children's perceptual biases due to their liking of TV characters.

67. The Effects of Varying Television Production and Transmission Techniques on the Perceptions and Cognitions of Selected Adolescents.* Hood, Marc Carrol, East Texas State University, 1979, 188p (7918455; Reprint: DC).

The purpose of this study was to measure the effects of varying production techniques on subjects' cognitive retention of a television program's content and on subjects' perceptions of the program narrator. This investigation proposed to answer the following questions:

1. Is there a significant difference in the cognitive retention scores as measured by test seven of the "California Short-Form Test of Mental Maturity" between those subjects viewing test narrative format I (formal) and those viewing test narrative format II (informal), and to what extent, if any, did the transmission of the content in color or monochrome contribute to this difference?

2. Is there a significant difference in the expressed viewer perceptions of the television program narrator as measured by the semantic differential scale between those subjects viewing test narrative format I (formal) and those subjects viewing test narrative format II (informal), and to what extent, if any, did the transmission of the content in color or monochrome contribute to this difference?

The instructional television production variables of camera shot, camera change, set design, lighting, and narration were polarized into two opposing production formats—formal and informal. In each format, the content and the individual narrating that content were the same. A narrative taken from test seven of the "California Short-Form Test of Mental Maturity" was used as the content of both television productions which were presented to selected junior high students.

Findings indicate that intimate production techniques may significantly affect junior high viewers' cognitive retention and perceptions with respect to televised narrators. Subjects viewing the informal format presentation scored significantly higher on a test that measured their cognitive retention of the program content. The use of intimate camera, design, and delivery techniques significantly enhanced subjects' perceptions of the narrator's activity, novelty, and receptivity. The transmission of the format presentations in color or monochrome had no measured effects on subjects. The results indicated advantages in the use of intimate as opposed to formal ITV production techniques when presenting a televised narration.

68. Exploring the Realities of Television with Children. Morison, Patricia et al., Harvard University, Cambridge, MA, Harvard Project Zero, 1978, 19p. Sponsoring agency: John and Mary R. Markel Foundation, New York, NY (ED 165 804; Reprint: EDRS).

A study proposing reality and fantasy discrimination of television content as a classificatory ability sought to identify differences between subjects who were able to make sophisticated reality-fantasy judgements and those who were not, and factors which might contribute to a subject's sophistication in discrimination. Open-ended and structured interviews were conducted with 36 children in grades one, three, and six; these interviews were scored and ranked according to the subject's sophistication with and tendency to use reality and fantasy concepts, sophistication in understanding the commercial broadcast television system, and degree of program familiarity. Results indicated that high scorers in reality-fantasy judgements were distinguished from their less sophisticated grade peers by their increased spontaneous use of reality-fantasy considerations. Also, the ability to assess the reality status of various types of television was relatively independent of the child's familiarity with a variety of television programs. The findings imply that efforts to teach children about the medium of television and its conventions could improve their skills in discriminating reality from fiction on television.

69. Eye Movements, Individual Differences, and Television-Viewing Patterns of Children. Baron, Lois J. Apr 1979, 17p. Paper presented at the Annual Meeting of the American Educational Research Association (San Francisco, CA, April 8–12, 1979) (ED 168 696; Reprint: EDRS).

This study investigates the perceptual processing capabilities by analysis of eye movement of children from differing levels of field independence/dependence. Forty nine field independent (24 girls, 26 boys) and 36 field dependent (19 girls, 17 boys) children in third grade were analyzed as they viewed either seven dynamic or seven static segments from the Children's Television Workshop program. It was hypothesized that both good readers and field independents would exhibit more sophisticated scanning strategies and that the dynamic mode of presentation would result in significant eye movement differences from those exhibited in the static mode. Regression analyses revealed that eye movements were rather stimulus specific. Supplantation of mental operation by the simuli was also an important consideration of this study.

70. Factors Which Predict the Credibility Ascribed to Television. Leifer, Aimee D. Sep 1976, 17p. Paper presented at the American Psychological Association (Washington, DC, September 5, 1976). Sponsoring agency: Office of Child Development (DHEW), Washington, DC (ED 135 332; Reprint: EDRS). For related document, see citation 457.

In an effort to identify critical evaluation skills, interview information is analyzed looking at four types of differences: differences between age groups, differences between children who did and did not change their attitudes after viewing an entertainment program, differences among those who ascribed varying degrees of credibility to television content, and differences among White, Black and Puerto Rican subjects. Disconfirmed hypotheses included the importance of the content decided about, the importance in itself of accurate knowledge of the television industry, the type of real/pretend decisions children make, and the adjudged accuracy of children's decisions. The five critical evaluation skills which are tentatively identified are (1) explicit and spontaneous reasoning, (2) readiness to compare television content to outside sources of information, (3) readiness to refer to industry knowledge in reasoning about television content, (4) tendency to find television content more fabricated or inaccurate, and (5) less positive evaluation of television content.

71. How Preschoolers Explore the Relationship between Television and the Real World. Technical Report No. 11. Jaglom, Leona M. et al. Harvard University, Cambridge, MA Harvard Project Zero, Sep 1979, 23p. Sponsoring agency: John and Mary R. Markel Foundation, New York, NY: National Institute of Education (DHEW), Washington, DC (ED 182 746; Reprint: EDRS).

Over 300 verbal and behavioral associations between television and real life were recorded by observing three preschool children for three years and gathering supplementary information from five other children. The children's associations to real life experience made during television viewing occurred consistently earlier than associations to television from the context of daily experience. Regardless of age and amount of television viewed, children consistently used real life as the background against which television was compared. Of the 11 types of associations that were documented, some were found to occur regardless of age, including children commenting on the similarities/differences between television and real life, their requests for televised objects, and their imitation of television characters. Two-year-old children did not perceive the two worlds as separate, and were confused as to the nature of the boundary between the two realms. When the children were four years old, they demonstrated a clearer understanding of the boundary, but they also tended to be overly rigid about the unreality of televised material. At five years of age, the children understood the principal kinds of relationships between television and the rest of their experience, but they were still insensitive to certain connections.

72. Parents, Adolescents & Television: Culture, Learning, Influence: A Report to the Public. Summary of Findings. Tierney, Joan D. May 1978, 18p. Sponsoring agency: Canadian Radio-Television Commission, Ottawa (Ontario) (ED 172 763; Reprint: EDRS).

Findings of television research conducted in Montreal and Windsor, Canada, in February–May 1978, that studied numerous aspects of the parent-adolescent-television relationship are summarized in this report. Particular emphasis is given to differences between ethnic and English families, differences in the ways adolescent boys and girls perceive values in programming, and the role of the family. General findings are briefly noted and explained, while 13 major findings are listed and expanded upon with discussion.

73. **Parents, Adolescents and Television: Part I. Adolescents and Television Heroes: The Perception of Social Values in Favorite Television Series.** Tierney, Joan D. Aug 1978, 17p. Report based on a paper presented at the Annual Meeting of the International Sociological Association (Uppsala, Sweden, August 17, 1978). Bibliography and tables removed due to poor reproducibility. Sponsoring agency: Canadian Radio-Television Commission, Ottawa (Ontario) (ED 172 747; Reprint: EDRS—HC not available; also available from Canadian Radio-TV and Telecommunications Commission, Ottawa, Canada).

The social values orientation of Canadian adolescents and preadolescents was analyzed to determine the effects of television choice on their values. Youth were randomly selected from ethnic and nonethnic populations in Montreal and Windsor by percentages of subgroups listed in "Statistics Canada" for each city. It was assumed that ethnic and nonethnic adolescents and pre-adolescents would differ in their value orientation, that social and moral values held by ethnic parents and youth would differ from those of nonethnic parents and youth, and that these differences would be reflected in perceptions about television heroes and content. The most important question was whether or not heroes transmit values or simply reinforce them. An initial questionnaire indicated family attitudes about a number of social interactions values, against which six weeks of observations of viewers was compared. Findings indicate that television viewing during adolescence for both ethnic and nonethnic groups appears to be related to personal need and identity, as well as to entertainment, and values appear to be reinforced by television.

74. **Parents, Adolescents and Television: Part II. Adolescents and Television Heroes: Conceptual and Methodological Considerations of Analysis of Responses and Information Processing Strategies.** Tierney, Joan D. Sep 1978, 20p. Report based on a paper presented at the Annual Meeting of the International Association for Mass Communication Research (Warsaw, Poland, September 7, 1978). Best copy available. Sponsoring agency: Canadian Radio-Television Commission, Ottawa (Ontario), (ED 172 748; Reprint: EDRS—HC not available; also available from Canadian Radio-TV and Telecommunications Commission, Ottawa, Canada).

The data analysis and findings of the first panel study of adolescents and pre-adolescents in Canada are described. This longitudinal study was designed to (1) gather data on television viewing of heroes and heroines in series in the home environment; (2) analyze verbal responses about television programs to determine values perceived and the cognitive processing strategies used by the two age groups, and (3) determine if biological predisposition of the sexes was a factor in information perceived and meanings assigned. Initial questionnaires were administered separately to children and parents to gather sociodemographic, cultural, media, and family relationship data prior to the experiment. Repeat questionnaires were administered after every two weeks of viewing of the child's favorite television show. Analyses of the responses to

measure age and sex differences on four dimensions—concrete/cognitive, concrete/affective, inferred/cognitive, and inferred/affective—show clearly and specifically on what dimensions differences occur in perception of content by boys and girls aged 10 and 14.

75. **A Part of Our Environment Left Unexplored by Environmental Designers: Television.** Ross, Rhonda P. Jun 1979, 20p. Paper presented at the Annual Meeting of the Environmental Design Research Association (10th, Buffalo, NY, June 1979). Sponsoring agency: Spencer Foundation, Chicago, IL (ED 184 526; Reprint: EDRS).

Research studies on the influence of the viewing environment on children's attention to television and the amount of television viewed are reviewed, as well as control of television viewing through environmental design and what is known about the kinds of environments depicted on television. How television can influence the development of our environmental preference and behavior-environment congruence is also explored.

76. **Recall of Television Content as a Function of Content Type and Level of Production Feature Use.** Calvert, Sandra; Watkins, Bruce, Department of Human Development, Kansas University, Lawrence, Mar 1979, 16p. Paper presented at the Biennial Meeting of the Society for Research in Child Development (San Francisco, CA, March 15–18, 1979). Figures may not reproduce clearly. Sponsoring agency: Spencer Foundation, Chicago, IL (ED 178 180; Reprint: EDRS).

This study investigated developmental changes in children's recall of televised central and incidental content. Central content was plot-relevant; incidental content was peripheral to the plot. Both content types were classified at two levels of production features, high salience and low salience. High salience features were high action, loud music or singing, and special effects. Low salience features were character dialogue and low action. Comprehension questions were generated to fit each of these four cells. One hundred and sixty children at two age levels, kindergarten and third/fourth grade viewed a prosocial cartoon in same-sex pairs. Children then participated in an immediate multiple choice test and returned 45 minutes later for a delayed test. Results indicated that older children are more selective in recall of central over incidental material than are younger children. Findings also showed that pairing content with highly salient production features improved central recall at both age levels, particularly for younger children.

77. **The Relation of Visual and Verbal Style of Television Presentation to Learning of Prosocial Content.** Susman, Elizabeth J. Mar 1977, 11p. Paper presented at the Biennial Meeting of the Society for Research in Child Development (New Orleans, LA, March 17–20, 1977) (ED 140 956; Reprint: EDRS).

The study assessed the effect of two stylistic features of a prosocial television program, visual focusing and verbal labeling, on learning and behavior. Forty male and 40 female preschool children viewed one of five versions of a children's quiz show. Camera zooms and verbal labels alone and in combination emphasized sharing in four prosocial versions of the program: (1) visual focusing (camera zooms) alone, (2) verbal labeling alone, (3) verbal labeling and camera zooms and (4) no camera zooms, no verbal labeling. Sharing was edited out of a fifth version (control). Sex differences were found. Results indicated that: symbolic codes of the media can be used as mediators of television content, and symbolic codes influence behavior more than learning measured by words and pictorial symbols. Results are discussed in terms of the developmental lag between motoric performance and the ability to manipulate abstract symbols representing an act.

78. Television and Growing Up: The Medium Gets Equal Time. Huston-Stein, Aletha. Aug 1977, 28p. Paper presented at the Annual Meeting of the American Psychological Association (85th, San Francisco, CA, August 26–30, 1977) (ED 148 462; Reprint: EDRS).

This paper presents a review of research on television viewing and child behavior. The first section of the paper presents a brief historical review of television research. This review includes research on the effect of television on people's lives, the effects of violent content on aggressive behavior and the possible harmful effects of advertising and social stereotypes as well as the beneficial effects of prosocial and educational content on children's attitudes and behavior. The second section of the paper reviews research on the visual and auditory form rather than the content of television programs. This research suggests that such features as nonverbal auditory effects, action, and rapid auditory or visual changes tend to elicit and hold children's attention. Visual camera effects such as zoom and pan techniques were less powerful in eliciting attention than similar auditory features such as sound effects and changes in auditory stimuli. The research cited suggests that formal, as opposed to content, features in general are especially influential with very young children and children with little television viewing experience. Comprehension of formal features was found to increase with age. It is also suggested that formal features may affect behaviors such as persistence, activity level, and aggression and may be more influential than violent content in eliciting certain behaviors. The paper suggests that more research in these areas is necessary to clarify these results.

79. Temporal Integration and Inferences About Televised Social Behavior. Collins, W. Andrew, Mar 1977, 12p. Paper presented at the Biennial Meeting of the Society for Research in Child Development (New Orleans, LA, March 17–20, 1977) (ED 140 962; Reprint: EDRS).

Discusses research on age-related aspects of children's processing and comprehension of the narrative content of family oriented television programs. In one study, the temporal integration necessary to make inferences about audiovisually presented information was examined in 254 second-, fifth- and eighth-grade children. Subjects were shown one of four versions of an edited television program, each presenting different processing demands in terms of the number and organization of scenes. Afterwards, memory for explicitly portrayed events and implied information was tested. Results indicated that older children made better use of information conveyed by order than younger children, especially younger boys. In a second study, second grade children were shown one of two family situation comedites: one portraying a working class family and one portraying a middle class family. Results of two memory tests indicated that children who saw the show that portrayed characters and settings similar to their own class background inferred emotional states and relations better than those for whom the show represented higher or lower class settings. Another study indicated that information integration was more difficult when a commercial separated an action and its consequences. Further research is suggested.

80. Two Dream Machines: Television and the Human Brain. Deming, Caren J. May 1979, 32p. Paper presented at the Annual Meeting of the International Communication Association (Philadelphia, PA, May 1–5, 1979) (ED 172 299; Reprint: EDRS).

Research into brain physiology and dream psychology have helped to illuminate the biological purposes and processes of dreaming. Physical and functional characteristics shared by dreaming and television include the perception of visual and auditory images, operation in a binary mode, and the encoding of visual information. Research is needed in the following areas: the effects of heavy television viewing on the brain's internal scanning mechanism or firing pattern; the effect of exposure to television's heavily saturated, luminous colors on the colors experienced in dreams; the relationship between experiences in dreaming and viewing by comparing electro-encephalographic recordings during rapid eye movement (REM) sleep and during television viewing; the capability of television viewing to stimulate a mental state between waking and dreaming; the relationship between perceptions in dreams and on television and its implications for visual literacy; comparison of dream content to television content; the programming; and the possibility that television is capable of bypassing conscious processing and implanting images directly into the unconscious.

BOOKS

81. Children Communicating: Media and Development of Thought, Speech, Understanding. Wartella, Ellen, ed. Beverly Hills, CA: Sage Publications, 1979, 286p (Sage Annual Reviews of Communication Research, Volume 7).

Investigations of the growth of children's communicative behavior and ability, in terms of their interactions with media and their communication with other people, are described in this book. The first chapter presents an overview of the studies, explains the developmental perspective that characterizes them, and identifies some issues fundamental to studying how children communicate as they grow older. The remaining eight chapters report research results relating to the following topics: children's comprehension of television content; the way media symbols partake in the development of children's abilities; children's television attention patterns; children's understanding of television characters; the development of communication in children; language and cognition in the developing child; a model for assessing mass media effects, and its application in determining how adolescents are affected by media content related to their stage in the life cycle; and the young child as a consumer.

82. The Television Experience: What Children See.
Winick, Mariann P.; Winick, Charles. Beverly Hills, CA: Sage Publications, 1979, 215p.

This study was undertaken in order to explore the television experience within a developmental framework. The kind and degree of similarities and dissimilarities between television viewing by adults and children of different ages (2–15), as reflected in what they see on the screen, provided age-stage related data in six areas: fantasy, believability, identification, humor, morality, and violence. As a means of maximizing the "ordinariness" of the situation, children were interviewed in their own homes, at a time generally used for viewing television.

The central finding is that on aspects of television experience, such as expectancy and developmental readiness to be aware of kinds of content, children differ from adults. Furthermore, children are not a single entity but a series of different groups with the four basic age breaks (preschool, 7–9, 10–12, 13+) representing one possible way of regarding the developmental progression. Because of the enormous range covered in the preschool years, further subdivision of it into two to three and four to six year old groups is useful. Differences among groups, or the maturational differential, apply to all the epochs studied. That approximately similar patterns of development were found in all the ethnic, racial, and socioeconomic groups studied provides additional clues to their possible validity.

THE IMPACT OF TELEVISION ON CHILDREN AND ADOLESCENTS

General Reports

JOURNAL ARTICLES

83. Anik I and Isolation: Television in the Lives of Canadian Eskimos—The Far North. Coldevin, Gary O. *Journal of Communication.* v27, n4, p145–53, Fall 1977 (EJ 200 969; Reprint: UMI).

Describes the impact of the expanded availability of television as a result of the Anik I satellite transmission system on the Canadian Eskimo. Adults are shown to have an increased knowledge of national and international affairs. Indicates critical social and psychological effects on Eskimo children, while adults have retained traditional social customs and environment.

84. Can Watching TV Be Good for Children? Quisenberry, Nancy L.; Klasek, Charles B. *Audiovisual Instruction.* v22, n3, p56–57, Mar 1977.

This is a critique of an article by Nancy Larrick (*Teacher*, Sep 1975, pp75–7) which identified characteristics of children who watch television. The authors insist that characteristics such as short attention span, love of noise, poor sleeping patterns, worldliness, and lack of respect for elders cannot be blamed solely on television.

85. Children and Television. Feinbloom, Richard I. *School Media Quarterly.* v5, n3, p171–74, Spr 1977 (EJ 168 237; Reprint: UMI).

Television in the home and its effects on violent behavior and faulty nutritional patterns as seen by a pediatrician.

86. Children and Television: The Electronic Fix. Kittrell, Ed. *Children Today.* v7, n3, p20,24–25,36–37, May–Jun 1978 (EJ 182 020; Reprint: UMI).

Compares the experience of television watching, especially by young children, with that of drug-taking. Both actions serve to remove children from their environment and both are basically passive states. Discusses the issues of television violence and advertising.

87. Children's Hypervideo Neurosis. Ferullo, Robert J. *USA Today.* v107, n2408, p56–58, May 1979 (EJ 212 003; Reprint: UMI).

Excessive television viewing in the formative years can complicate, if not paralyze, children's psychological development and educational achievement. It distorts their perceptions of reality and it causes them to be overactive, overanxious, and inattentive.

88. An Educator Looks at Home Television—TV or Not TV: That Is the Question. Wagner, Hilmar. *Education.* v99, n3, p303–08, Spr 1979 (EJ 203 595; Reprint: UMI).

The strengths and weaknesses of home television are examined from a developmental point of view, and recommendations for action by educators and parents are made. Strengths considered are educational growth, aesthetic development, and entertainment. Weaknesses discussed include television violence and aggressive behavior, passivity by viewer, and the limiting of socialization. Recommendations are made to parents and educators on improving television.

89. Fearing Television: A Short History of Media Criticism Gone Awry. Morrow, James. *Media and Methods.* v16, n2, p24–26, Oct 1979 (EJ 209 307; Reprint: UMI).

Argues that television viewing may not be as harmful to children as its critics imply. Reviews earlier, similar criticisms of comic books, radio, and motion pictures to illustrate the point.

90. How Television Is Changing Our Children. Chamberlin, Leslie J.; Chambers, Norman. *Clearing House.* v50, n2, p53–57, Oct 1979.

The effects of television on young viewers has assumed immense importance due to the central role of viewing in their lives. This article examines the results of an in-depth exposure of young children to television viewing in terms of knowledge, school achievement, social attitudes, self image, socialization, desensitization to violence, and increased aggression.

91. The Impact of Television on American Institutions. Comstock, George. *Journal of Communication.* v28, n2, p12–28, Spr 1978 (EJ 193 841; Reprint: UMI).

Reviews the influence of 25 years of television on family life and the socialization of children; church and religion; enforcement of laws and norms; mass media and leisure; public security; and politics and public affairs.

92. The Impact of Television Usage on Emerging Adolescents. Van Hoose, John H. *High School Journal.* v63, n6, p239–43, Mar 1980 (EJ 226 971; Reprint: UMI).

The author presents ways in which media, especially television, affect social processes in early adolescence (ages 10 to 15). Research is reported which substantiates social characteristics which may emerge as a direct result of media influence.

93. The Medium and the Message: Effects of Television on Children: ERIC/RCS Report. Dietrich, Daniel; Ladevich, Laurel. *Language Arts.* v54, n2, p196–204, Feb 1977.

This review describes findings about the nature of the television viewing experience, details some of the harmful effects which television can have on children, discusses research on the beneficial effects of several specific educational programs, and suggests directions for teacher action.

94. TV's Effect on Children: An Opinion Survey of Pediatricians. Bruyn, Henry B. *Journal of School Health.* v48, n8, p474–76, Oct 1978 (EJ 197 186; Reprint: UMI).

The results of a mail survey of northern California pediatricians' views of TV programing policy as it relates to children are reported.

95. Television and the Urban Child: Some Educational Policy Implications. Berry, Gordon L. *Education and Urban Society.* v10, n1, p31–54, Nov 1977.

This paper looks at the nature and needs of the inner-city child, the inner-city school, and the effects of commercial television on the self-concept and social values of the urban, disadvantaged child. Educational policy and curricular efforts are recommended for helping these children to understand and deal with television.

96. Television: The Preschooler's First Classroom. Graves, Sherryl Browne. *Phaedrus.* v5, n1, p5–8, Spr 1978.

Notes television's potential educational and socializing effects on children in light of the amount of children's viewing time and their sensitivity to nonverbal communications; the ease with which these factors influence children is considered. The effects of commercials and televised violence are cited, as is television's ability to influence behavior and cognitive functioning.

97. Video Valhalla and Open Education. Whaley, Charles R.; Antonelli, George A. *Phi Delta Kappan.* v61, n3, p171–72, Nov 1979 (EJ 210 981; Reprint: UMI).

When parents and educators are dismayed by the younger generation's declining skills, future orientation, and interest in success; they should direct their concern to the interplay between "video Valhalla," narcissistic consumerism, and open education in today's enculturative processes.

98. What Parents Say about Children's TV. Safran, Claire. *Redbook.* v153, p50,155–58,162, Oct 1979.

More than 6,000 parents answered "Redbook's" questionnaire about children's television. This article summarizes their responses about what's right and what's wrong with TV commercials and programs, and how they deal with it.

99. The World through Five-Year-Old Eyes. Van Camp, Sarah S. *Childhood Education.* v54, n5, p246–50, Mar 1978 (EJ 178 109; Reprint: UMI).

Presents results from interviews with kindergarten children about their television program preferences and their understanding of the news, and reactions from the teachers of these children. Also discusses some effects of violence in television programming and comments on how parents and teachers can counter these effects.

MICROFICHE

100. Children's Television Programming and Public Broadcasting: An Analysis and Assessment of Needs, Final Report. Seaver, Judith W.; Weber, Stephen J., Market Facts, Washington, DC, Jan 1979, 264p. Sponsoring agency: Corporation for Public Broadcasting, Washington, DC. (ED 178 046; Reprint: EDRS). Executive Summary available as ED 178 047, 43p.

Designed to serve as a resource book to promote informed decision making by Corporation for Public Broadcasting (CPB) staff and advisory panels, this study reviews and analyzes the topic of children's public television viewing. Both instructional and more general types of programming for children are examined; however, information relevant only for commercial children's television is excluded. Information was collected through interviews, site visits, and reference research; and data are displayed in tabular form throughout the report. Five broad content topics comprise the body of the report: children and television-content analysis; television series for children; program utilization and needs assessment; constituent concerns; and alternatives and options for CPB action. Information sources are listed, and the appendices include a course distribution comparative survey of five national agencies.

101. Children's Television: The Best of ERIC. Clark, Richard E., Syracuse University, NY. ERIC Clearinghouse on Information Resources, 1978, 76p. Sponsoring agency: National Institute of Education (DHEW), Washington, DC (ED 152 254; Reprint: EDRS; also available from Syracuse University Printing Services, 125 College Place, Syracuse, NY 13210).

This is the most recent in a series of retrospective bibliographies on television and children. It includes an annotated listing of research reviews, position papers, and planning documents entered in the ERIC system in the years 1974–1977. Over 100 documents are listed in 14 categories: helping children to learn from television, new experimental programs, the effects of television on the learning of social behaviors, cognitive effects of television on children, effects of televised commercials, current issues in research design and methodology, useful reviews of research and bibliographires, using television in the classroom, current television treatment of minorities and women, television in helping children learn to read, consumer action group activities, current federal policies, children's television outside the United States, and television and the handicapped or gifted child. Cross references are provided at the end of each section.

102. The Impact of Television: A Natural Experiment Involving Three Communities. Williams, Tannis MacBeth. May 1979, 27p. Paper presented at the Annual Meeting of the International Communication Association (Philadelphia, PA, May 1–5, 1979) (ED 172 293; Reprint: EDRS).

The five research papers that comprise this document report on research into the impact of the inception of television reception on residents of a Canadian town, "Notel." The introductory section tells how Notel and two other similar Canadian towns that already had television reception were studied just before Notel received television reception in 1973, and again two years later; the section also explains the cross-sectional and longitudinal comparisons that were made in the research. The research papers separately outline findings on the impact of television on children's aggressive behavior, reading skills, cognitive development, and sex role perceptions, as well as on residents' participation in community activities. The findings presented suggest that television viewing may result in the following: increases in children's physical and verbal aggression; decreases in reading skills, varying by sex and grade level; decreases in some cognitive skills; formation of more traditional sex role attitudes; and decreases in participation in community activities.

103. TV and Kids, Parts I and II. National Public Radio, Washington, DC, Aug 1978, 38p. Programs No. 127 and 128 (ED 165 776; Reprint: EDRS).

In this series of National Public Radio interviews, individuals from education and television broadcasting discuss the use and abuse of television by schools and the influence of television on children in home viewing. It is asserted that television is and will continue to be watched, and therefore it is necessary to learn how to deal with it. By having children view programs, create programs, and read scripts, schools do use television to help teach organizational, creative writing, and reading skills, in addition to critical viewing skills. These interviews noted that: (1) teachers feel that television produces unrealistic competition between the teacher and entertainer; (2) children are able to learn at varying rates from instructional television; (3) children are influenced by television; (4) violence in the media has been replaced by sex, which has proved to be difficult to define; (5) broadcasting networks argue that television productions and stereotypical characters merely reflect social issues; (6) the Parent Teachers Association has issued viewing guides to help parents select productions; and (7) despite discriminatory selection, too much television viewing has an effect on children's ability to develop cognitively or to develop complex skills.

104. Television and Its Viewers: What Social Science Sees. Comstock, George, Rand Corporation, Santa Monica, CA, May 1976, 28p. Paper presented at the Annual Meeting of the Association for Educational Communications and Technology (Anaheim, CA March 28–April 2, 1976). Sponsoring agency: John and Mary R. Markle Foundation, New York, NY (ED 125 573; Reprint: EDRS). For a related document see citation 115.

In light of procedural problems of the social sciences, what is known about television and human behavior was reviewed. It was found that the relevant literature included over 2,300 items of great variety. From the diversity of information considered, the report focused on specific themes which included: (1) the role of television in behavior modification; (2) the influence of television on the way people spend their time; (3) the contribution of television to politics; and (4) what the American public thinks of television. It was concluded that television's effects are many, typically minimal in magnitude, but sometimes major in social importance. Extensive references are also included.

105. Television and the Teacher. Comstock, George, Rand Corporation, Santa Monica, CA, Oct 1976, 19p. Sponsoring agency: John and Mary R. Markle Foundation, New York, NY (ED 134 163; Reprint: EDRS).

Television is a large part of growing up in America, and a part that meshes in various ways with other influences. Teachers should understand it, and as the occasion requires, confront, correct, or take advantage of it. Research on television viewing yields five lessons: (1) Television experience is an individual one, although there are definite patterns related to sex, age, ethnicity, and socioeconomic status; (2) viewing often serves quite specific needs, including information and escapism; (3) the role of television and other mass media changes as children grow; (4) there is evidence that television can influence behavior; and (5) television's influence is at least partly contingent on other communication reaching the young viewer. The weight of evidence is that television is one of many factors that influence the child, and a teacher cannot ignore it. Needed now is research concerning the ways in which teachers might intervene more effectively in the communication between the child and the medium to turn its teachings to constructive ends.

106. Television in American Culture. Hartman, Hermene D. Aug 1977, 17p. Paper presented at the National Teacher Corps Conference (Washington, DC, August 6, 1977) (ED 150 958; Reprint: EDRS).

What is television doing to our society and our culture? What has it done to education? Television has had a great impact on human behavior but rather than communicating, it dictates a philosophy of life, moral judgments and a lifestyle. Television presents a violent image of society where fantasy and reality are often confused. It is a system controlled by only a few, yet the impact of their decisions reaches millions. The most important component, the viewer, is the least heard and the most unrecognized. A constant diet of television affects the cognitive process by eliminating creativity. Commercials preach a philosophy totally unrelated to realistic aspirations. Television has contributed to illiteracy by eliminating critical analysis and original thought. It creates and perpetuates stereotypes. Television news has become a visual newspaper but without the depth necessary for a comprehensive understanding of current events. The general public, and especially parents, have to become aware of the dangers of television. Most important, educators need to demand intelligent programming from the Federal Communications Commission and the stations themselves. Educators must also learn to compete successfully with television in the schools.

107. Trends in the Study of Incidental Learning from Television Viewing. Comstock, George, Syracuse University, NY. ERIC Clearinghouse on Information Resources, 1978, 61p. Sponsoring agency: National Institute of Education (DHEW), Washington, DC (ED 168 605; Reprint: EDRS; also available from Syracuse University Printing Services, 125 College Place, Syracuse, NY 13210 (Order no. IR-30).

Research on incidental learning by children from television is both a cause and effect of the increasing attention being given by social and behavioral scientists to the influence of mass media. Laboratory-type experiments and data collected from everyday life are consistent in their findings, providing convincing evidence that television can influence the immediate behavior of children. When this altered behavior is carried over into social interaction, the foundation is established for more far-reaching influence. Television also has varied cognitive and attitudinal effects on children, e.g., it is their principal source of information on public affairs. Television designed to convey information can be quite effective, and entertainment programs occasionally provide instruction, but their impact is sometimes limited by redundancy with one another. Commercials also instruct children by influencing preferences for the value placed upon products. Tastes and preferences in programing and time spent with the medium change along with individual interests and needs as young people grow older. The study of television's influence requires both laboratory-type experimentation and the collection of data from real life, the former to establish the possibility of causation and the latter to confirm the presence in real life of experimental findings.

BOOKS

108. Children and Television. Brown, Ray, ed. Beverly Hills, CA: Sage Publications, 1976, 368p.

Designed as an overview or text, this volume presents 16 papers representing the last two decades of research on children and television in three areas of inquiry: children's use of television and program preferences; factors which influence the viewing experience; and the impact of television on children's behavior and attitudes. Research methodology is also discussed.

109. Children's Television: An Analysis of Programming and Advertising. Barcus, F. Earle; Wolkin, Rachel. New York: Praeger Publishers, 1977, 218p.

The studies reported in this book are content analyses of children's television and attendant advertising. Following an introductory statement, chapters present data about children's commercial television on the weekends, children's commercial television after school, and the seasonal variations in television advertising to children. A concluding statement says that change is needed and that the industry and the public must question the failure of television to live up to its potential. Nine appendixes of information related to the studies and 122 tables of data are included.

110. Effects and Functions of Television: Children and Adolescents. A Bibliography of Selected Research Literature 1970–78. Meyer, Manfred, Comp.; Nissen, Ursula, Comp. New York: K. G. Saur Publishing, Inc., 1979, 172p (Communication Research and Broadcasting Series, No. 2).

This bibliography of selected television research lists 914 references to English, French, and German publications (empirical studies, research reviews, and summarizing literature) which deal with the use of television and its various functions for children and adolescents and particularly with the effects of television on children's personality and socialization. All of the studies were published from 1970 to about March 1978. Titles of each entry are in English. Contents in 12 sections cover a wide range of topics: bibliographies, mass communication research, general introductory works and literature reviews, studies on the uses and functions of television and other media (including comparisons of various age groups, developmental studies), studies on cognitive and emotional effects and studies on aspects of socialization (including socialization and interaction in the family context). Also cited are studies on the effects of TV violence on social behavior (including the research program of the Surgeon General's Scientific Advisory Committee on Television and Social Behavior), studies of the effects of prosocial content, formative and summative research on television series for children (Sesame Street, The Electric Company, Around the Bend, Carrascolendas, and other series), studies on the effects of news and information programs, studies on the effects of television advertising, and research agenda and recommendations. Entries are indexed by author and subject.

111. **Public Perceptions of Television and Other Mass Media: A Twenty-Year Review 1959–1978.** Roper, Burns W. New York: The Television Information Office, 1979, 24p.

This synopsis of 20 years of media study examines public preferences for different news media, belief in media credibility, use of media in election years, and attitudes toward TV commercials and programing. Results show that television is holding its lead position with the American public in terms of its credibility and choice as a news source. Little favor was found for government control of television and little evidence of an increase in criticism of children's programing and advertising.

112. **Remote Control: Television and the Manipulation of American Life.** Mankiewicz, Frank; Swerdlow, Joel. New York: Times Books, 1978, 308p.

This book examines the distortions and dysfunctions commercial television has introduced into American life. Through both anecdotal and scholarly evidence, it describes how television teaches crime and violence, how the "family hour" is a network sham, how television news invents priorities, how it has first promoted then repressed racial and sexual liberation, how it positively and negatively affects reading and school achievement, how TV commercials create consumers, and, finally, how TV news distorts perceptions of social reality.

113. **The Show and Tell Machine: How Television Works and Works You Over.** Goldsen, Rose K. New York: Dial Press, 1977, 427p.

The pervasiveness and sameness of television tend to numb individual consciousness and present fragmented, standardized cultural perceptions. The author's analysis is largely based on a content study of the 1974–75 television season. Data are provided in extensive appendices.

114. **Television and Children.** Howe, Michael J. London: New University Education, 1977, 157p.

In seven chapters, the author collates and examines available evidence from British and American studies about television's various influences on children: their viewing habits, the kind of world which is presented to them, informal learning from viewing, violence, programs for children, television as a teaching aid, and problems which have arisen from the effects of television viewing.

115. **Television and Human Behavior.** Comstock, George et al. New York: Columbia University Press, 1978, 510p. For a related document see citation 103.

To compile a comprehensive review of English language scientific literature regarding the effects of television on human behavior, the authors of this book evaluated more than 2,500 books, articles, reports, and other documents. The book discusses television research according to the following topics: an overview, past and future; content analysis of various program types; audience analysis; television in everyday life; the effect of television on children and other specific audiences; television in politics and advertising; the psychology of behavioral effects; and the future of television. In addition to a lengthy reference section, the book provides a name and subject index.

Television as a Behavior Model: Sex and Violence or Prosocial Learning?

JOURNAL ARTICLES

116. **Aggression on TV Could Be Helping Our Children.** Lopiparo, Jerome J. *Intellect.* v105, n2383, p345–46, Apr 1977 (EJ 165 217; Reprint: UMI).

The author asserts that the experience of aggression is a necessary part of child development; that all humans have a potential for violence, with or without TV; and that the expression of this aggression is not only normal but, in many respects, beneficial.

117. **Children's Emotional Reactions to TV Violence—Effects of Film Character, Reassurance, Age, and Sex.** Surbeck, Elaine; Endsley, Richard D. *Journal of Social Psychology.* v109, n2, p269–81, Dec 1979.

Sixty-four American children, 32 between four and six years of age and 32 between eight and eleven years of age, were each shown two three-minute video episodes containing exactly the same series of violent acts. However, one of the violent episodes (HV) involved human actors while the other

(PV) involved puppets. The results clearly indicated that HV was judged to be "scarier" than PV. Girls also reported being more scared by both episodes, particularly HV, than the boys. Verbal reassurance proved effective in reducing the HV and PV scariness ratings made by the older children. However, with the younger children, reassurance entered into a complex interaction with the orders of presenting the two episodes.

118. Children's Perceptions of "Comic" and "Authentic" Cartoon Violence. Haynes, Richard B. *Journal of Broadcasting*. v22, n1, p63–70, Win 1978 (EJ 183 874; Reprint: UMI).

Results of this study indicate that violent content in comic cartoon programs is recognized as violent by children and not regarded as merely humorous.

119. Children's Television Viewing Habits and Prosocial Behavior: A Field Correlational Study. Sprafkin, Joyce N.; Rubinstein, Eli A. *Journal of Broadcasting*. v23, n3, p265–76, Sum 1979 (EJ 209 910; Reprint: UMI).

Questionnaires were given to second, third, and fourth graders examining relationships between television viewing habits and prosocial behavior. Results indicated the fewer programs watched and the more prosocial their content, the more likely a child was to exhibit prosocial behavior. Each variable accounted for about 1 percent of the variance.

120. A Consumer Model for TV Audiences: The Case of TV Violence. Robinson, Deanna C. et al. *Communication Research—An International Quarterly*. v6, n2, p181–202, Apr 1979.

Explores attitudes toward television violence and censorship, using a consumer behavior model. Findings suggest that support for the anti-television-violence campaign is not universal and that excessive violence is only one of four distinct viewer complaints about television programs.

121. Cultural Indicators: Violence Profile No. 9. Gerbner, George et al. *Journal of Communication*. v28, n3, p176–207, Sum 1978 (EJ 195 924; Reprint: UMI).

Describes the most recent phase of the long-range research called "cultural indicators" which yields an annual television violence profile. This report stresses methodology, current (1977) findings on the distribution of power in the world of television drama, and some behavioral and attitudinal correlates of viewing.

122. The Demonstration of Power: Violence Profile No. 10. Gerbner, George et al. *Journal of Communication*. v29, n3, p177–96, Sum 1979 (EJ 217 491; Reprint: UMI).

Annual progress report sums up findings suggesting that fear and inequity may be television's most pervasive lessons. 1978 Index shows violence up in children's hours.

123. Desensitization to Portrayals of Real-Life Aggression as a Function of Television Violence. Thomas, Margaret H. et al. *Journal of Personality and Social Psychology*. v35, n6, p450–58, Jun 1977.

In two separate experiments, the hypothesis that exposure to violence in the context of television drama decreases subjects' emotional responsivity to portrayals of real-life aggression was tested. Subjects were shown either an excerpt from a violent police drama or a segment of an exciting but nonviolent volleyball game before watching a videotaped scene of real aggression. Emotionality was measured by changes in skin resistance. In Experiment One, subjects were eight- to ten-year-old children and the real aggression was a film of an argument and fight between two preschoolers. In Experiment Two, reactions to real aggression were measured while college students watched scenes from news films of the riots at the 1968 Democratic National Convention. With the exception of adult females, subjects who previously had viewed the aggression drama were less aroused by the scenes of real aggression than were subjects who had seen the control film. Further support for the hypothesis was provided by the finding that for most groups of subjects, the amount of television violence normally viewed was negatively related to responsivity while viewing aggression.

124. Differential Racial Patterns of School Discipline during the Broadcasting of "Roots." Ryback, David; Connell, Robert H. *Psychological Reports*. v42, n2, p514, Apr 1978.

Two Georgia high schools were surveyed about disciplinary problems before, during, and after the broadcast of the Black history drama "Roots." Detentions of Black students increased significantly during the broadcast.

125. Does Television Violence Enhance Program Popularity? Diener, Ed; DeFour, Darlene. *Journal of Personality and Social Psychology*. v36, n3, p333–41, Mar 1978.

Two studies were conducted to explore the effects of fictional television violence on adventure show popularity. In Study One the amount of violence occurring within 62 episodes of 11 programs was correlated with the national Nielsen viewer index. A very low and nonsignificant relationship emerged. In addition, student raters' perceptions of the programs were factor analyzed. A violence factor emerged, but reported liking for programs did not load substantially on this factor. Study Two was an experiment in which an adventure program ("Police Woman") was presented to subjects either uncut or with the violence deleted. Although the uncut version was perceived as significantly more violent, it was not liked significantly more. The violence condition accounted for approximately 1 percent of the variance in reported liking. There is presently little evidence indicating that violence enhances program popularity.

126. The Effect of Television Violence on the Perceptions of Crime by Adolescents. Teevan, James J.; Hartnagel, Timothy F. *Sociology & Social Research.* v60, n3, p337–48, Apr 1976.

It is hypothesized that individuals who prefer violent television shows will perceive more real-life crime and react more defensively to protect themselves from that crime than individuals who choose less violent shows. These effects should be greater for those people who not only watch but also perceive their favorite shows as violent. The data from secondary students give only weak support to these hypotheses. Several reasons for the weak relationships are discussed.

127. The Effects of Commercial Interruption of Violent and Nonviolent Films on Viewers' Subsequent Aggression. Worchel, Stephen et al. *Journal of Experimental Social Psychology.* v12, n2, p220–32, Mar 1976.

Aggressive responses of college students following the viewing of violent and nonviolent films were studied. Groups of subjects saw one of three full-length films: (1) a staged violent film, (2) a realistic violent film, or (3) a nonviolent film. For half of the groups of subjects, films were interrupted periodically by sets of commercials. Results confirmed predictions that aggressive responses will be greater after viewing aggressive films than nonaggressive films, and that aggressive responses will be greater if films are interrupted by commercials than when not interrupted. No differences in aggressiveness following presentation of realistic and staged violent films were found.

128. The Effects of Televised Consequences of Aggression upon Physiological Arousal (Heart Rate). Wotring, C. Edward; Porter, D. Thomas. *Communication Quarterly.* v26, n2, p57–63, Spr 1978 (EJ 193 892; Reprint: UMI).

Describes a study using heart rate as an index of autonomic arousal to measure the effects on television viewers of depicting the consequences of violence, violence with no consequences, and nonviolence. Supports the conclusion that specific content manipulations of aggressive stimuli affect levels of arousal: viewing consequences significantly inhibited arousal, while viewing violence without consequences or viewing nonviolence significantly increased arousal.

129. The Effects of Television on the Prosocial Behavior of Young Children. Moore, Shirley G. *Young Children.* v32, n5, p60–65, Jul 1977.

Reports research on the effects of television, particularly educational shows such as ''Sesame Street'' and ''Misterogers' Neighborhood,'' on the prosocial behavior of young children.

130. The Effects of TV Program Pacing on the Behavior of Preschool Children. Anderson, Daniel R. et al. *AV Communication Review.* v25, n2, p159–66, Sum 1977 (EJ 166 429; Reprint: UMI).

Assertions that television shows (''Sesame Street'' in particular) produce hyperactivity, impulsivity, disorganized behavior, and shortened attention spans in preschool children were investigated. No evidence was found that rapid television pacing has an immediate negative impact on behavior of preschool children.

131. An Examination of Three Models of Television Viewing and Aggression. Watt, James H., Jr.; Krull, Robert. *Human Communication Research.* v3, n2, p99–112, Win 1977.

Three general models of the relationship between television viewing and aggressiveness are described: the facilitation model, featuring learning or legitimization of aggression from television violence; the catharsis model, or the reduction of innate aggressive drives through vicarious participation in television violence; and the arousal model, which considers television programing as an agent of arousal, generating a drive toward activity, with the nature of the activity determined by situational factors. The arousal model is further discriminated into an emotional arousal model and form arousal model. The facilitation, catharsis, and form arousal models are contrasted on a sample of 597 adolescents. The results indicate independent facilitation and form arousal processes occur. A rather startling result is the finding that levels of aggressiveness can be predicted as well by examining only the form of programing as they can by examining only the violent content. Age and sex differences are associated with different strengths of facilitation and/or form arousal effects, indicating possible socialization or maturation processes affecting the response of adolescents to programing.

132. Favorite TV Characters as Behavioral Models for the Emotionally Disturbed. Donohue, Thomas R. *Journal of Broadcasting.* v21, n3, p333–45, Sum 1977 (EJ 190 915; Reprint: UMI).

Discusses research on how television affects standards of conduct and behavior. Overall finding is that television provides mostly innocuous behavioral models for emotionally disturbed children, supporting the notion that emotionally disturbed children are less inclined than normal children to accept adult or authoritarian figure influence.

133. The Gerbner Violence Profile. Blank, David M. *Journal of Broadcasting.* v21, n3, p273–79, Sum 1977 (EJ 190 911; Reprint: UMI).

Reviews the current ''Violence Profile'' (number 8) which reports on fall 1976 television network programing. The discussion includes comment on the violence index and the risk ratio sections of the profile, but does not cover the third section of Gerbner's profile, the cultivation index.

134. The Gerbner Violence Profile—An Analysis of the CBS Report. *Journal of Broadcasting.* v21, n3, p280–86, Sum 1977 (EJ 190 912; Reprint: UMI).

The Cultural Indicators Research Team's analysis of the CBS report suggests that the Gerbner violence profile is defined too broadly and composed of an arbitrary set of measures;

employs faulty units of analysis; is inadequate on the basis of time sampled; and measures relative rather than absolute victimization, which probably does not correspond to viewers' perceptions.

135. The Great American Teaching Machine—Of Violence. Skornia, Harry J. *Intellect*. v105, n2383, p347–48, Apr 1977 (EJ 165 218; Reprint: UMI).

The author believes that commercial television is a dangerous, criminal, and inexcusable threat to America, responsible for many of the disasters our nation is experiencing. He calls the U.S. Surgeon General's report on television and violence a ''scandal'' and suggests that citizens combat TV violence through consumer boycotts of violent television shows.

136. How to Cope with Violence on the Tube. Patterson, Amos C.; Neustadter, Cheri. *Audiovisual Instruction*. v23, n6, p40–42, Sep 1978 (EJ 187 107; Reprint: UMI).

Discusses relevant theories and research on the effects of television violence on child behavior. Six measures which a media specialist may take to assure that this complex, controversial issue is examined properly in the school environment are discussed.

137. Mass Media and Psychiatric Disturbance. Frazier, Shervert H. *Psychiatric Journal of the University of Ottawa*. v1, n4, p171–72, Dec 1976.

This examination of the relationship between television and violence suggests that children may be more disturbed by violence on news broadcasts than by fictional violence, since the former is often local, involves real people, and rarely shows the aggressor being punished, as television drama usually does.

138. Perceived TV Reality as a Predictor of Children's Social Behavior. Reeves, Byron. *Journalism Quarterly*. v55, n4, p682–89,695, Win 1978 (EJ 201 122; Reprint: UMI).

Results of a study conducted with 721 fourth, sixth, and eighth graders did not support certain assumptions about the impact of exposure to television on children's social behavior: Perceiving TV programs to be real increased the incidence of prosocial behavior and decreased the incidence of antisocial behavior.

139. Perceptions of TV Program Violence by Children and Mothrs. Abel, John D.; Beninson, Maureen E. *Journal of Broadcasting*. v20, n3, p355–63, Sum 1976.

A survey of 235 fifth- and sixth-grade children and their mothers gathered data to compare children's perception of television violence with that of their mother.

140. Physical Contact and Sexual Behavior on Prime-Time TV. Silverman, L. Theresa et al. *Journal of Communication*. v29, n1, p33–43, Win 1979 (EJ 207 857; Reprint: UMI).

Presents data on the kinds of physically intimate and sexual behaviors dealt with on prime-time television during the 1977–78 season. Results indicate an increasing tendency to tease the audience behaviorally (through flirting), verbally (through innuendo), and visually (through contextually implied intercourse).

141. Portrayal of Prosocial and Aggressive Behaviors in Children's TV Commercials. Schuetz, Stephen; Sprafkin, Joyce N. *Journal of Broadcasting*. v23, n1, p33–40, Win 1979 (EJ 203 513; Reprint: UMI).

Presents a content analysis of the prosocial and aggressive content of a sample of child-oriented television commercials and compares the results with a similarly conducted study of child-oriented television programs.

142. Prime Time Television: A Profile of Aggressive and Prosocial Behaviors. Harvey, Susan E. et al. *Journal of Broadcasting*. v23, n2, p179–89, Spr 1979 (EJ 205 228; Reprint: UMI).

Analyzes the manner in which prosocial behaviors are currently presented on entertainment television, including various categories of prosocial behavior in a detailed profile of a sample week of prime-time television, and seeks to determine the positive behaviors performed, their frequency, on what types of programs, on what time slot, on which networks, and by what character types.

143. Problem-Solving in TV Shows Popular with Children: Assertion vs. Aggression. Dominick, Joseph R. et al. *Journalism Quarterly*. v56, n3, p455–63, Fall 1979 (EJ 214 185; Reprint: UMI).

A content analysis of the 23 prime-time and Saturday morning television programs most popular with children suggested that in prime-time programs assertive and helping behavior were more frequent than aggression in efforts to solve problems, but that the rate of aggression was higher in Saturday programs.

144. Relationship of TV-Viewing to Violence and Aggression. Quisenberry, Nancy L. et al. *Childhood Education*. v55, n1, p59–64, Oct 1978.

This review of research literature on violence and television details some major studies and attempts to clarify some of their contradictory findings. Considered are effects on children's aggressive behavior, with special attention to cartoons and socioeconomic factors, and the catharsis theory, which postulates that viewing violence reduces aggression in the observer.

145. Research: Television Violence and Aggressive Behavior. Wurtzel, Alan. *ETC.: A Review of General Semantics*. v34, n2, p212–25, Jun 1977 (EJ 209 349; Reprint: UMI).

Summarizes the major research findings on the relationship between television violence and aggressive behavior, concluding that the evidence points strongly to a link between the two.

146. Resolving Conflict: Methods Used by TV Characters and Teenage Viewers. Roloff, Michael E.; Greenberg, Bradley S. *Journal of Broadcasting.* v23, n3, p285–300, Sum 1979 (EJ 209 912; Reprint: UMI).

Tested hypotheses that action/adventure characters are perceived by teenagers as likely to engage in antisocial conflict resolution; situation comedy/family drama characters, in prosocial modes. Also tested was hypothesis that, as favorite character's perceived use of a mode increases, so does the viewer's intention to use the same mode.

147. Sex and Violence: Can Research Have It Both Ways? Dienstbier, Richard A. *Journal of Communication.* v27, n3, p176–88, Sum 1977 (EJ 165 686; Reprint: UMI).

Using a social learning model the author analyzes the conflicting findings of the Surgeon General's Scientific Advisory Committee on Television and Social Behavior and of the Commission on Obscenity and Pornography. The former commission reported that overexposure to violence in the media increased aggression in children. The latter group found that known sex offenders generally experienced underexposure to sexually explicit materials and sexual knowledge during adolescence.

148. TV Violence and Viewer Aggression: A Cumulation of Study Results 1956–1976. Andison, F. Scott. *Public Opinion Quarterly.* v41, n3, p314–31, Fall 1977 (EJ 173 391; Reprint: UMI). For a related document see citation 206.

Supports the view that television violence increases viewers' levels of aggression, advocating the reduction in amounts of violence portrayed on television programs. A chart summarizes 23 studies in chronological order.

149. TV Violence Assailed. *NJEA Review.* v50, n5, p12–13,44, Jan 1977.

Does watching violence on the television screen teach children to be violent? More and more people think it does. Protests by the PTA and other national organizations are cited.

150. Teenage Violence and the Telly. Muson, Howard. *Psychology Today.* v11, n10, p50–51, 53–54, Mar 1978. For a related document see citation 206.

A six-year study of 1,565 teenage boys in London, conducted by William Belson and sponsored by CBS, found strong links between long-term exposure to television violence and delinquent behaviors. Television stories presenting violence in a very realistic fashion tended to increase actual violence.

151. Televised Violence and Paranoid Perception: The View from Great Britain. Wober, J. J. M. *Public Opinion Quarterly.* v42, n3, p315–21, Fall 1978.

Fails to replicate in Great Britain the results of a United States study showing "paranoid perception"—the association

by teenagers and adults of lifelike television violence with the real world state of affairs. Raises doubts about the original (American) studies.

152. The Television and Delinquency Debate. Murdock, Graham: McCron, Robin. *Screen Education.* n30, p51–67, Spr 1979.

Discusses the continuing debate about the effects of televised violence on viewers, particularly children, in terms of aggressive behavior. The two opposing views, the psychological and the relational, are each supported by research which, in turn, affects the use of censorship.

153. Television Violence and Its Effect on the Young. Styles, Ken; Cavanah, Gray. *California English.* v15, n1, p4–5, Jan 1979.

While science cannot definitively measure the relationship, common sense tells us that, by its ubiquity, by its production techniques, and by its implicit and explicit messages, television can be a powerful force in shaping the viewer's values, including those relating to violence. Censorship has no place in the adult world, but some control is necessary over what is fed the juvenile mind.

154. Television Violence and Viewer Aggression: A Reexamination of the Evidence. Kaplan, Robert M.; Singer, Robert D. *Journal of Social Issues.* v32, n4, p35–70, Fall 1976 (EJ 166 960; Reprint: UMI).

This paper should not be interpreted as stating that TV violence can not cause aggression; rather, it argues that no such link has been demonstrated to date. Further, it questions the applicability of laboratory experimentation for this policy related issue.

155. Television Violence—Reactions from Physicians, Advertisers, and Networks. Feingold, Murray; Johnson, G. Timothy. *New England Journal of Medicine.* v296, n8, p424–27, Feb 24, 1977.

In response to a call for correspondence on television violence, the authors received more than 1,500 letters from physicians. Seventy-two percent of the leading television advertisers responded to a subsequent letter requesting a description of their policies regarding content of the programs they sponsor. Their responses included exculpating factors such as lack of control over programing, the limited amount of available advertising time, and censorship. These responses were presented to network representatives, who commented on the difficulty of defining violence, the current decrease in the amount of violence shown, and their activities in response to this issue.

156. Television Violence, Victimization, and Power. Gerbner, George et al. *American Behavioral Scientist.* v23, n5, p705–16, May–Jun 1980.

The independent contribution of television to the cultivation of assumptions can best be seen in those aspects in which television presents a pattern different from or more extreme than other sources. One such area is of course violence. The results of adult and child surveys show consistent learning and children's particular vulnerability to television. These results also confirm that violence-laden television not only cultivates aggressive tendencies in a minority but, perhaps more important, generates a pervasive and exaggerated sense of danger and mistrust. Heavy viewers revealed a significantly higher sense of personal risk and suspicion than did light viewers in the same demographic groups, exposed to the same real risks of life.

157. Television's Impact on Emotionally Disturbed Children's Value Systems. Donohue, Thomas R. *Child Study Journal.* v8, n3, p187–201, 1978 (EJ 192 901; Reprint: UMI).

This investigation studied the influences of television's behavioral models on institutionalized, emotionally disturbed children between the ages of 6 and 11. Investigated were children's perceptions and judgments of right and wrong, appropriate and inappropriate behaviors by their favorite TV characters, themselves, their friends, and their families.

158. Television's Trying Times. Meyer, Karl E. *Saturday Review.* v5, p19–23, Sep 16, 1978.

Notes the growing trend toward lawsuits against television, as epitomized by the "Born Innocent" case, in which a rape victim's mother sued the network claiming that her daughter's attackers had learned their crime from that television drama. Potential effects of this legal trend on free speech and creativity in television are discussed.

MICROFICHE

159. An Assessment of Variables Associated with Television Viewing and their Influence on Aggressive Behavior of Third Grade Children.* Reynolds, Jean Ellen, Southern Illinois University at Carbondale, 1978, 90p (7908074; Reprint: DC).

Null hypotheses were tested to determine the significance of the effects of each of the following factors on aggressive behavior of third grade children: violence on television, amount of television viewed, Saturday morning cartoons, sex, socio-economic level, and family status. The sample included 108 third grade children. An individual aggression index was determined by having teachers and peers evaluate each child in the classroom on eight behavior items by ranking them on a scale from 0–5.

A listing of weekly television programs was constructed to give hours of viewing. Subjects were interviewed regarding the programs regularly viewed each week. A total score in hours gave the amount of viewing for one week for each child. Separate totals showed hours spent viewing cartoons on Saturday morning.

A violence rating was determined for each child by totaling the hours spent watching violent programs as measured by a combination of national violence ratings and a supplementary list obtained from opinions of a panel of raters. Other information pertinent to the study came from a questionnaire completed by parents.

The factors considered in the study were found to be significant predictors of aggressive behavior in third grade children when considered altogether, but whenever assessed singly there were no significant findings. Data also revealed that third grade children watch an average of 38.1 hours per week, with 3.72 hours of this time spent viewing Saturday morning cartoons. Since none of the single factors assessed in this study was found to contribute significantly to aggressive behavior of third graders, it was concluded that other factors should be considered in future research. It may be implied from the results that such things as parental influence and other environmental contributors are important in developing children's attitudes and behavior.

160. Beyond Entertainment: Television's Effects on Children and Youth. Television and Socialisation Research Report No. 1. 1976, 29p (ED 131 856; Reprint: EDRS).

Recent worldwide studies on the viewing habits of children emphasize the large amount of time spent viewing television and the potential influence that television has to shape the behavior of children. Extensive research has investigated the short- and long-term effects of viewing television violence, and the results, though complex, suggest that children do learn interpersonal behaviors by observing models presented in television programs. Combined with some fundamental principles of social learning, these findings have led to the design and production of interventions aimed at promoting specific educational and social skills. Results of using such interventions show that social behavior can be enhanced by exposure to appropriate role models via television programing.

161. Cartoon Violence and Children's Aggression: A Critical Review. Hapkiewicz, Walter G., Aug 1977, 17p. Paper presented at the Annual Meeting of the American Psychological Association (85th, San Francisco, CA, August 26–30, 1977). Best copy available (ED 147 008; Reprint: EDRS).

This paper reviews 10 studies on the effects of television cartoon violence on aggressive behavior in children and discusses possible reasons for the inconsistent results. Methodology and results of field and laboratory studies are compared and study limitations are noted. The impact of cartoons is discussed in terms of human v animal characters and real v animated filming. In four of these studies, the predicted antisocial effect of viewing violent cartoons was not confirmed. A review of the remaining reports indicated that there may be plausible alternatives to the interpretations suggested by the investigators. Problems associated with interpreting research on children's viewing of aggressive cartoons are discussed.

162. Content Analysis: Television. Williams, Tannis MacBeth et al. May 1979, 24p. Paper presented at the Annual Meeting of the International Communication Association (Philadelphia, PA, May 1–5, 1979) (ED 172 291; Reprint: EDRS).

Content analyses of the depiction of aggression and images of reality on Canadian television were performed on 109 program tapes of top-rated Toronto programs. Content was coded in terms of global messages communicated, character portrayals, context and setting of the program, amount and nature of conflict portrayed, and detailed information on incidents of aggression. Aggression was defined as any behavior that could inflict either physical or psychological harm, and included explicit and implicit threats, nonverbal behaviors, and verbal abuse. Results were as follows: there were 18.5 acts of aggression per program hour; situation comedies led in nonphysical aggression, which, portrayed as funny, excessively distorted patterns of human interaction; aggression was incidental to plot; physical consequences of aggression were seldom shown; aggression, violence, and certain methods of conflict resolution were portrayed almost exclusively and milder forms of conflict and more constructive methods of resolution were rarely seen; characters were most often male, white collar, socially isolated, White, English-speaking North Americans; and police officers were commonly depicted engaging in violent behavior. In comparison to United States findings, Canadian programing was less aggressive in general but slightly higher in verbal/psychological aggression.

163. Crime News Coverage in Perspective. Graber, Doris A. Oct 1977, 33p. Paper presented at the Annual Meeting of the Midwest Association for Public Opinion Research (Chicago, IL, October 27–29, 1977) (ED 151 842; Reprint: EDRS).

According to one sociological model, news is a product of socially determined notions of who and what is important and the organizational structures that result for standardizing news collection; events that deviate from these notions are ignored. This report describes a study of crime news coverage in the media that used this model to examine the determinants of newsmaking, frequency of presentation, prominence of placement, and source of news flow. The data for this study came from a year-long content analysis of six daily newspapers, one weekly paper, and nightly newscasts on three national and two local television stations. The analysis reveals that individual crime receives three to four times as much attention as other issues in all of the news sources considered. The study then evaluated the vast amount of crime news coverage according to three norms: the hierarchy of social significance, the hierarchy of audience preference, and the mirror of society concept. Nine data tables and extensive notes accompany the report.

164. Cultural Pollution and the Productivity of Violence. Gandy, Oscar H., Jr.; Signorielli, Nancy. Aug 1979, 32p. Paper presented at the Annual Meeting of the Association for Education in Journalism (62nd, Houston, TX, August 5–8, 1979) (ED 177 568; Reprint: EDRS).

A study was conducted in which half-hour segments of prime-time network dramatic programing were tabulated for such violence-related items as: the seriousness and significance of violence, the number of violent actions in the program, and the duration of violence. Other factors considered were: audience size, share of audience, program duration, program type, program tone, format, and time of broadcast. This consideration of how one dimension of program content (violence) affects audience size indicated that violence measures accounted for little more than 5 percent of the variance in audience shares, an additional 4 percent during nonfamily hour programs, and 55 percent when the focus was only on feature films.

165. The Effects of Action and Violence in Television Programs on the Social Behavior and Imaginative Play of Preschool Children. Huston-Stein, Aletha et al. Mar 1978, 18p. Paper presented at the meeting of the Southwestern Society for Research in Human Development (Dallas, TX, March 1978).

The independent contributions of action and violence in television programs to children's attention and social behavior were investigated. Pairs of preschool children were assigned to one of these television conditions: (1) high action-high violence, (2) high action-low violence, (3) low action-low violence, or (4) no television. Action was defined as rapid movement by characters or objects; violence was physical aggression by characters. Visual attention was greater in high action than in low action programs; there were no differences in attention as a function of violence when action was controlled. Children were observed in free play sessions before and after viewing. Those who saw low action-low violence television or no television increased in imaginative, fantasy play: those who saw high action-high violence decreased in imaginative play; the high action-low violence group fell in between. There was some tendency for aggressive behavior to follow the opposite pattern—higher aggression following high action-high violence or high action-low violence than after low action-low violence or no television. There were no differences in activity level as a function of treatment. These results were interpreted as supporting arousal theory more strongly than observational learning theory.

166. Effects of Peer Pressure and Prosocial/Antisocial Television Content on Children's Prosocial Behavior. Tannenbaum, Barbara Irene, University of Massachusetts, 1976, 122p (77-6430; Reprint: DC).

This study measured the effects on children's behavior of peer influence and prosocial and antisocial television messages. The subjects, 120 children in second, third, and fourth grades, were placed in different situations: one in which no television was viewed, one in which an excerpt from a television program portraying violence was viewed, and one in which an excerpt from a television program with a prosocial message was viewed. For each of the three viewing situations, four variables of peer influence were tested: no peers present, peers present but silent, peers encouraging prosocial behavior, and peers encouraging antisocial behavior. Analysis of the findings indicated that the highest level of prosocial responses occurred in the group seeing the prosocial television segment with peers encouraging the prosocial response and that the lowest level of prosocial responses occurred in the group seeing the antisocial television segment with peers encouraging the antisocial response.

167. Emotion as a Means of Dramaturgy. (Summary of Prix Jeunesse Seminar, Munich, Germany, June 18–20, 1979). Jun 1979, 59p. Sponsoring agency: Prix Jeunesse Foundation, Munich, Germany (ED 175 561; Reprint: EDRS).

This collection of seminar papers is concerned with the presentation of emotions on the screen, the emotional impact of such presentations on young children, and the use of children's televised drama to foster the development of emotional sensitivity. Also considered are differences in the violence depicted on Japanese and American television, and areas in which researchers and producers can cooperate to reach common objectives. Two of the papers present analyses of a children's cartoon serial named "Heidi" and the real-life film titled "Big Henry and the Polka Dot Kid." One of the analyses is an interaction analysis of social behavior and the other is a psychological analysis. Other papers present a developmental view of the impact of television on children's emotions; a discussion of the differences between real drama and kitsch; a description of the use of children's television drama in the East German television organization to develop and educate children's emotions; a comparison of pain, aggression, and identification with aggressors and victims on television in Japan and America, accompanied by a discussion of possible reasons for the differing crime trends in the two countries; and an outline of emerging areas for cooperation between educators and television producers. A brief summary of the main points of the group discussions in the seminar is provided, along with a list of the participants and their addresses.

168. Emotional Effects of Televised Violence.† Geen, Russell G., Missouri University, Columbia, Department of Psychology; National Science Foundation, Washington, DC, Engineering and Applied Science, Nov 1978, 39p (PB 80-174451; Reprint: NTIS).

A series of experiments was conducted to test for possible effects of TV violence on emotions and verbal-attitudinal behavior motivated by emotional reactions. In three of these studies, some support was found for the hypothesis that exposure to TV violence set in a realistic contemporary urban setting can elicit emotional arousal attributable to socially conditioned fear.

169. Equilibration and Sensory Overload in the Pre-School Child: Some Effects of Children's Television Programming. Miller, Thomas W., Sep 1979, 20p. Paper presented at the Annual Meeting of the American Psychological Association (87th, New York, NY, September 1–5, 1979) (ED 179 286; Reprint: EDRS).

This paper reports an attempt to research sensory overstimulation in a variety of children's television programs by rating the level of visual sensory stimulation, auditory sensory stimulation, verbal response patterns and nonverbal response patterns in 45 television programs designed for preschool children. The television rating inventory (TVRI) was designed to objectively assess these four dimensions on a 7-point Likert-type scale ranging from helpful to harmful. Programs were assessed by four independent raters. A comparison was made among programs of the following types: (1) cartoon-animal characters ("Pink Panther"), (2) cartoon-individual characters ("Fat Albert"), (3) cartoon-group or family characters ("Addams Family"), (4) human live-action ("The Three Stooges"), and (5) educational programs ("Misterogers' Neighborhood"). Results suggest that significant mean differences exist between the types of programing offered through educational children's programs and cartoon features, with the education programs being rated as more helpful than

harmful to the preschool child. Assessment and brief suggest that significant mean differences exist between the types of programing offered through educational children's programs and cartoon features, with the education programs being rated as more helpful than harmful to the preschool child. Assessment and brief discussion include issues and implications related to adversary roles, sexual stereotyping, aggressive behavior, identification and role models, and likely outcomes in observed children's behavior as a result of television viewing.

170. The Evidence on Television Violence. Comstock, George, Rand Corporation, Santa Monica, CA, Oct 1976, 18p. Paper presented at National Homicide Symposium (San Francisco, CA, October, 1976). Sponsoring agency: John and Mary R. Markle Foundation, New York, NY (ED 134 162; Reprint: EDRS).

To some degree television is the current inheritor of anxiety over the effects of communications from outside the home, and is not alone among mass media in presenting sizeable amounts of violence. However, the accessibility, pervasiveness, and very character of television make it the ultimate mass medium, and hence a cause for concern. Television violence is likely to be a continuing phenomenon because it is the product of the medium's response to its competitive environment, and it fits well its particular story telling needs. Experiments have found that the likelihood of aggression is increased by exposure to televised violence, and under certain conditions this likelihood is increased further. However, there is little evidence to support the claim that television violence desensitizes viewers to real-life violence. It has been found among adults that heavier viewers consistently perceive a world more in line with that portrayed in television drama than lighter viewers. The evidence on desensitization and fearfulness is too limited to draw broad conclusions. The evidence on aggressiveness is much more extensive but does not in itself support a conclusion of increased antisocial aggression.

171. The Fantasy-Reality Distinction in Televised Violence: Modifying Influences on Children's Aggression. Sawin, Douglas B. Aug 1977, 12p. Paper presented at the Annual Meeting of the American Psychological Association (85th, San Francisco, CA, August 26–30, 1977). Sponsoring agency: Texas University, Austin, Research Institute (ED 151 073; Reprint: EDRS).

This study involving 120 fifth grade and 120 kindergarten children (all middle class) was designed to assess the extent to which children's understanding of observed violence as fantasy (fictional), as opposed to real (documentary), influences their subsequent aggressive behavior. Children were exposed to a violent televised episode that was introduced as a fictional portrayal (fantasy condition) or as a news broadcast (reality condition). Additional groups were given no information (no instructional set condition) about the violent stimulus or were not exposed to the violent episode (no-TV condition). Aggressive responses and helping responses were recorded immediately following exposure. Boys were most aggressive in the reality and no-TV conditions. They were less aggressive in the no-instructional set condition and least aggressive in the fantasy condition. In almost direct contrast, girls were most aggressive in the fantasy and no-instructional set conditions and least aggressive in the reality and no-TV conditions. These effects held for both older and younger children. The findings are discussed in terms of differences in the socialization of boys and girls for real and fantasy aggression.

172. Five Year ABC Research Project "Anti-Social and Pro-Social Effects of Television on Children." Summary. American Broadcasting Co., New York, NY, 1976, 43p (ED 126 850; Reprint: EDRS). For the full report see citation 191.

This report summarized the results of a five-year research investigation of the anti- and prosocial effects of television on children. At the outset of the investigation the focus of emphasis was on analyzing the possible antisocial effects of television on children, but about midway through the project the research was expanded to include possible prosocial effects of television on children. In the study, roughly 10,000 children in the 8 to 13 year-old-age range from a wide range of socio-economic backgrounds were used as subjects in a variety of experiments using altered program formats and varied actors. The net conclusion of the antisocial experiments was that under certain conditions and depending on the types of violence portrayed, exposure to televised violence is capable of producing increased inclination toward aggression in children.

173. Habituation and Sensitization to Filmed Violence. Gange, J. J. et al. 1976, 14p. Paper presented at the Midwestern Psychological Association (Chicago, IL, May 6–8, 1976) (ED 134 890; Reprint: EDRS).

In an extension of an earlier study by Cline, Croft, and Courrier (1973), the effects of amount of television viewing and preference for televised violence upon autonomic responses to violent and nonviolent videotaped movie sequences were examined. Thirty-six male undergraduates watched a six-minute portion of a boxing film and a six-minute portion of a nonviolent sporting events program. Heart rate and skin resistance were monitored and the highest, lowest, and average skin resistance and the number of skin resistance responses for each of the 12 30-second segments of each film were obtained. Subjects were divided into the following four groups on the basis of preexperimental questionnaires and logs they had kept of their TV viewing behavior: high/low viewing time × high/low preference for violent programing. The results supported the study's hypotheses: heart rate and average skin resistance differed between high and low viewing time and viewing preference groups, and the effects were stronger in response to the violent than to the nonviolent film. For the boxing film, both heart rate and average skin resistance were greater for low viewing time and high preference for violence subjects. The directions of the findings are interpreted within a habituation-sensitization inverted "U" model. The implications of the findings for human aggression and their relationship to aggression research done by experimental social psychologists are discussed.

174. Identification and Imitation in Children. Hoffman, Martin L., Mar 1979, 57p. Paper presented at the Biennial Meeting of the Society for Research in Child Development (San Francisco, CA, March 15–18, 1979). Best copy available (ED 175 537; Reprint: EDRS).

The psychoanalytic theory of identification and the cognitive-developmental and social-learning theories of imitation are briefly described. Pertinent empirical research in the following areas is summarized and critically evaluated: imitation in infants, observational learning, clinical use of modeling, and the relation of imitation to aggression, prosocial behavior, and self-control. Among the author's general conclusions: (1) identification appears not to be an all-encompassing unitary process; (2) children's general cognitive levels affect what they can learn by observing models; (3) children are active cognitive processors of the model's words and actions; (4) Piaget's work with infants is the closest approach to date of a stage analysis of imitation; (5) young children may acquire, from brief periods of observation, certain motor and verbal behaviors that appear to be associated with aggression in real-life situations; (6) the results of research on the long-term effects of television violence are equivocal; (7) experimental studies of observational learning of sharing behavior indicate that models do increase prosocial behavior in children; (8) prosocial behavior, however, does not seem to be enhanced by watching television programs with prosocial content; (9) exposure to models who perform a prohibited act and are not punished has a disinhibiting effect on children; the effects of exposure to models who resist temptation, however, is less clear due to demand characteristics of laboratory research.

175. The Impact of Violence on Television on Children: A Review of Literature. Crawford, Patricia et al., North York Board of Education, Willowdale, Ontario, Jan 1976, 26p (ED 127 975; Reprint: EDRS).

Based on a review of relevant literature, a report was prepared which examines the impact of viewing violence on television on the social behavior of the viewer. A definition of violence and proposes reasons why violence may appeal to viewers. The remainder of the text examines three major research questions: (1) the effects of television violence; (2) viewing patterns of children; and (3) the content of television programs.

176. An Investigation of the Relationship between Children's Television Viewing Habits and Their Behaviors in Unstructured Activities.* Walther, A. Ruth, Southern Illinois University at Carbondale, 1979. 115p (7916094; Reprint: DC).

This study assessed the broad range of behaviors of two groups of kindergarten children and correlated these findings with the variables of social position, sex of the child, number of hours of television viewing, and the interaction of television viewing and the sex of the child. Parents of the 51 children in this study were interviewed to determine the number of hours that their children viewed television per week. The interview also yielded information regarding the occupation and educational status of the head of the household. Each child was observed in unstructured activities in the classroom and on the playground for a total of one hour. Behaviors were recorded every 10 seconds of a two-minute observational period. A total of 360 behaviors were recorded for each child.

The findings indicated that the 51 children watched an average of 38.10 hours of television per week.

A significant negative correlation was found between the frequency of inappropriate behaviors in unstructured activities and the total amount of time spent viewing television. The total amount of time spent viewing television did not adversely affect the number of inappropriate behaviors; the children who were heavy viewers displayed few inappropriate behaviors in the school setting. The research further revealed that children who watched large amounts of television also displayed many desirable behaviors in unstructured activities.

There was no significant relationship between the frequency of inappropriate behaviors and the sex of the child. There was no significant relationship between the frequency of inappropriate behaviors and the interaction of the total hours of television viewing and sex by interaction after adjusting for social position.

177. A Laboratory/Field Study of Television Violence and Aggression in Children's Sports. McCabe, Ann E.; Moriarty, Richard J. Mar 1977, 23p. Paper presented at the meeting of the Society for Research in Child Development (Biennial, New Orleans, LA March 1977) (ED 159 130; Reprint: EDRS).

A study on the effect of viewing violence on television on children's behavior was conducted within the context of sport activity. Three sports—baseball, hockey, and lacrosse—were chosen. Teams of children from three different age groups were the subjects. Within each of the age levels in each sport, teams were selected and assigned to prosocial, antisocial, and control treatment conditions. Experimental television inputs were selected from available recordings of actual athletic events and edited to be relatively antisocial, prosocial, or neutral for the appropriate treatment groups. Observations of players' behavior included measures of physical, verbal, and nonverbal symbolic aggression, and prosocial behavior. The most notable finding was that exposure to prosocial media presentations appeared to consistently reinforce prosocial behavior on the part of the subjects. It is concluded that relationships that may exist between media aggression and viewer's aggression were not detected. Mean values for age and treatment conditions in each sport are presented in tabular form.

178. Legitimatizing Violence: Audience Judgments of Television Situations. Johnson, Mark. 1978, 16p (ED 164 704; Reprint: EDRS).

This document examines some of the factors involved in individual judgments of television portrayed violent behaviors in an attempt to determine how and why people attach aggressive labels to behaviors and to assess the impact of such decisions. A review of related literature is provided to point out the lack of substantial attention in such research to this area. This report then describes a study of 40 adolescents undertaken to test two hypotheses: (1) there is a positive relationship between indices of viewers' aggressive behavior and aggressive character and program preferences, and (2) there is a positive relationship between indices of viewers' aggressive behavior and the frequency with which individuals will approve of televised

aggression. Data from the study indicate that the first hypothesis was not supported whereas the second hypothesis was strongly supported. Total aggression score, group membership, sex, and approval of specific situations where television characters used violence were used as the predicting variables. Based upon these findings, it is argued that a new definition of television impact is required and that it must be the basis for understanding the complex interactional and cognitive processes stimulated by television viewing and, in particular, televised violence.

179. Media Research and Media Education—Controversy, Contradiction, and Complement. Schneller, Raphael. 1978, 37p (ED 178 063; Reprint: EDRS).

Recent research on mass media, with a particular emphasis on television, is reviewed for the effects that the media has on behavior and the use of media in educational endeavors. Although a very pessimistic view is taken concerning the contribution of specific research studies, it is emphasized that one should not underestimate their importance, for research is seen to have contributed some very important general concepts. The view that television and other mass media have been the irresistible dominators of socialization is heavily exaggerated; psychological, societal, and environmental influences are also factors. Many of mass media's possibilities, intentions, and limitations could be clarified by understanding not only the media's messages but also their structure and process through professional, political, and economic considerations.

180. Mitigating the Impact of Televised Violence through Concurrent Adult Commentary. Horton, Robert W.; Santogrossi, David A. Aug 1978, 19p. Paper presented at the Annual Convention of the American Psychological Association (Toronto, ON, August, 1978) (ED 177 412; Reprint: EDRS).

The effects of 80 second- through fifth-grade boys and girls of three types of adult commentary (antiaggressive, nonaggressive, neutral), presented during a violent TV show, were examined and compared to a nonviolent control film group. Subjects' latency in seeking responsible adult assistance when witnessing "real" aggression among other children was measured. In addition, a paper and pencil response hierarchy measure was employed to assess subjects' solutions to hypothetical conflict situations. Results indicated that antiaggressive and nonaggressive commentary subjects were faster in the summoning of help than were neutral commentary subjects. Neutral commentary children were significantly slower than control film subjects in summoning the experimenter. For the response hierarchy measure, the experimental groups did not differ significantly.

181. Moderators of Boys' Aggressive Reactions to Violence: Empathy and Interest. Steinman, David R.; Sawin, Douglas B. Sep 1979, 10p. Paper presented at the Annual Meeting of the American Psychological Association (87th, New York, NY, September 1–5, 1979) (ED 178 206; Reprint: EDRS).

First- and fifth-grade boys' interest in a televised portrayal of violence and their expressions of empathic pain in response to the victims' pain cues were examined as variables moderating their aggressive behavior toward a peer. The 27 subjects viewed a violent videotaped stimulus which consisted of a fight between two men and which included vocalizations of pain as well as close-up shots of the victims' facial expressions of pain. In order to assess the subjects' affective reactions, video recordings of their faces were made as they viewed the televised stimulus. Following the televised violence and the recording of the facial expressions, the subjects' willingness to behave aggressively toward a peer was assessed using a modified version of Liebert and Baron's "Help/Hurt" apparatus. The subjects were put in a position of being able to hurt or help another child's chances of succeeding on a difficult task. Regression analyses indicated that empathic expressions of pain recorded on the faces of the older boys while viewing a victim's pain was negatively correlated with subsequent aggression toward a peer. In contrast, expressions of interest and pain during the high-violence segments of the televised violence significantly predicted higher levels of aggression toward a peer by the younger boys. These results are discussed in terms of older boys' ability to monitor their emotional arousal and to use arousal cues in the control of their aggressive behavior.

182. Network Prime-Time Violence Tabulations for 1976–77 Season. Klapper, Joseph T., Columbia Broadcasting System, Inc., New York, NY, Office of Social Research, May 1977, 24p (ED 148 317; Reprint: EDRS).

An annual report on violence in prime-time television. The tabulations, based on the monitoring of 13 weeks of programs on three networks, indicate that CBS was the lowest of the three networks in violence, though at the same level as the previous year. ABC remained the same level as last year, while NBC increased. Both the number of incidents and the rate of violence for all networks combined has increased since last season. A new measure, duration of violence, introduced to this year's study, indicates a substantial relationship between the total number of minutes devoted to violence and the number of incidents of violence. Data from this survey and from previous years are presented, and the appendices include definitions of terms used in the study.

183. Parent and Adult Mediation of Television Programming and Peer Presence: Their Effects on Children.* Fontes, Brian Frederick, Michigan State University, 1977, 235p (7810048; Reprint: DC).

Research has shown that comments made by experimenters before and during the viewing of antisocial television programing can reduce postviewing aggression and can also increase the amount of information gained from educational programing. This study examines the effect of mother and adult comments and peer presence on children's ability to (a) recall pictorial content, (b) recall consequences of violent behavior, (c) recall verbal content, (d) perceive violence as inappropriate, and (e) demonstrate postviewing cooperation.

An experimental posttest only control group design was employed. Subjects were randomly assigned to one of the following conditions: (1) mother providing comments about TV

programing while viewing with her child, (2) mother viewing with her child but providing no comments, (3) a female adult providing comments about TV programing while viewing with a child, (4) a female adult viewing with a child but providing no comments, (5) a child viewing with a peer, with no comments provided, and (6) a child viewing alone.

Comments described what occurred in the stimulus and condemned violence.

The stimulus depicted shooting scenes taken from two movies shown on network television during 1976–77.

Children (N = 132) six–eight years of age participated in the experiment. Each treatment condition contained 11 males and 11 females.

After viewing the stimulus each subject played a game in which he/she could either help or not help someone. A post-viewing cooperation measure of duration and frequency for helping and nonhelping behavior was obtained. Subjects were then interviewed to determine how much of the stimulus could be recalled and if they perceived violence occurring in the stimulus as inappropriate.

Subjects participating in the parent and combined parent/adult "comment" conditions were able to recall more: (1) pictorial content, (2) consequences of violent behavior, and (3) verbal content than those subjects participating in the parent and combined parent/adult "no comment" conditions.

There were no differences between treatment conditions or combinations of treatment conditions for the dependent measure of postviewing cooperation when controlling for sex.

184. Parental Mediation of Children's Social Behavior Learning from Television. Atkin, Charles K.; Greenberg, Bradley S. Aug 1977, 29p. Paper presented at the Annual Meeting of the Association for Education in Journalism (60th, Madison, WI, August 1977) (ED 151 808; Reprint: EDRS).

A study was conducted to explore the relationship between a child's exposure to television content portraying various levels of physical aggression, verbal aggression, altruism, and affection, and that child's enactment of these four types of behavior under different conditions of parent-child coviewing and discussion of the television content. Seven hundred twenty-one children in grades four, six, and eight responded to a questionnaire listing 29 television programs appearing in one season and indicated the frequency of viewing for each program. In addition, an index of social behavior was constructed to rate each child on the four areas of behavior under consideration, and a random subsample of 293 mothers of these children participated in the study by viewing television with their children. Results of the study show that parental comments, in parent-child coviewing of television, can shape the child's response to television messages by reducing the negative effects of physical and verbal aggression and increasing the effects of altruism and affection.

185. **Pro-Social and Anti-Social Behaviors on Commercial Television in 1975–76. Report No. 1.** Greenberg, Bradley S. et al., Michigan State University, East Lansing, Department of Communication, Feb 1977, 78p. Project CASTLE: Children and Social Television Learning. Sponsoring agency: Office of Child Development (DHEW), Washington, DC (ED 178 031; Reprint: ERDS).

This study investigates prosocial and antisocial behaviors portrayed on prime time and Saturday morning television during the 1975–76 season. An initial review of relevant research in this behavioral area is followed by a description of the basic content categories for prosocial and antisocial behaviors, motives and consequences of these behaviors, the measurement of act intensity, coder training program, coder reliability estimative procedures, and samples of television content. A total of 92 programs comprising 68.5 hours of viewing were analyzed for this study and results are discussed for a variety of frequency and time categories. Appendices include intensity of acts, shows by program type and representative intensity levels for both pro- and antisocial acts.

186. **Results of a Survey of Pupils and Teachers Regarding Television.** Crawford, Patricia; Rapoport, Max, North York Board of Education, Willowdale, Ontario, Apr 1976, 61p (ED 127 976; Reprint: EDRS).

To test the validity of hypotheses regarding television violence and social behavior of viewers, a survey was conducted of a large stratified sample of sixth-grade and kindergarten pupils and of teachers. The student survey identified: (1) frequency with which pupils watch television; (2) parental control of television viewing; (3) family activities; (4) reasons for watching television; (5) degree of selectivity of programs; (6) student perception of televised violence; and (7) favorite programs. The survey of teachers identified: (1) the extent to which teachers used television in their classrooms; (2) teacher perceptions of violence on television; (3) teacher views on the impact of television violence; and (4) student behaviors which teachers identified as directly attributable to television violence. Sample questionnaires are included.

187. **Seeking Solutions to Violence on Children's Television.** Committee on Children's Television, San Franciso, CA, Feb 1977, 24p. Transcripts from a Strategy Workshop (San Francisco, CA, May 5, 1976) (ED 142 300; Reprint: EDRS—HC not available; also available from Committee on Children's Television, Inc., 1511 Masonic Avenue, San Francisco, CA 94117).

This document contains the transcripts from a workshop to investigate strategies to use in dealing with violence on children's television. The papers given by outside experts include: (1) "Effect of Television Violence on Children and Youth" by Michael Rothenberg, (2) "Implications of the Psychological Effects of Television Programming on Black Children" by Carolyn Block, (3) "Towards a More Daring Middle Ground" by Peter Almond, and (4) "The Role of Fantasy and Play in Child Development with Implications for

the Current Generation of Television Watchers" by John Sikorski. An article on television violence is also reprinted from the Congressional Record. A final paper by Sally Williams of the Committee on Children's Television addresses the workshop's major thrust: seeking solutions to the problem of violence on children's television. A bibliography, a resource list of organizations, and a list of publications available from the Committee on Children's Television are also included.

188. **Selective Exposure to Televised Aggression. Report No. 7.** Atkin, Charles K. et al., Michigan State University, East Lansing, Department of Communication, Feb 1978, 16p. Project CASTLE: Children and Social Television Learning. Sponsoring agency: Office of Child Development (DHEW), Washington, DC (ED 178 032; Reprint: EDRS).

This two-wave panel survey of young people was conducted to explore the relationship between attitudes and viewing over time, examining aggressiveness and viewing of programs portraying physical and verbal aggression. Questionnaires were administered to 227 children in the fourth, sixth, and eighth grades in 1976 and again one year later. The pertinent variables in this analysis are exposure to physically and verbally aggressive programing and reports of physical and verbal aggressiveness. Of secondary importance are measures of program prohibition, grade, and sex. This study provides supportive evidence for selective exposure to aggressive television entertainment programing which is compatible with aggressive attitudinal predispositions. Even with a conservative regression analysis that controls for grade, sex, and initial viewing patterns, a significant relationship remained between prior orientations and subsequent program choices. Findings of this study suggest that a portion of the basic relationship between viewing and aggressiveness may be attributable to selective exposure rather than the reverse viewing-causes-aggression sequence.

189. **Sex and Violence on TV: Hearings before the Subcommittee on Communications of the Committee on Interstate and Foreign Commerce. House of Representatives, 94th Congress, Second Session, July 9, August 17–18, 1976. Serial No. 94-140.** Congress of the United States, Washington, DC. House Committee on Interstate and Foreign Commerce, 1977, 381p. Not available in hard copy due to marginal legibility of original document (ED 136 321; Reprint: EDRS—HC not available).

This volume contains the proceedings of hearings concerning the issue of televised violence and obscenity. Transcripts of statements given by individuals involved in various aspects of television and other communication media are included. In addition, other material (such as letters from concerned individuals) which was submitted for the record is provided.

190. Sex and Violence on TV. Hearings before the Subcommittee on Communications of the Committee on Interstate and Foreign Commerce, House of Representatives, 95th Congress. First Session on the Issue of Televised Violence and Obscenity. Serial No. 95-130. Congress of the United States, Washington, DC. House Committee on Interstate and Foreign Commerce, Mar 1977, 485p. Not available in hard copy due to small print (ED 168 547; Reprint: EDRS—HC not available; also available from Superintendent of Documents, US Government Printing Office, Washington, DC 20402).

These transcripts of statements on televised violence and obscenity, presented by government officials and representatives from universities, national organizations, and the television industry, include an outline of the proposed Murphy Bill. This bill would limit the control of the three networks over television programing and promote competition in the production, sale, and distribution of programs for television broadcasting. Additional materials submitted for the record by concerned groups are included, i.e., publications, program reports, exchanges of letters, journal articles, additional statements, and letters directed to the committee or its chairman.

191. Studies in Violence and Television. Heller, Melvin S.; Polsky, Samuel, American Broadcasting Co., New York, NY, 1976, 529p (ED 126 850; Reprint: EDRS—HC not available). For a summary report see citation 172.

The complete reports of the research efforts on the effects of televised violence on children sponsored by the American Broadcasting Company in the past five years are presented. Ten research projects on aggression and violence are described which examined primarily the effect of television on children who were emotionally disturbed, came from broken homes, or were juvenile offenders. In addition to complete documentation on each of the studies, guidelines for viewing and programing of televised violence are given. General implications for the broadcasting industry in light of the findings of the studies are also included. Data collection instruments are appended.

192. Styles of Parental Disciplinary Practices as a Mediator of Children's Learning from Antisocial Television Portrayals. Korzenny, Felipe et al. 1977, 25p. Best copy available (ED 178 094; Reprint: EDRS—HC not available).

This study examines the effect of parental socialization forces on children's learning of antisocial behavior from television portrayals. The intervening variables are the patterns of parental disciplinary practices and general interactions with their children in their everyday life. Two types of parental styles were identified: induction, characterized by a loving attitude, based on reason, explanation, and pointing out the consequences of the child's actions on others; and sensitizing parental behaviors, those that focus on external consequences of social behaviors without providing the child with a cognitive frame of reference for internalizing moral guidelines. Three types of antisocial behaviors are studied: physical and verbal aggression and deceit. The relationship between watching these types of behavior on television and the child's own antisocial predispositions were studied for different combinations of parental styles. The results indicate that children of those parents who are highly inductive and who only occasionally resort to sensitizing techniques are the least affected by physical and verbal aggression on television. In the case of physical aggression, children whose parents are mostly sensitizing and seldom use inductive techniques tend to be the most affected. Although the differences among correlation coefficients were not statistical significant, the trends encountered rendered encouraging support to the theoretical expectations. Data tables and a list of references are attached.

193. Substance Use and Sexual Intimacy on Commercial Television. Report No. 5. Fernandez-Collado, Carlos et al., Michigan State University, East Lansing, Department of Communication, Oct 1977, 26p. Project CASTLE: Children and Social Television Learning. Sponsoring agency: Office of Child Development (DHEW), Washington, DC (ED 178 033; Reprint: EDRS).

This study reports a content analysis of 1976–77 commercial television programing for incidents of alcohol, drug, and tobacco use and sexual behavior. The analysis included one episode of each prime time and Saturday morning dramatic series, comprising 77 programs and 58 hours of television viewing. A concurrent survey among 300 fourth-, sixth-, and eighth-grade children identified the series viewed by 40 percent or more of these children. Substance use and sexual behavior are defined as they relate to this study and findings are discussed. A 23-item bibliography is attached.

194. Television and Violence: Methodological Issues for Future Research. Hollenbeck, Albert R.; Susman, Elizabeth J. Sep 1978, 10p. Paper presented at the Meeting of the International Society for Research on Aggression (Washington, DC, September 23, 1978). Sponsoring agency: National Institute of Mental Health (DHEW), Rockville, MD (ED 168 708; Reprint: EDRS).

This paper identifies limitations of previous investigations of the relation between televised violence and viewer aggression and suggests a framework for future research concerning the effects of media viewing on child development. It is suggested that typical research is short-term, cross-sectional, and laboratory based. Factors which mediate the effects of televised violence, such as gender differences, habitual levels of aggression, motivational states, age, portrayal of motives, format of the program and parental approval/disapproval, remain relatively unexplored. While studies indicate that positive behaviors increase in children after these behaviors are viewed on television, processes involved in prosocial behavior effects are unclear. Effects of prosocial television on children should be investigated. A framework for redirecting research efforts comes from life-span and ecological perspectives of developmental psychology. Longitudinal design permits the identification of cohort and time of measurement variables which are especially important in the assessment of media effects. Cumulative effects of exposure to media violence can be identified. Cohorts of children, with siblings used as matched controls, can be studied naturalistically in the family setting. Although risky and expensive, collaborative use of both life-span and ecological perspectives should yield vital information about the impact of television on the lives of children.

195. Television Portrayal and Aggressive Behavior.
Comstock, George, Rand Corporation, Santa Monica, CA, Dec 1976, 17p. Sponsoring agency: John and Mary R. Markle Foundation, New York (ED 145 800; Reprint: EDRS).

This is a review of research relating to the attributes of portrayals which play a role in affecting aggressive behavior. The effects of portrayal can occur at any of three successive stages: acquisition, disinhibition/stimulation/arousal, performance. The older the individual, the more likely the influence is to be in all three stages of influence. Yet much research with young viewers fails to consider the latter stages of influence and perhaps the larger effects. Evidence which does consider such stages suggests: (1) portrayals of violence can lead to aggressive performance; (2) repeated exposure to portrayals of violence may increase the likelihood of aggressive performance; (3) aggressive performance is not dependent on a typical frustration; (4) whether aggressive effects may also mean antisocial effects remains to be shown; (5) factors in a portrayal which increase the likelihood of aggression suggest that aggression is justified, socially acceptable, motivated by malice, or pays off; (6) exposure to portrayals of violence may desensitize young persons to responding to violence in their environments. Related effects of aggressive portrayals on two other behaviors (rule violation and self-harm) are summarized.

196. Television Viewing and Cultural Indicators: Some Notes on Theory and Measurement.
Hawkins, Robert P.; Pingree, Suzanne. May 1980, 24p. Paper presented at the Annual Meeting of the International Communication Association (Acapulco, Mexico, May 18–23, 1980) (ED 185 608; Reprint: EDRS).

Two underlying assumptions of the cultural indicators approach to television research were examined, using data on the television viewing habits of 76 second-grade, 150 fifth-grade, 509 eighth-grade, and 350 eleventh-grade students in Perth, Australia. The assumptions were that commercial television presented an organically composed total world of interrelated stories produced to the same set of market specifications, and that television audiences viewed largely nonselectively and by the clock rather than by the program. The evidence on selection and habit in television viewing countered a "purely ritual" overstatement of the cultural indicators assumption. Two of the three content types most related to social reality (crime adventure and cartoons) were quite predictable from viewing habits. But habitual television watching itself did not account for all content-specific relationships, because viewing comedy and news programs related to other viewing habits without being related to beliefs about social reality. This evidence pointed to content differences (selection) as a key factor in television viewing even though habit could be considered an important antecedent to much of

the viewing that produced the cultivation of a biased conception of the real world. Greater than average viewing times for cartoons and game shows were associated with perceiving the world as relatively mean and violent, while the reverse was true for drama and news viewing.

197. Television-Viewing and Imaginative Play in Pre-Schoolers: A Developmental and Parent-Intervention Study. Progress Report No. 2.
Singer, Jerome L.; Singer, Dorothy G., Yale University, New Haven, CT, Department of Psychology, May 1978, 187p. Sponsoring agency: National Science Foundation, Washington, DC (ED 168 576; Reprint: EDRS). For a related document see citation 198.

This study examined the patterns of ongoing play manifested over a year's time by 141 three- and four-year-old boys and girls at nursery schools and day-care centers. The relationships between such play and concurrent language usage and the child's patterns of television viewing at home were examined during this period. Parents of the children were also randomly assigned to one of three intervention groups or to a control group. Intervention groups received training either in stimulating the children's imaginative play, stimulating the child's cognitive and language development, or in controlling the child's television-viewing frequency and encouraging more discriminating use of the set. The control group merely kept logs of children's viewing as did the other parents. Based on this research, eight recommendations were made. Family interview data relating to home organization, daily routines, patterns of discipline, parental aggressive behavior, and traumatic events or stress suggest that the laxity of control over TV viewing and a general lack of alternative interests by the family may expose children to greater influence by the TV programing and yield the danger of more initiative aggressive or hyperactive behavior.

198. Television Viewing, Family Style and Aggressive Behavior. Singer, Jerome L.; Singer, Dorothy G., Yale University, New Haven, CT, Family Television Research and Consultation Center, 1979, 48p. Paper presented at the Annual Meeting of the American Association for the Advancement of Science (Houston, TX, 1979). Sponsoring agency: National Science Foundation, Washington, DC. Filmed from best available copy. (ED 176 847; Reprint: EDRS—HC not available). For a related document, see citation 197.

As part of a larger one-year examination of the relationship between television viewing patterns and spontaneous play in nursery school, this study focuses on (1) the correlation between children's television viewing patterns in the home and their level of aggression in nursery school, and (2) specific factors within family settings that might determine this correlation. The major sources of data were daily logs kept by parents of the type and frequency of programs watched by their children over two-week periods four different times during the year; concurrent observations and ratings of overt physical aggression directed toward other children on property during free play in nursery school; and family interview questionnaires concerning daily routines in the home, patterns of discipline, leisure activities, TV viewing habits, and indications of family difficulties. Data from the parent logs and observations were based on a sample of 141 three- and four-year-olds, while the interviews were given to a subset of four groups of children (N = 10 per group) who represented the extremes in both TV viewing and aggression. Correlations between weekly TV viewing and aggression (r = .35) were significant, even with the effects of socioeconomic status, ethnicity, and IQ partialed out. Further analyses suggest a causal direction from heavy TV viewing to aggressive behavior. Results of the family interview study indicated significant differences among the groups of extremes on the level of order and organization in the family, and on the degree of outside activities engaged in by the family.

199. Television's Action Arsenal: Weapon Use in Prime Time. Higgins, Patricia B.; Ray, Maria W., United States Conference of Mayors, Washington, DC, 1978, 68p. Sponsoring agency: George Gund Foundation, Cleveland, OH (ED 155 573; Reprint: EDRS).

Weapon use was chosen as the topic of this study not only because it is a manageable component of the entire television violence issue, but because it is one that is clearly subject to modification by the broadcast industry. Weapons are not behavior, attitudes, or values that can be altered by a camera stance; they are instruments which are supplied to or withheld from the actors to develop a story line. Because they are essentially action props, weapons can be added to or subtracted from a scene. In short, someone controls the flow. This report suggests that weapon use on television is excessive and uncomfortably antiseptic. Little bloodletting or suffering accompany the weapon use. Thus, the severity of the results of the weapon use is ignored. This report must be regarded as a first step. While it has made a significant contribution to the understanding of the nature of television violence, it has more often pointed out the need for additional research.

200. Testimony. Statements made at the National Congress of Parents and Teachers National Hearing on Television Violence. Chicago, January 25, 1977. Heintz, Ann Christine; Conley, Elizabeth. Jan 1977, 10p (ED 141 812; Reprint: EDRS).

The first statement in this testimony points out the need for groups to define "violence" before taking any action against violent television programs, since violence means different things to different people. Many of the studies on violence use a narrow and simplistic definition of violence which does not take into account the effects of violence on different individuals. For example, programs which portray emotional violence, rather than physical violence, have been found to be very upsetting to adolescents. Through discussing concepts of violence in home, school, and community, we can provide ourselves with a broader base for making decisions about our personal selection of programs, and we can encourage each other to communicate with local television stations, networks, and producers about broadcasts both good and bad. The second statement deals with ways in which parents can mediate the effects of television violence on their children. Parents can discuss with their children the television shows they watch, using them as starting points for discussions of moral and social issues. They can discuss the violence in television

shows in an abstract way, in order to demystify violent shows and to help children become aware of the barrage of violence to which they are exposed.

201. Trends in Network Television Drama and Viewer Conceptions of Social Reality, 1967–1976. Violence Profile No. 8. Gerbner, George et al. Pennsylvania University, Philadelphia, Annenberg School of Communications, Mar 1977, 12p. Sponsoring agency: National Institute of Mental Health (DHEW), Rockville, MD (ED 139 395; Reprint: EDRS).

Trends in violence in television drama were measured from 1967 to 1976. In 1976, 89.1 percent of programing contained violent episodes, as opposed to 78.4 percent in 1975. The increase in violence was not due to changes in context of dramatic programing. The National Broadcasting Company (NBC) contained the most violence overall in children's and late evening hours. The American Broadcasting Company (ABC) was middle in overall violence due to a decline in late evening violence and despite increases in family and children's hours. The Columbia Broadcasting System (CBS) held the lowest family, late evening, and overall violence scores. Persons most frequently victimized were children; old, unmarried, non-White or lower class women; and non-Whites. Children and adult viewer responses to questions about social reality confirmed previous findings that heavy exposure to violence in television drama may cultivate fear and mistrust. Tables showing trends of overall violence, violence for different viewing hours, and violence for each network from 1967 to 1976 are included.

202. Violence and the Ratings: A Comparison for 1975's "Second Season." Doolittle, John. 1976, 16p. Paper presented at the Annual Meeting of the International Communication Association (Portland, OR, April 1976) (ED 127 655; Reprint: EDRS).

Violence ratings for 49 second-season (January to April 1975 prime-time network programs were obtained from 48 high school juniors and seniors. Audience ratings for the same shows were obtained from the Nielsen ratings. No relationship was found between ratings of violence levels and average audience ratings. Violent shows tended to be longer than nonviolent shows, however, and longer shows tended to have poorer audience ratings. Given that the violent program has to compete with similar programs and keep its audience for longer times, this type of programing may be performing relatively well in the ratings.

203. Violence on Television: Report Together with Additional, Dissenting, and Separate Views by the Subcommittee on Communications of the Committee on Interstate and Foreign Commerce, House of Representatives, Ninety-fifth Congress, First Session, September 29, 1977, Washington, DC. Congress of the United States, Washington, DC, House Committee on Interstate and Foreign Commerce, Sep 1977, 39p. Not available in hard copy due to marginal legibility of original document; several pages contain light type (ED 149 385; Reprint: EDRS—HC not available).

This subcommittee report presents a history of congressional action regarding violence on television and then outlines conclusions and recommendations for legislative consideration. Acknowledging that excessive viewing of violence may have harmful effects on children, the report places responsibility for program content on the networks and advocates industry self-regulation as an effective means of limiting televised violence. There are avenues consistent with the First Amendment through which the government and the public can address the problem. However, this study concludes that parents are the most powerful agents in curbing this problem. Three ways are suggested: parents should (1) monitor more closely the viewing habits of their children, (2) participate in a positive and active way in their children's television viewing, and (3) write to local broadcasters and networks to register complaints about offensive programs. Several dissenting and separate views on the issue accompany the report.

204. **Violence Profiles for Fall Programming.** National Citizens Committee for Broadcasting, Washington, DC, 1976, 35p. Several tables may not reproduce well due to poor type (ED 141 837; Reprint: EDRS).

This document presented by the National Citizens Committee for Broadcasting at a 1976 press conference provides an assortment of materials concerned with violence in television. Among the materials included are "Who Sponsors the New Fall Violence?" by Nicholas Johnson, a description of and rationale for the study of advertisers who sponsor television violence, and a statement by Richard E. Palmer, president of the American Medical Association, concerning that organization's commitment, in the form of a $25,000 grant, to encourage media reform. Definitions are provided of the measures used to evaluate the level of violence in various programs. In addition, "An Evaluation of a System for the Continual Monitoring and Periodic Reporting of the Commercial Sponsorship of Television Violence" summarizes the findings of a study to analyze the reliability of two measures of television violence:

the number of violent actions and the total time of violence in the prorgram. This analysis was conducted on a sample of 23 prime time network television programs aired during November 1976; examples of data tabulation methods are included.

BOOKS

205. **Symposium on Television Violence (Colloque sur la Violence a la Television); Queen's University, Kingston, Ontario, Canada, August 24–26, 1975.** Canadian Radio-Television Commission, Ottawa, ON. Ottawa, Canada: Supply and Services Canada Publishing Center, 1976, 252p.

This book presents material from a symposium on television violence that was organized by the Canadian Radio-Television Commission. Part 1, "The Public Issue," discusses the social effects of mass media and violence as a dramatic convention. Part 2, "The Social Effects of Television Violence," provides experiments, research, and patterns in research. Part 3, "The Industry Perspective," discusses the quality and economics of Canadian television production. Part 4, "Control and Improvement," presents the legal and social implications of control mechanisms as they relate to mass media and summarizes the symposium. Lists of the background papers presented at the symposium, their bibliographies, and the names of symposium participants are appended. Some of the papers are printed in both French and English.

206. **Television Violence and the Adolescent Boy.** Belson, William H. Hampshire, England: Saxon House, and Lexington, MA: D.C. Heath, 1978, 529p. For a related document see citation 148.

This eight-year study, based on self-reports from 1565 London boys, finds a direct link between watching violent TV programs and committing serious acts of violence.

Stereotypes on Television: Social Role Learning

JOURNAL ARTICLES

207. **Androgyny on the TV Screen? An Analysis of Sex-Role Portrayal.** Peevers, Barbara Hollands. *Sex Roles: A Journal of Research.* v5, n6, p797–809, Dec 1979.

Characters in 1975 "family time" television programs and 1976 programs shown after the "family time" concept had been legally challenged were rated on sex role portrayal. A

significant relationship among viewing time, program type, and sex of character suggested that content considered acceptable for children emphasized stereotypic female roles.

208. **Dramatic TV Content and Children's Sex-Role Stereotypes.** Miller, M. Mark; Reeves, Byron. *Journal of Broadcasting.* v20, n1, p35–50, Win 1976.

Prime-time television dramas were analyzed to isolate counterstereotypical sex-role portrayals, and children were surveyed to determine the impact of these portrayals on sex-role perceptions. The appeal of male and female television characters as role models was also tested.

209. The Effects of Television Cartoons on Sex-Role Stereotyping in Young Girls. Davidson, Emily S. et al. *Child Development.* v50, n2, p597–600, Jun 1979 (EJ 211 475; Reprint: UMI).

Thirty-six five- to six-year-old girls viewed one of three television network cartoons, either high or low stereotyped or neutral. They were then tested for sex-role stereotyping on a 24-item measure, each measure showing a male and a female and asking a question about them. Results indicate that girls who viewed the low-stereotyped program received lower sex-role stereotype scores than did girls in the high and neutral conditions, who did not differ from each other.

210. The Effects of Television on Children's Stereotyping of Women's Work Roles. O'Bryant, Shirley L.; Corder-Bolz, Charles R. *Journal of Vocational Behavior.* v12, n2, p233–43, Apr 1978.

Elementary school students (N = 67) from three ethnic groups were systematically exposed, over a one-month period, to specially produced television commercials. Results indicate children do learn about occupations from television content and they also learn to stereotype or nonstereotype various occupations based on sex of the TV model.

211. Fantasy and Culture on Television. Stein, Ben. *Society.* v16, n3, p89–94, Mar–Apr 1979.

Television shows on prime time are a new folk culture contending with the time-honored wisdom of the folk. TV presents a unified picture of life in the United States, consisting of standardized environments and standardized views of particular social groups. What makes television culture different from previous popular cultures is that it does not arise from national dreams and nightmares, but from the views of a small group of writers and producers in Los Angeles. Although the power of television mass culture is evident, its consequences are not yet clear.

212. From "Bionic Woman" to "Ultra Man": TV's New Stereotypes. Wiles, Jon; McNamera, Donna. *National Elementary Principal.* v56, n3, p60–61, Jan-Feb 1977.

The major problem with the media's accepted sex role models is that they are totally unrealistic, out of keeping with today's social values, and, therefore, utterly unacceptable. A new, singular ideal of self-sufficiency and aggression is replacing traditionally defined male and female roles. This new ideal even more rigidly limits the range of behaviors allowed men and women in our society.

213. Girls' Favorite TV Females. Lull, James. *Journalism Quarterly.* v57, n1, p146–50, Spr 1980.

This study documents some of the ways in which a sample of 200 high school girls perceive many female television characters viewed in recent years. Their ratings are listed for those characters they believe are like themselves, wish to emulate, perceive as "in control," and believe are "typical."

214. Impact of Television on Children's Social Development. Liebert, Robert M.; Sprafkin, Joyce N. *School Media Quarterly.* v5, n3, p163–70, Spr 1977 (EJ 168 238; Reprint: UMI).

Discusses the three-stage observational learning process of exposure (amount of contact and type of content), acquisition (what is learned), and acceptance (how much affects attitudes and actions), with emphasis on racial and sexual stereotypes.

215. The Mass Media and Youth Culture. Altheide, David L. *Urban Education.* v14, n2, p236–53, Jul 1979 (EJ 208 992; Reprint: UMI).

The immediate, direct effects of the mass media upon individuals are obscure but the indirect effects are substantial in creating and disseminating a separate youth culture and life-style.

216. Racial Stereotyping on Television: A Comparison of the Behavior of Both Black and White Television Characters. Reid, Pamela Trotman. *Journal of Applied Psychology.* v64, n5, p465–71, Oct 1979.

Television is a source of information that influences the formation of attitudes toward minority groups through its characterizations of them. This study investigated the behavior of both Black and White characters on comedy programs to determine whether there were differences in their portrayal. It was hypothesized that Black characters would differ from White ones along several dimensions, for example, activity level and dominance, and that White characters on Black programs would behave differently from Whites on White or mixed programs. Three episodes each of Black, White, and mixed comedy programs were videotaped. Raters tallied the behavior of 110 different characters on 12 types of behavior. A two-way analysis of variance, sex × race, indicated that racial stereotypes and sex role stereotypes were the bases for character portrayals on television. The differences between Black female and White female characters seemed crucial to the depiction of the races. In addition, the portrayal of White characters on Black programs was negative.

217. Sex Bias on Children's Television Programs. Nolan, John et al. *Journal of Psychology.* v96, pt2, p197–204, Jul 1977.

Shows that Saturday morning television programs covertly teach children that boys are more significant persons than girls.

218. Sex on TV and Adolescent Sexual Self-Image. Baran, Stanley J. *Journal of Broadcasting.* v20, n1, p61–68, Win 1976.

A study of sex as seen on television and as it relates to adolescent sexual self-image demonstrates that a relationship exists between perceptions of television portrayals of sex and initial coital satisfaction. Satisfaction with being a virgin was unrelated to perceptions of television sex.

219. Sexism's Universal Curriculum. Bonk, Kathleen; Gardner, JoAnn Evans. *American Education*. v13, n6, p15–19, Jul 1977 (EJ 165 336; Reprint: UMI).

Television's combination of wide appeal and potential for distortion is giving advocates of equality for the sexes concern about its influence in perpetuating sexist notions.

220. Some Antecedents of Children's Sex-role Stereotypes. Perloff, Richard M. *Psychological Reports*. v40, n2, p463–66, Apr 1977.

A study which investigated children's observational learning of sex-role stereotypes from parental and televised models. Children's stereotypes tended to be similar to their parents' stereotypes, and children whose mothers were employed outside the home had less stereotyped sex-role perceptions than children whose mothers did not work outside the home. The results also indicated that heavy television viewers did not have more stereotyped sex-role perceptions than moderate or light viewers. Implications of the findings are discussed.

221. TV Beauty Ads and Role Expectations of Adolescent Female Viewers. Tan, Alexis S. *Journalism Quarterly*. v56, n2, p283–88, Sum 1979 (EJ 207 940; Reprint: UMI).

A study of the responses of 56 high school girls shows the cultivation effects of television beauty-related commercials on the girls' perceptions of the importance of sex appeal, youth, and beauty to women in four different aspects of their lives: success in careers; success as wives; popularity with men; and personal satisfaction.

222. TV Comedy: What It's Teaching the Kids. Waters, Harry F. et al. *Newsweek*. v93, p64–68, 71–72, May 7, 1979.

This article examines the situation comedies of the 1979 network television season, noting that most of the shows are directed toward children, on the theory that the family's major consumer—the mother—will watch what the children want to see. It points out some of the dubious messages offered by these "kidcoms": the adult is a dolt; dumb is cool, smart is square; the working class is pure; the rich are corrupt; and the real world looks like Los Angeles.

223. Television's Impact on Preferences for Non-White Playmates: Canadian "Sesame Street" Inserts. Goldberg, Marvin E.; Gorn, Gerlad J. *Journal of Broadcasting*. v23, n1, p27–32, Win 1979 (EJ 203 512; Reprint: UMI).

This study of the capacity of television to influence children's attitudes and behavior towards other racial groups examined children's playmate preference after viewing racially integrated television programs. Testing for delayed effects and generalization of effects extended previous work in the area.

224. Television's New Sex Education. Levinsohn, Florence Hamlish. *School Review*. v85, n3, p439–44, May 1977 (EJ 163 665; Reprint: UMI).

The author is concerned with sexual identity as it may be being learned by youngsters (including her youngster) from their TV screens. She is concerned that young people are viewing as natural and normal the presentation of sex on television as a routine, affectless experience in which women are the objects of men's lust.

MICROFICHE

225. An Analysis of the Portrayal of the Elderly in Television Commercials Viewed by Children.* Serock, Kathryn Ellen, University of Maryland, 1979, 188p (8002059; Reprint: DC).

The purpose of this study was to examine the portrayal of the elderly in television commercials viewed by children during evening prime time and Saturday mornings. This was accomplished by determining (1) the frequency of appearance of the elderly in television commercials viewed by children and the amount of exposure they were given during times when children watch television; (2) the manner and commercial context in which the elderly were portrayed in the commercials; (3) the differences in the portrayal of the elderly in the commercials on the basis of sex and race of the elderly; and (4) the personality profile of the elderly in comparison to the personality profile of persons on other age groups appearing in the commercials.

Results of the study were:

1. The elderly were very underrepresented in weeknight commercials. Elderly men were portrayed twice as often as elderly women. Elderly minorities were virtually absent; only two elderly Blacks were viewed in weeknight commercials. While commercials portraying the elderly were seldom repeated in the weeknight sample, repeated exposure in Saturday commercials was very evident.

2. Elderly persons in television commercials viewed by children appeared significantly more often in one manner and commercial context. In weeknight commercials the elderly were real persons, not giving an argument for a product, seldom interacting with children, and exhibiting passive behaviors, while in Saturday commercials the elderly were animated characters, having credibility as authorities on the products, interacting with children, and exhibiting active behaviors. Most weeknight commercials with the elderly were serious in tone, while the Saturday commercials were humorous. Age-related remarks were few in number and seldom derogatory.

3. There were significant differences in the portrayal of the elderly in television commercials viewed by children on the basis of sex of the elderly. Elderly women were most often associated with domestic roles, while men were associated with professional roles. Men were rated significantly higher than the women on the personality profile in terms of acceptability.

4. When age groups were compared, children received higher ratings in terms of effectiveness, whereas the elderly received higher ratings in terms of autonomy. Children and elderly not interacting were rated significantly higher in terms of effectiveness, than those who interacted.

The results indicate that the elderly in commercials viewed by children were portrayed inaccurately and unrealistically. This was particularly true for elderly women and minorities. How such portrayals of the elderly affect children's perceptions and attitudes toward the elderly should be considered in future research.

226. Children and Parents in our Television Programmes. Homberg, Erentraud, Comp., Prix Jeuenesse Foundation, Munich, Germany, Jun 1977, 26p (ED 161 456; Reprint: EDRS).

Researchers and practitioners of commercial television met for three and a half days for an international seminar to examine the portrayal of the relations between children and parents in television programing, and the effects of television on the family unit. This report provides abstracts of the lectures by nine researchers and producers addressing such issues as psychology of styles in television media usage, effects of television on the family, dissemination of educational ideologies, and emotional reactions of children to television programs. In addition to the lectures, excerpts showing family scenes characteristic of television programs in each country were screened by producers from Sweden, Hungary, the USA, Japan, England, Germany, and Iran. Participants in group discussions, despite the differences in their cultural backgrounds, seemed to share some major areas of concern in programing, including (1) avoiding overidealization and overdramatization in programing; (2) not shattering conventional family structures, but carefully altering them; (3) showing reality with its conflicts; (4) conveying self-confidence, security, and mental stimuli to underprivileged children; and (5) conveying democracy and solidarity to the family. Some suggestions for dealing with such concerns are included.

227. Children's Impressions of Television Families. Wartella, Ellen, 1978, 25p. Sponsoring agency: John and Mary R. Markle Foundation, New York, NY (ED 168 681; Reprint: EDRS).

This research study examines the types of social behaviors portrayed by families in various television series and explores children's impressions of the TV family members. Content analysis of nine family-oriented TV series was employed to describe the ranges of behaviors of fathers, mothers and children on television. Eleven shows from each series was taped. Behaviors portrayed were coded as being either prosocial or antisocial. Survey data were collected from 388 children in second, fifth and eighth grades. Each child interviewed was asked to "describe a (character) so that someone would know what he was like and why he was like that" in order to elicit children's impressions of father, mother, and child characters from two series. Results of the analyses indicated that depictions of families on television are fairly prosocial. Fathers' and children's behaviors were mixed, while mothers' behaviors were consistently prosocial. Children at all three ages fairly accurately perceived TV characters' behavior patterns. Both father and child characters were uniformly well liked by the children regardless of their behavior patterns, while mother characters were less well liked overall. It is suggested that future research should investigate how TV character portrayals might build children's expectations of how people should behave.

228. The Demography of Fictional Television Characters in 1975–76. Report No. 2. Simmons, Katrina Wynkoop et al., Michigan State University, East Lansing, Department of Communication, Feb 1977, 39p. Project CASTLE: Children and Social Television Learning. Sponsoring agency: Office of Child Development (DHEW), Washington, DC (ED 178 030; Reprint: EDRS).

This study examines the messages presented by fictional characters during the "family hour," later prime time, and Saturday morning television in the 1975–76 season. Demographic variables of program attributes include type of program—family or medical drama, situation comedy, or action-crime; attributes investigated for the fictional characters include sex, age, national origin, accent, ethnic identity, socio-economic status, occupation, program role of the character, and minority characteristics. Findings of the study are presented and discussed, together with some of their implications. A list of references is provided.

229. Formal Attributes of Television Commercials: Subtle Ways of Transmitting Sex Stereotypes. Welch, Renate L. et al., Kansas University, Lawrence. Department of Human Devlopment, Mar 1979, 16p. Paper presented at the Biennial Meeting of the Society for Research in Child Development (San Francisco, CA, March 15–18, 1979). Sponsoring agency: Spencer Foundation, Chicago, IL (ED 171 424; Reprint: EDRS).

Differences in formal aspects of television commercials aimed at boys and those aimed at girls were investigated. Formal attributes were defined as production techniques such as action, pace, visual effects, dialogue and narration, background music and sound effects. Two aspects of content were also examined: aggressive behavior and the gender of the narrator. Sixty toy advertisements were selected from videotaped records of Saturday and weekday morning children's programing. Twenty of the commercials contained all male characters, 20 contained all female characters, and 20 contained characters of both sexes. These were scored by blind observers for types of formal attributes used and type of aggression portrayed. Compared to female and mixed gender ads, male and mixed gender ads had higher levels of cuts and of male narration. Female ads had higher levels of fades and dissolves, of female narration, and of background music. There were no differences among the three types of commercials in levels of action by characters, total pace, and total dialogue. These findings are interpreted as indicating subtle sex stereotyping: production techniques in male ads convey action, speed and toughness, while in female ads they convey softness, gentleness and inactivity.

230. Impaired View: Television Portrayal of Handicapped People.* Leonard, Bonnie Downes, Boston University School of Education, 1978, 218p (7819756; Reprint: DC).

The universe of data sampled were the adult dramatic shows on Boston television's three major networks: NBC, CBS, and ABC, during prime time (8–11 p.m.). A preliminary base-line study collected data on the percentage of handicapped characters portrayed on prime-time dramatic shows by screening a sample of composite week of prime-time programs. An in-depth study of the depiction of handicapped characters examined another sample of dramatic shows in which handicapped characters appeared. This second sample was videotaped and included 26 programs of 34 hours aired over a period of four months. The total number of characters for this sample was 365 (316 nonhandicapped and 49 handicapped).

The base-line study of the composite week of television yielded data that reflected a discriminatory view of handicapped people. The percentage (3 percent) of handicapped characters on television did not even approximate the percentage (20 percent) of handicapped people that exists in the population at large.

The in-depth study of the depiction of handicapped characters, which utilized a content analysis approach, presented further evidence of discriminatory portrayal. On almost every dimension examined, handicapped characters were distinguished from nonhandicapped characters to a significant degree.

Race and gender were the only demographic dimensions that did not differentiate handicapped from nonhandicapped. With regard to age, 40 percent of the handicapped characters were depicted as children and, unrealistically, no handicapped characters were portrayed as over 65. Social class and occupation were distinguishing variables. Handicapped characters were portrayed more often as lower class, unemployed and in low status occupations when at work. However, they were generally not depicted at work or at home, but in institutions and schools. Handicapped characters were excluded from important roles in family life. They were not portrayed as fathers and mothers, or husbands and wives, but as sons and daughters with many portrayed as single, regardless of age.

In their life-stories or dramatic roles, handicapped characters were depicted as victims: of humor, of ridicule, and of verbal and physical violence. Hero status was denied handicapped characters. Story ending also distinguished handicapped from nonhandicapped, since fewer handicapped characters were given neutral endings. Positive endings sometimes had the disquieting effect of removing the character from the ranks of the handicapped by means of a miracle cure, thus denying the chronicity of the treatment of disability. The large percentage of negative endings for the handicapped reaffirmed their role as victim.

The analysis of the interaction of handicapped characters with nonhandicapped characters around the needs of affiliation, nurturance, and power revealed awkward, dependent, and important social relationships.

The findings of physical and personality traits of handicapped characters provided the final strokes of a grim portrait. They were depicted as uncultured and stupid, with little to say. They were presented as defensive, lacking in self-confidence, and dependent. Physically, they were shown as passive and weak in comparison to their nonhandicapped counterparts. The handicapped on television were seen as impatient and selfish. Identified also as sloppy in dress, the only unpleasant descriptors they avoided were ugly, fat, clumsy and bad.

231. The Language of the Saturday Morning Ghetto.
McCorkle, Suzanne. Feb 1980, 34p. Paper presented at the Annual Meeting of the Western Speech Communication Association (Portland, OR, February 16–20, 1980) (ED 184 161; Reprint: EDRS).

A content analysis was conducted to assess the verbal climate of Saturday morning television programs, the types of verbal aggression that appear in them, and the way verbal responses relate to other program variables. Three content analysis tools were developed and applied to 10 half-hour program blocks drawn randomly from the regularly scheduled programs broadcast in the Denver, Colorado, area by the three network affiliates. Among the conclusions were that the White male adult was vocally and visually dominant in the programs and that several social stereotypes were reinforced. Television characters usually operated from a neutrally valued verbal cluster (stating feelings and opinions, observing, describing, or instructing), but when the dominant mode of verbal response was not used, the verbal behavior became more defensive, personally attacking, and commanding. The programs exhibited less positively valued communication behavior by attractive than by unattractive characters, and they implied that supportive communication does not help, and defensive communication does not really hinder, problem resolution. Although defensiveness was associated with less "real" character types (animated characters and nonhumans), the extent to which young children attend to nonhuman characters is not known at this time.

232. Learning about Minorities from Television: The Research Agenda.
Greenberg, Bradley S.; Atkin, Charles K. Apr 1978, 53p. Paper presented at the conference "Television and the Socialization of the Minority Child," convened by the Center for Afro-American Studies, University of California at Los Angeles, April 27–28, 1978. Not available in hard copy due to marginal legibility (ED 166 712; Reprint: EDRS).

Several research studies that have compared the effects of television viewing on economically disadvantaged Black children with its effects on White children indicate that the Black children tend to allocate more time to television, are less selective in choosing content, and are more likely to accept fictional stories as reality. In addition, the Black children use television to learn information, display a high level of involvement in television content, and are likely to identify with the portrayal of Black characters (Black people appear on about half of the fictional programs). Isolating these critical factors concerning television viewing and the minority child clarifies new research issues for the future such as exploring the consequences of the child's social role attitude and the expectations that the child develops about specific role behaviors. A research model based on social learning theory offers a theoretical approach for examining such key variables as child attributes, message content factors, and social influences.

233. The Relationship between Sex-Role Stereotyping in TV Programming and Children's Autonomy.
Olsen, Judith E. Nov 1979, 33p. Paper presented at the Annual Meeting of the Speech Communication Association (65th, San Antonio, TX, November 10–13, 1979) (ED 180 040; Reprint: EDRS).

Six classes with 20 students per class participated in a study to determine the effects of television programing's stereotyped images on children's autonomy (independence of thought and action). Classes of first and second-grade students and two classes of fifth-grade students were the experimental groups, while the third- and sixth-grade classes served as control groups. A pretest, the games and activities checklist, was used to control the number of subjects both high and low in sex-role stereotyping. The experimental subjects observed videotapes of either traditional or nontraditional female television characters. The children's dependency scale was used as the posttest. The results supported three of six hypotheses that were proposed: boys got significantly higher scores on the autonomy scale than girls; fifth-grade students scored higher for autonomy than first and second-grade children; and fifth-grade students who observed nontraditional female roles scored higher than children in other age or treatment groups. The hypotheses that were not supported were that higher scores would occur for children in the nontraditional setting, for boys observing the nontraditional roles, and for fifth-grade boys.

234. The Relationship of Demographic Variables and Racial Attitudes to Adolescent Perceptions of Black Television Characters.* Dates, Jannette Lake, University of Maryland, 1979, 113p (7925740; Reprint: DC).

This study focuses on the research question: are any differences that exist in adolescent perceptions of Black television characters related to differences in race, sex, socioeconomic status, academic achievement, amount of time spent viewing Black television characters and general racial attitude?

The sample subjects were 11th-grade students from the Baltimore City Public School System in 1978–79. Eight public high schools were used to collect data on 207 subjects. The subjects reflected the general adolescent population with regard to sex, race, socioeconomic level, academic achievement, television viewing time and racial attitude.

The study used the California Achievement Test, which gave students' recent achievement test scores, a questionnaire developed by the investigator (based on the semantic differential technique), and a measure of general racial attitude (the Multifactor Racial Attitude Inventory).

Analysis of the data revealed:

1) There was an inverse relationship between general racial attitude and perceptions of Black television images. Youngsters with positive racial attitudes had more negative perceptions of Black television characters. As viewer racial attitudes became more positive, fewer people believed that Black television characters reflected reality.

2) There were significant differences between Blacks and non-Blacks in their perceptions of Black and non-Black television characters. Black viewers were the heavy viewers of Black television shows and rated Black television characters more positively than did non-Blacks. Blacks believed Black television characters represent real-life.

3) High academic achievers had positive racial attitudes and low academic achievers had negative racial attitudes.

4) There was no significant negative relationship bewteen racial attitudes and the extent to which students identified with black television characters.

5) There were significant differences between males and females in their evaluative perceptions of Black and non-Black television characters and in their perceptions of the reality of Black television characters.

6) There were no significant differences between low and high socioeconomic status youngsters in their perceptions of Black television characters.

7) No significant relationship was found between academic achievement and evaluative perceptions.

235. Sex Roles on TV: More Than Counting Buttons and Bows. Williams, Frederick. Oct 1978, 7p. Paper presented at the Annual Convention of the American Psychological Association (Toronto, ON, Canada, August, 1978) (ED 172 106; Reprint: EDRS).

The problem of sex-role stereotyping on television has been studied by trying to develop television materials that are explicitly counterstereotypic in terms of sex roles. The development of a new television series "Freestyle," aimed at 9–12-year-old children and their families, has led to some important observations about children's perceptions of sex-role portrayals. Children look past gender to the qualities of the individual; they hold stereotypes but not unalterable ones. Children view cartoon characters enthusiastically but skeptically. Sex-role attributes seem to be the last things in the children's minds when discussing these characters. On the other hand, children seem to view extreme sex-role stereotypes as so unreal as to be taken no more seriously than Bugs Bunny. Characterizations of real-life individuals, whether male or female, who mix those qualities of personality and behavior which make them "good people" are most attractive to children.

236. TV Stereotyping: "How to Keep 'em Down on the Farm." Top, N. Ferris, Apr 1977, 8p. Paper presented at the annual meeting of the Association for Educational Communications and Technology (Miami Beach, FL, April 26, 1977) (ED 143 322; Reprint: EDRS).

The modeling theory of aggressive behavior being promoted by violence on television points to more serious implications, that is, the molding of a national consciousness laden with 19th century values and stereotypical characterizations of reality. Since students are not taught how to watch television, they use it as a perception of reality. Because commercial television tries to please all people all the time, it finds the lowest common denominator. It portrays people in overgeneralized stereotypical and unreal ways. We must recognize that television offers a variety of products and we must educate the television consumer on how to choose these products, particularly the children, who learn from it early in their lives.

237. Television and Children's Images of Occupational Roles.* Heald, Gary Robert, Michigan State University, 1977, 175p (77-18, 487; Reprint: DC).

This study examines the occupational socialization phenomenon by focusing on organizing principles that lead to consistency in the ways that individuals perceive work roles, and by exploring some of the effects of learning about occupational roles from "primary" as opposed to "secondary" information sources. Primary information sources are those sources that are shared by large societal aggregates (e.g., mass media), with the primary sources providing largely undifferentiated messages. In contrast, secondary sources (e.g., family, friends) are more idiosyncratic and individualized thus allowing diverse, specialized information to be learned.

The essay begins with a discussion of "incidental learning" as it relates to children and adolescents. Learning in this paradigm centers on the acquisition of *images*, not isolated fact, about occupational roles. Special attention is given the part that the self-concept plays in image perception. Ten hypotheses are drawn out of this as to specific personal, relational and material characteristics that individuals use to distinguish occupational roles. The theoretic section then addresses the consequences of learning about work roles from a shared, primary source such as television. Hypotheses are offered as to the effects of this primary information source on cultural homogenization, occupational stereotyping, status conferral and individual perceptions of work role distributions.

The research hypotheses were tested through a survey of 210 fourth-, sixth- and eighth-grade students. Using a combination of paired-comparison and unidimensional measures, fifteen occupational roles were studied. Seven occupations were chosen due to their emphasis in the television medium; the remaining eight, while not emphasized in TV programing, were chosen owing to their use in previous research.

Multivariate analyses revealed that eight of the ten hypothesized attributes were as predicted in contributing to occupational images held by children. Counter to expectations, examination of the occupational images held by male versus female, and lower as opposed to upper socioeconomic children revealed no consistent patterns. Also contrary to hypotheses are the results indicating that learning about occupational roles from primary as compared to secondary information sources does not lead to greater cultural homogenization. The hypothesis of a stereotyping effect received mixed, inconclusive support. There is evidence, however, that persons receiving a proportionally larger part of their information from primary sources tend to have more stereotypic views of occupational roles. The hypothesis of a status conferral effect traceable to receiver dependence on primary information sources was not sustained. Predictions that primary sources can influence perception of occupation role distributions were confirmed. Conditional analyses further demonstrated partial support for predictions that this effect is greatest where secondary information about work roles is relatively absent.

238. Television and Social Reality: The Influence of Direct and Indirect Information on Adolescent Perceptions of Law Enforcement.* Slater, Dan, University of Oregon, 1977, 167p (7802571; Reprint: DC).

In recent years research on the effects of television viewing has begun looking at perceptual effects. Prior research concentrated on behavioral effects, that is whether specific content, such as TV violence, leads to specific acts of antisocial behavior. The perceptual effects research is concerned instead with whether viewers are absorbing distorted images of the world from television entertainment programing and whether those images are perceived as reality.

One institution in our society with which relatively few have had direct contact is law enforcement. As a result, most rely upon television as a primary source of indirect information about police, crime, and law enforcement activities. This dissertation tested the effects of television on perceptions of law enforcement among an adolescent sample.

Three groups with differing levels of direct contact with police were sampled: average high school students with little or no direct contact or experience with police, high school students with a high-positive level of contact with police via enrollment in a high school course in law enforcement, and high school students with a high-negative level of contact with police as a result of arrest, conviction, and probation.

A questionnaire was administered to a total of 557 high school students in California and Oregon, covering TV viewing habits, favorite programs, and the perceived reality of programs. Also included were questions designed to elicit the subjects' knowledge of law enforcement statements designed to indicate the extent to which subjects reify, that is believe the stereotyped police behaviors seen on television, and questions relating to demographic information.

The student groups formed the three levels for the independent variable, degree of direct information. The total sample was also divided into thirds according to their level of viewing law enforcement programs to form the other independent variable, degree of indirect information. Dependent variables included degree of perceived fidelity (reality) of TV law enforcement programs, degree of familiarity with observable facts (knowledge), and degree of perceived group reification (stereotyped TV behaviors). No interaction between independent variables was found for any of the dependent variables reported.

It was hypothesized that as direct information increased, perceived fidelity of police programs and reification would decrease and that knowledge would increase. It was also hypothesized that as indirect information, the viewing of police programs, increased, perceived fidelity and reification would increase and knowledge would decrease.

For each dependent variable a two-way analysis of variance is reported along with a table of means. The hypotheses concerning perceived fidelity and reification were supported, although only partially for direct information. In that latter case, the juvenile offender group departed from the predicted direction and exhibited higher levels of perceived fidelity and reification. The hypotheses relating to knowledge were not supported. The subjects in the police classes were less likely to perceive the programs as real and to reify, but mean scores for four of the five most popular police-crime programs tested revealed that even subjects in the police classes see the programs as more realistic than unrealistic.

239. Women and Minorities in Television Drama, 1969–1978. Gerbner, George; Signorielli, Nancy, Pennsylvania University, Philadelphia, Annenberg School of Communications, Oct 1979, 67p (ED 185 178; Reprint: EDRS).

This report presents an analysis of the characters created for prime time and weekend daytime network television drama and viewer conceptions associated with exposure to television. Data was gathered through 10 years of monitoring television programs, analyzing characters, and conducting surveys of child and adult viewers. Trends in representation of women and minorities (non-Whites, Hispanics, young and old people), findings on role characterizations and occupations, a measure of violence as a demonstration of power, and associations between television exposure and viewer conceptions of social reality are discussed. Television drama is found to underrepresent women and minorities. Typecasting of women is seen to restrict opportunities. Women and minorities are characterized as more vulnerable than their majority counterparts and are more frequently depicted as victims of violence. A positive and statistically significant relationship was found between the time an individual spends watching television and the individual's stereotyping of the role of women and the aged. Younger viewers born into a television world are found to be more imbued with its depiction of people and less likely to express an independent view of reality. Graphs and tables of data are included in the report.

BOOKS

240. Promise and Performance: Children with Special Needs. Harmonay, Maureen. Cambridge, MA: Ballinger Publishing Company, 1977, 255p.

This Action for Children's Television report examines the way that television treats handicapped children, both as subjects and viewers. It makes proposals to improve television both about and for those with disabilities.

Television News and Political Socialization

JOURNAL ARTICLES

241. The Adolescent and Television News: A Viewer Profile. Prisuta, Robert H. *Journalism Quarterly.* v56, n2, p277–82, Sum 1979 (EJ 207 939; Reprint: UMI).

A survey of more than 600 Michigan high school students suggests that adolescents who prefer television news and public affairs programs tend to feel their families, friends, and schools think public affairs are important; tend to be older; and tend not to be from a minority racial background.

242. Child and Adolescent Television Use and Political Socialization. Rubin, Alan M. *Journalism Quarterly.* v55, n1, p125–29, Spr 1978 (EJ 183 137; Reprint: UMI).

A study of the relationships between television use and political socialization indicated that lower levels of political information and understandings of the workings of government are associated with increased quantities of television viewing, but that positive political attitudes and higher levels of political knowledge are associated with public affairs viewing.

243. Children's Viewing Patterns for Television News. Egan, Lola M. *Journalism Quarterly.* v55, n2, p337–42, Sum 1978 (EJ 192 325; Reprint: UMI).

Reports that young children (ages 6–11) characterized as high or medium news watchers probably watch the news with their parents, watch more as they grow older, have a fairly good idea of the scope and usefulness of television news, prefer stories about topics appearing in popular entertainment programs, particularly crimes, murders, and disasters, and tend to see television news as being about bad or sensational events.

244. "Learned Helplessness" and the Evening News: T.V. News. Levine, Grace Ferrari. *Journal of Communication.* v27, n4, p100–05, Fall 1977 (EJ 200 963; Reprint: UMI).

Presents a study examining current network television newscasts to determine the extent to which "helplessness" models are depicted. Concludes that there is little variation between the networks and that, in some ways, the rendering of the story rather than the event itself produces the "helplessness" model.

245. Learning from a Television News Story. Drew, Dan; Reeves, Byron. *Communication Research—An International Quarterly.* v7, n1, p121–35, Jan 1980.

Studies the relationship between children's perceptions of the news and learning, and the effect of televised news story context on their perceptions. Explores the effect of news story context on learning through perceptual variables: liking the story, liking the program, believing the story, and understanding the function of the story.

246. TV News Is First Choice in Survey of High Schools. Atkins, Paul A.; Elwood, Harry. *Journalism Quarterly.* v55, n3, p596–99, Fall 1978 (EJ 197 770; Reprint: UMI).

A survey of more than 200 students in six high schools in West Virginia and Pennsylvania revealed that television was favored as a news source by a wide margin over newspapers, radio, and news magazines in three areas: general preference, believability, and preference should the consumer be limited to one news source.

247. TV Newsmen—Stop Cheating My Children. Sullivan, James Michael. *Intellect.* v106, n2395, p393–94, Apr 1978 (EJ 182 845; Reprint: UMI).

Examines the dangers and disappointments of television journalism, which suffers from lack of time, and a "tell them what they want to hear" syndrome, and focuses on a few core issues that point out what is keeping TV news from becoming that positive social force that it has the potential to become.

248. Television News and Political Socialization. Atkin, Charles K.; Gantz, Walter. *Public Opinion Quarterly.* v42, n2, p183–98, Sum 1978.

Elementary school children frequently watch child-oriented news segments on Saturday morning television and they occasionally view network newscasts. News viewing is mildly associated with political knowledge and public affairs interest for older children, but younger viewers learn little. Parent/child discussions of news are also related to newscast exposure.

MICROFICHE

249. Political Advertising Effects on Voters and Children. Atkin, Charles K. Sep 1976, 29p. Paper presented at Annual Meeting of the American Psychological Association (Washington, DC, September 3–7, 1976) (ED 147 200; Reprint: EDRS).

The document examines the influence of political television commercials on voting behavior. In addition, the paper reports new data concerning the role of voter-oriented ads in socializing children to the political environment. Part I characterizes political ads and presents findings and conclusions of three voter surveys recently published in "Public Opinion Quarterly." The method used in the reported surveys was to conduct interviews with 835 representative voters in Wisconsin, Colorado, and Michigan gubernatorial and congressional campaigns. Findings indicated that significant cognitive changes occurred among voters who watched political TV ads, but that attitude changes were related to preexisting ideological orientations and to the degree of attention paid by the voter to the ads. Relationships among voter attitudes, knowledge, exposure and attention to political ads, and voter turnout are discussed. Part II focuses on the relationship between campaign advertising and political socialization of children. It was hypothesized that children who view political commercials would know more about a candidate and like the candidate better than children who were less exposed to the messages. Findings from a survey of 120 elementary school students indicated moderate to strong relationships between viewing of political ads and knowledge about and positive attitudes toward the advertised candidate. It was concluded that campaign advertising directed at adult voters may play a significant role in socializing children to the political environment.

Television Commercials: Consumer and Health Learning

JOURNAL ARTICLES

250. American Research on T.V. Advertising's General Impact on Children. Rossiter, John R. *Australian Journal of Early Childhood.* v3, n1, p15–19, Mar 1978.

Reviews literature on cognitive, attitudinal, and behavioral effects of television commercials on children. Both cumulative exposure and heavy viewing effects are discussed.

251. Children's Perception of the Value of an Advertised Product. Sheikh, Anees A.; Moleski, Martin. *Journal of Broadcasting.* v21, n3, p347–54, Sum 1977 (EJ 190 916; Reprint: UMI).

A study compared the perceived value of a product by children who had viewed a commercial with that of others who had examined the product. Data indicate that, when television commercials exaggerate the virtues of the products, boys are more apt to be misled by the advertising claims than girls.

252. Children's Responsiveness to Commercials. Robertson, Thomas S.; Rossiter, John R. *Journal of Communication.* v27, n1, p101–106, Win 1977.

This study of 289 first-, third-, and fifth-grade boys examined susceptibility to toy advertisements in relation to the amount of TV exposure, the child's age, level of peer integration, and parent education background. Age was the most important dispositional factor influencing the effects of advertising on the children. Heavy viewers were also more "persuasible." Strong peer and/or parent mediation reduced the impact of commercials.

253. Children's Viewing of Television and Recognition Memory of Commercials. Zuckerman, Paul et al. *Child Development.* v49, n1, p96–104, Mar 1978 (EJ 178 179; Reprint: UMI).

Videotapes of elementary school children watching a standard 15-minute television presentation were analyzed for attention to television, viewing patterns, and alternate activities. Recognition memory of auditory and visual contact of the commercials and of the products was tested. Children's behavior during the program and during the commercials was compared. Evidence for rapid habituation to the content of commercials was obtained.

254. Conflict in the Family over Commercials.
Sheikh, Anees A.; Moleski, L. Martin. *Journal of Communication.* v27, n1, p152–57, Win 1977.

This study of 48 White upper-middle class elementary students examined their purchase requests in response to television commercials and, particularly, the likelihood of unpleasant reactions to their parent's refusal to comply. Unpleasant affect was found to peak in grade 3 and to be more pronounced in girls.

255. Effects of Drug Commercials on Young Viewers.
Atkin, Charles K. *Journal of Communication.* v28, n4, p71–79, Fall 1978 (EJ 204 406; Reprint: UMI).

Discusses children's television viewing, particularly their exposure to advertisements for proprietary drug products, and relates this to their views of the amount of sickness in society and the reliance on medicine. Draws a tentative profile of the type of preadolescent who tends to be more influenced by over-the-counter drug commercials: a bright, higher status male or female who is usually healthy and whose parents disapprove of medicine usage.

256. Effects of Television Commercial Disclaimers on the Product Expectations of Children. Liebert, Diane E. et al. *Journal of Communication.* v27, n1, p118–24, Win 1977.

This study found that the standard disclaimer used in two different TV toy commercials, "Some assembly required," was totally ineffective in communicating to children in the age range for which it was intended. Children exposed to the modified disclaimer, "You have to put it together," showed twice as much understanding, demonstrating the importance of wording appropriate to young children.

257. The Experts Look at Children's Television.
Culley, James D. et al. *Journal of Broadcasting.* v20, n1, p3–21, Win 1976.

A study of attitudes of government spokesmen, industry spokesmen, and consumer groups toward advertising on children's television programs.

258. How Black Children See TV Commercials.
Meyer, Timothy P. et al. *Journal of Advertising Research.* v18, n5, p51–58, Oct 1978.

The purpose of this study was to assess the cognitive responses of 205 inner-city Black children, varying in age from 5 to 12, to TV advertising. Findings indicate that low-income Black children have a very low degree of consumer understanding in this area—no more than 56 percent of the sample had any awareness of the purpose of a TV commercial, compared to 85–90 percent in a study of White middle-class children. The Black children were also more likely to believe that TV commercials always tell the truth. Implications for advertising and consumer education are discussed.

259. The Impact of Television Advertising on Children from Low Income Families. Gorn, Gerlad J.; Goldberg, Marvin E. *Journal of Consumer Research.* v4, n2, p86–88, Sep 1977.

A study on TV advertising and low-income boys, ages 8–10, suggested that even one exposure to a commercial produced favorable attitudes towards the advertised product. Additional exposures were necessary, however, to influence the children to expend more effort than the control group to obtain the advertised product.

260. Integrating Results from Children's Television Advertising Research. Resnik, Alan J. et al. *Journal of Advertising.* v8, n3, p3–12, Sum 1979 (EJ 214 155; Reprint: UMI).

Presents a model of the way children process television advertising.

261. Language in Children's Television Commercials: A Sociolinguistic Perspective. Bloome, David; Ripich, Danielle. *Theory into Practice.* v18, n4, p220–25, Oct 1979 (EJ 220 206; Reprint: UMI).

The use of language in television commercials to promote products and the use of deceptive language in commercials addressing young children are discussed. It is suggested that such language may not only influence children's consumer behavior but may also be providing them with poor models of social interaction and language use.

262. Parental Concern about Child-Directed Commercials. Feldman, Shel et al. *Journal of Communication.* v27, n1, p125–37, Win 1977.

This article reports some pilot work conducted in Philadelphia during 1974 on questions relating to the extent of parental concern over child-directed commercials and possible relationships between parent demographics, parental concern, and parental preferences among regulatory options.

263. Parental Mediation of Television Advertising Effects. Robertson, Thomas S. *Journal of Communication.* v29, n1, p12–25, Win 1979 (EJ 207 855; Reprint: UMI).

Reviews the current research on the effects of television advertising on children and the interaction between parent and child regarding the child's consumer behavior. Suggests areas for future research.

264. Race as a Dimension in Children's TV Advertising: The Need for More Research.
Barry, Thomas E.; Sheikh, Anees A. *Journal of Advertising.* v6, n3, p5–10, Sum 1977 (EJ 169 683; Reprint: UMI).

States that most of the current research in the area of television advertising for children excludes Black subjects; reviews major studies of television and children and Black v White child development.

265. The Relationship between Television Advertising and Drug Abuse among Youth: Fancy and Fact.
Payne, Donald E. *Journal of Drug Education.* v6, n3, p215–19, Fall 1976.

Television advertising of over-the-counter drugs has been suspected of being a contributing factor in drug abuse among youth. Recent research suggests that these suspicions are ill founded. What is worse, they focus attention, effort, and resources on a factor which is simply irrelevant to the problem.

266. Reliability of a Short Test Measuring Children's Attitudes toward TV Commercials. Rossiter, John R. *Journal of Consumer Research.* v3, n4, p179–84, Mar 1977.

This article presents a short objective test for measuring children's attitudes toward television commercials. The test is shown to have high internal-consistency reliability and satisfactory test-retest reliability for a sample of 208 children. Extension of the test for use with younger children and its modification for measurement of children's attitudes toward other forms of advertising are discussed.

267. Some Unintended Consequences of TV Advertising to Children. Goldberg, Marvin E.; Gorn, Gerlad J. *Journal of Consumer Research.* v5, n1, p22–29, Jun 1978.

This study of 50 preschoolers (ages 4–5) investigated some potential unintended consequences of TV advertising on a child's reaction to both parents and peers and on personal feelings when denied a request for a toy. To the extent the operationalized measures reflect these broad concerns, the results generally support the hypothesis that TV advertising may: (a) lead the child to select material objects over more socially oriented alternatives, (b) potentially increase parent-child conflict, and (c) lead to a more disappointed, unhappy child.

268. TV Messages for Snack and Breakfast Foods: Do They Influence Children's Preferences? Goldberg, Marvin E. *Journal of Consumer Research.* v5, n2, p73–81, Sep 1978.

When offered a choice of highly sugared or more wholesome snack and breakfast foods, first graders' choices reflected their TV exposure experience. Those who viewed commercials for highly sugared foods opted for more (advertised and nonadvertised) sugared foods. Those who viewed pronutrition public service announcements chose more fruits, vegetables, and other more nutritious foods. A 24-minute animated program ''Junk Food'' was most effective in reducing the number of sugared foods selected.

269. Television and Interpersonal Influences on Adolescent Consumer Learning. Churchill, Gilbert A., Jr.; Moschis, George P. *Journal of Consumer Research.* v6, n1, p23–35, Jun 1979.

This article offers a framework for organizing and conceptualizing variables in the study of consumer socialization, applies the general notion of socialization to the specific context of consumer socialization, and empirically tests the resulting model with a sample of 806 Wisconsin adolescents. Results failed to support the model with respect to several key relationships but television, family, and peers did appear as important sources of consumer information, with the impact of television being mitigated by parent intervention.

270. Television—Health Education or Mental Pollution? Price, James H. *Health Education.* v9, p24–26, Mar–Apr 1978 (EJ 186 084; Reprint: UMI).

Studies are cited demonstrating that television programs and commercials present erroneous ideas about nutrition, health products, sex, and family life. Suggestions are offered to reduce the level of cerebral pollution emitted by the television.

271. Television: The Anti-Wellness Tool. Leary, John E. *Health Education.* v10, n5, p16–18, Sep–Oct 1979 (EJ 216 879; Reprint: UMI).

The influence of television pervades American society to the extent that it seriously interferes with the development of desirable attitudes towards sexuality, nutrition, exercise, nonviolence, and general human wellness.

272. The Unhealthy Persuader: The Reinforcing Value of Television and Children's Purchase-Influencing Attempts at the Supermarket. Galst, Joann Paley; White, Mary Alice. *Child Development.* v47, n4, p1089–96, Dec 1976.

This study collected behavioral data on the relationship between children's attentiveness to television commercials and their product requests, using the techniques of operant conditioning and direct observation. Cereals and candy were the most heavily requested items and the food items most frequently advertised in commercials directed at children. As advertisements for sugared-cereals outnumber those for unsugared cereals by 3 to 1 during programing directed at children, the results were discussed in terms of TV's contribution to unhealthy eating patterns.

273. Why Television Advertising Is Deceptive and Unfair. Goldsen, Rose K. *ETC.: A Review of General Semantics.* v35, n4, p354–75, Win 1978 (EJ 209 363; Reprint: UMI).

Discusses many topics, including proposals to limit television advertisers' access to children; the dependence of television commercials on involuntary, mnemonic learning; the way television commercials' bypassing of rationality is aided by cognitive processing of music, rhythms, and familiar sensory events; and ideas for correcting the damage caused by deceptive, unfair television advertising.

MICROFICHE

274. Black and White Children's Perceptions of the Intent and Values in Specific Adult and Child Oriented Television Commercials. Donohue, Thomas R. et al. 1977, 16p. Paper presented at the Annual Meeting of the International Communication Association (Berlin, Germany, May 29–June 4, 1977) (ED 139 056; Reprint: EDRS).

The purpose of this study was to identify the effect of television advertising on different types of children—specifically, the cognitive responses and extra-product expectations fostered by television commercials in both White and Black children. The subjects, 52 middle-class White children and 30 inner-city Black children ranging in age from six to eight years, were asked to describe a television commercial, and then were shown two McDonalds commercials in color, and finally were asked questions about the commercials. Analysis of results showed that White children indicate significantly higher levels of awareness than do Black children and that older children demonstrate significantly higher levels of understanding than do younger children. Several disturbing health and nutritional implications are discussed, and the study concludes that it is important to know the extent to which subtle or implied appeals are internalized by children of various levels of cognitive development.

275. Children and Advertising: A Bibliography.
Council of Better Business Bureaus, Inc., New York, NY. Clearinghouse for Research on Children's Advertising. Jun 1978, 57p (ED 170 777; Reprint: EDRS; also available from Children's Advertising Review Unit, National Advertising Division, Council of Better Business Bureaus, 845 Third Avenue, New York, NY 10022).

More than 600 entries are contained in this annotated bibliography of materials concerning the effects of television advertising on children. Entries are alphabetized by author and are divided into the following categories: special interest articles; general interest articles; books and pamphlets; government publications; transcripts of oral presentations; completed research, studies, and reports; research proposals and research-in-progress; unpublished works; bibliographies on children and advertising; and references of related interest.

276. Children's Attitudes Towards Television Commercials: Methodological Considerations and Implications.* Riecken, William Glen,
Virginia Polytechnic Institute and State University, 1979, 232p (8007946; Reprint: DC).

The purpose of this study was to evaluate the reliability of selected attitude measuring devices and to use the data obtained to derive implications for research methodology, public policy, and advertising strategy.

Five problem areas were included: (1) reliability evaluation of the original scale modified to reflect towards commercials for cereals, proprietary medicines, and toys, (2) reliability evaluation of the original scale, (3) comparison of attitude scores produced, (4) examination of attitude scores by demographic characteristics of respondents, and (5) examination of the relationship between commercial attitudes and specific brand evaluations.

Some children in the Piaget's concrete operational stage of cognitive development who attended one school in Muncie, IN were chosen as respondents. The questionnaire was administered at two points in time. Younger children had the questionnaire read to them by their teachers; older children self-administered the questionnaire.

Both the original and modified scales produced reliable measures; the interitem and item-total coefficients fit the guidelines, the alpha measures were high, and the test-retest correlations were generally significant at $p < .001$.

All commercials were looked at negatively but toy commercials somewhat less so. Attitudes were found to be independent of either age or sex and brand evaluations were found to be independent of commercials attitudes as well.

In terms of research methodology, some implications are: (1) agreement/disagreement scales generate reliable attitudinal data, and (2) both general and specific attitudes can be measured.

In terms of public policy, the findings suggest that children are capable of evaluating commercials and are able to form evaluations of brands independently from commercials attitudes. Thus regulation involving banning commercials for all products when children comprise a certain percentage of the television audience may not be necessary. Instead, a selective regulation approach may be more appropriate.

In terms of advertising strategy, the results indicate that advertisers should attempt to design commercials that will gain more favor with children—particular attention should be paid to the truth of commercials and to ensuring that product performance matches advertising claims. Each industry needs to determine why children view those particular commercials in a negative manner.

277. Children's Conceptions of Proprietary Medicines: The Role of Television Advertising.†
Robertson, Thomas S. et al., Wharton School, Philadelphia, PA, Center for Research on Media and Children; National Science Foundation, Washington, DC, Applied Science and Research Applications, 1978, 163p (PB-287 551/6ST; Reprint: NTIS).

This project is designed to assess the effects of televised medicine advertising on children. The sample is comprised of 673 children (ages 8–13) and their parents. The sample composition includes boys and girls and spans a socioeconomic range from disadvantaged to upper-middle class. The project objective is to provide an analysis of the relationship between proprietary medicine advertising and children's beliefs, attitudes, and behavior toward proprietary medicines. Results suggest that televised medicine advertising performs only a limited role in the formation of children's beliefs and attitudes toward medicines. In the short run, it produces a modest increase in beliefs and attitudes. In the long run, this increase is overshadowed by a significant decline in children's attitudes and beliefs as a function of age, and thus cognitive development and experience. Further, the study indicates a lack of relationship between advertising and usage (which is controlled by parents) and finds no support that children abuse proprietary medicines. Usage levels are moderate and the extent to which parents allow children to self-administer medicines is relatively low.

278. Children's Interactional Experience with Television Advertising as an Index of Viewing Sophistication: A Symbolic Interactionist Study.
Reid, Leonard N.; Frazier, Charles F. Aug 1979, 23p. Paper presented at the Annual Meeting of the Association for Education in Journalism (62nd, Houston, TX, August 5–8, 1979) (ED 174 996; Reprint: EDRS).

After seven judges had ranked 30 families for observed parental consumer teaching orientations and family television viewing habits, one family was selected for each cell of a 3×3

factorial design for age of children (3 to 5, 6 to 8, 9 to 11) and family consumer teaching orientation (high, moderate, low). These nine family groups were observed over three months in family group viewing situations. The observational records supported the view that children, including preschoolers, are potentially sophisticated viewers, able to deal with television advertising and affected by the family group's particular consumer-related skills and knowledge. The findings challenged the view that a child's ability to understand television advertising is determined at age-graded stages of cognitive development. As skilled interactants at easly ages, children identify and define the nature of television commercials in relation to consumer-related levels of interaction with parents, make demands and requests of parents and others in relation to the character of viewing situations, seek out information about commercial content and other social events, plan future social actions toward and through television commercials, and negotiate various joint acts with others while situated in front of the family television set.

279. Edible TV: Your Child and Food Commercials.
Choate, Robert B., Comp.; Engle, Pamela C., Comp., Council on Children, Media, and Merchandising, Washington, DC, Jun 1977, 105p (ED 143 420; Reprint: EDRS). For a related document see citation 293.

This document reports on the impact of television food commercials on children under 12, focusing specifically on how commercials influence children's food preferences and concepts, how they affect children's knowledge of nutrition, and how they contribute to obesity. Part I is a compilation of short excerpts from relevant testimony before the Federal Trade Commission (FTC), 1976–77. Included are witnesses' remarks on the above issues and comments concerning ways to make television a more educational medium in matters pertaining to food selection. Part II contains (1) a synopsis of the 1976 testimony of Robert B. Choate dealing with the frequency and content of food commercials directed toward children, and (2) a report on a developmental study of the use of graphics to convey nutritional information to children aged 4 to 10.

280. The Effects of Adult-Oriented Advertising on First, Second, and Third Grade Children across Socioeconomic Bounds.
Lucas, Richard Jay, University of Massachusetts, 1976, 247p (77-6429; Reprint: DC).

The purpose of this study was to examine the socializing effect the viewing of adult-oriented commercials has on young children of differing socioeconomic backgrounds. The subjects, 227 children in the first, second, and third grades, included 109 lower-socioeconomic-level Black children and 118 White children representing upper-middle-income families. After viewing a half-hour television program that included six commercials, the children were interviewed about their recall of the commercials and their attitudes toward them. Analysis of the results indicated that the White middle-class children understood commercial intent significantly more often than did children in the other group. The White children were more skeptical of commercials' truthfulness and rejected the idea that people need products or money to be happy. The lower-socioeconomic-level Black children did not seem to understand

commercial intent, and they perceived commercials as truthful. They tended to recall lifestyle details portrayed in the commercials more than did the White children, and they strongly agreed that products and money are necessary to happiness.

281. The Effects of Televised Advertising on Mother-Child Interactions at the Grocery Store.
Reeves, Byron; Atkin, Charles K. Aug 1979, 22p. Paper presented at the Annual Meeting of the Association for Education in Journalism (62nd, Houston, TX, August 5–8, 1979) (ED 181 474; Reprint: EDRS).

One hundred mother/child dyads were involved in a study to provide empirical evidence on parent/child interaction in grocery stores and on the contributions of Saturday morning television commercials to those interactions and to the purchase of candy and cereals. Data were collected in 15 supermarkets in two midwestern cities. First, the mother/child dyads were unobtrusively observed during the purchase of candy and cereal. After the observation, children were interviewed concerning the frequency of their exposure to Saturday morning television while mothers responded to a written questionnaire about their children's reactions to television advertising. The results indicated that children took the initiative for purchases of candy and cereal a majority of the time and that regardless of who initiated the interaction, the other party would likely comply with the request. Amount of exposure to Saturday morning television immediately prior to a shopping trip was the only statistically significant predictor of whether children would initiate a product request.

282. The Effects of Televised Drug Commercials on Children.
Sheiman, Deborah Lovitky. 1977, 7p (ED 178 052; Reprint: EDRS)

This paper addresses the issue of nonprescription drug commercials appearing on commercial television and the impact that they have on children. Self-regulatory standards set by the National Association of Broadcasters are cited, and the lack of definitive research concerning children and drug commercials is discussed. A brief bibliography is attached.

283. Influence of Television Commercials on Young Children.
Lam, Pamela Y. May 1978, 77p. Master's thesis, North Texas State University (ED 156 326; Reprint: EDRS).

This study investigated the influence of television commercials for toys and cereals on young children. Forty-four children, ranging in age from four to seven years, were interviewed regarding their television viewing habits, their attitudes toward television commercials, their demands for their mothers to buy cereals and toys, and their interpretation of the reality of commercials. The mothers of these children completed a questionnaire about their children's television viewing habits, their own attitudes toward commercials, and their reactions to their children's demands for advertised products. The data were analyzed by computing percentages and the results revealed several trends. The more television the children watched, the more they demanded advertised products. Most of the time, mothers did not yield completely to their children's demands for advertised products. Children were able to name their specific preferences and dislikes for television commercials and they tended to prefer commercials which were related to their interests. Parental discussion on the content and selling techniques of television advertisements reduced the extent of children's demands for advertised products and the extent of parental yielding to demands. Boys and girls did not show particular differences in responding to television commercials.

284. Mass Media and Interpersonal Influences on the Acquisition of Consumer Competencies. Moore, Roy L. et al. Apr 1978, 21p. Paper presented at the Annual Meeting of the International Communication Association (Chicago, IL, April 25–29, 1978) (ED 158 343; Reprint: EDRS).

To achieve competency as consumers in the marketplace, young people need to acquire specific consumer skills. To determine the influence of such socialization agents as television, family, peers, and school on the acquisition of these skills, 607 middle and high school students in Kentucky and North Carolina completed self-administered questionnaires which focused on four variables relevant to the consumer role: brand knowledge, price accuracy, consumer affairs knowledge, and socially desirable consumer role perceptions. The results indicated that consumer skills varied according to the age, sex, and social class of the respondents. Older adolescents were found to possess these skills to a greater extent than younger adolescents. Males could more accurately price products and services, had greater consumer affairs knowledge, and were more aware of socially desirable consumer behaviors than females; but females were more aware of available brands. Upper-class adolescents scored higher in all four skills than lower-class adolescents. Peers and television were the most influential socialization agents. From their peers adolescents apparently learned about the availability of brands and about consumer matters, while from television they learned perceptions of effective consumer behavior. Parents and schools, however, contributed little to the acquisition of these skills, highlighting the need for evaluating current consumer education materials and practices at school and suggesting that some consumer education efforts could be aimed at adults.

285. Mediating Role of Parental Influence in Children's Response to Television Commercials: An Exploratory Study. Prasad, V. Kanti et al., Aug 1977, 20p. Paper presented at the Annual Meeting of the American Psychological Association (85th, San Francisco, CA, August 26–30, 1977). Sponsoring agency: National Institute of Mental Health (DHEW), Rockville, MD (ED 145 937; Reprint: EDRS).

This study investigated, in a laboratory experimental framework, the relative influences of television commercials and parental counter-commercial advocacy on children's consumption choice behavior. Sixty-four 8- to 10-year-old boys were randomly assigned to one of three treatment groups: (1) no counter commercial advocacy (control group), (2) power-assertive type of parental counter-commercial advocacy, (3) reasoning type of parental counter-commercial advocacy. Subjects viewed a 20-minute children's television program that contained three repetitions of commercials for one of two toys. (The toys had been selected in a pilot study from a group of

toys not yet introduced in the area which had had statistically equal appeal to boys of the subjects' age.) After viewing the commercials, the subjects were placed in a room with their mothers who had been instructed to exhibit one of the three advocacy conditions. Children then played a game with the experimenter in which they were allowed to win tokens which they exchanged for one of the two toys. Product choice and decision time were the dependent variables. Results partially supported the hypothesis that a reasoning style rather than a power assertive style of parental counter-commercial advocacy would be more effective in counteracting the influence of television commercials, but did so only in the situations in which the advertising induced temptation was not very high to begin with.

286. Research on the Effects of Television Advertising on Children; A Review of the Literature and Recommendations for Future Research. Adler, Richard P. et al., National Science Foundation, Washington, DC, RANN Program, 1977, 230p. Some pages of document may be marginally legible due to size of type (ED 145 499; Reprint: EDRS; also available from Superintendent of Documents, US Government Printing Office, Washington, DC 20402, Stock no. 038-000-00336-4).

This report summarizes the present state of knowledge about the effects of television advertising on children. After a discussion of children's television viewing patterns, the report reviews the existing research relevant to such issues as children's ability to distinguish commercials from program material; the influence of format and audiovisual techniques on children's perceptions of commercials; the effects of characters in commercials, self-concept appeals, premium offers, food advertising, the volume and repetition of commercials, and medicine advertising; violence and unsafe acts in commercials directed to children; the effects of television advertising on consumer socialization; and television advertising and parent/child relations. The report then makes recommendations for future research. Appendixes present evaluations of 21 individual studies, a statistical profile of the national research resources currently available for relevant studies, and the children's advertising guidelines issued by the National Association of Broadcasters Code Authority. A bibliography of relevant publications is included.

287. Preschoolers' Discrimination of Television Programming and Commercials. Levin, Stephen R. et al. Mar 1979, 12p. Paper presented at the Biennial Meeting of the Society for Research in Child Development (San Francisco, CA, March 15–18, 1979) (ED 171 426; Reprint: EDRS).

This study used a recognition procedure to directly assess preschool children's ability to discriminate between programs and commercials in an actual viewing situation. Seventy-two children, equally grouped by sex and age (three, four, and five years) were individually presented with three videotapes. Each tape contained a sample of 48 10-second segments of TV programs and commercials; one tape was in a video-only mode, one in audio-only mode and the third in both video and audio. Results indicated that accuracy increased with age, but that even three-year-olds could discriminate commercials from programs.

Errors appeared to be in the direction of misidentifying TV program segments as commercials rather than vice-versa. There were fewer errors for commercials directed at children than for those directed at adults. The effect of mode interacted with age: four-year-olds discriminated best in the audio-video mode while the three- and five-year-olds discriminated equally well in all three modes. The influence of three individual difference characteristics on recognition abilities was additionally investigated: age, children's intellectual skills, the Peabody Picture Vocabulary Test, and parents' estimates of children's exposure to television. Age and PPVT scores were positively correlated with discrimination scores, but TV exposure was negatively correlated with discrimination scores.

288. Socialization Influences of Television Commercials on Preschool-Age Children.*
Valdez, Armando, Stanford University, 1979, 325p (7912417; Reprint: DC).

This study examines the long-term socialization effects of television commercials on preschool-age children. Television commercials are conceptualized as cultural artifacts and like all cultural products reflect the world-views of the sociocultural system that produces them. The socialization effects of television commercials are thus examined as a social process within the broad parameters of the entire social structure. This perspective posits concentric spheres of influence on the child. The child is seen as interacting with and being correspondingly influenced by his immediate family and by television, in that order.

The analysis of preschooler exposure patterns revealed that the majority of preschooler's viewing occurs during certain peak periods. The largest preschool audience occurs on Saturday mornings, followed by weekend evenings. Preschoolers' viewing was found to be highly correlated to the viewing patterns of their 6-to-11-year-old siblings. The content analysis of television commercials to which preschoolers are commonly exposed revealed that role portrayals of males and females reflected the traditional roles of male dominance and female subordinance. Imbedded in many commercial messages were the overriding emphasis on resolving problems through the consumption of goods and services. These commercials stressed the purchase of commodities as a problem-solving strategy that unequivocally led to a desirable outcome. Food ads stressed self-indulgence and immediate gratification; however, this theme was evident in ads for other products as well. The nutritional information conveyed by food ads was sparse and often bordered on deception. Consequently, preschoolers for whom television ads constitute the sole source of nutritional information may in fact be nutritional illiterates.

The field study of preschooler television households revealed a very stable and predictable pattern within each preschool television household; however, the pattern itself was not the same across all preschooler households. A preliminary typology of preschooler television households demonstrated that preschooler viewing patterns were a useful indicator for household viewing patterns and family structure as well. Factors such as family size and number of older siblings were reflected in the preschooler's viewing behavior. Perhaps the most important finding was a preschooler pattern which showed television viewing as an activity-surrogate rather than as a caretaker, i.e., babysitter or pacifier, as is commonly presumed.

The institutional analysis of the children's television market identifies the enormous importance of economic factors which propel the images and messages that find their way to the television screen and ultimately to the children viewers. The marketing function of television and the high levels of economic concentration were found to be the motive force and thus two defining features of the children's television market.

289. Structural and Situtional Effects on Mothers' Responses to Children's Purchase Requests.*
Popper, Edward Thomas, Harvard University, 1978, 3760 (7818834; Reprint: DC).

This dissertation examined the ways that families make purchase decisions, with special attention being given to parent-child purchase interaction. A conceptualization of the family decision process was developed based on a synthesis of the literature in family decision making, family behavior, and organizational buyer behavior. From this conceptualization, the following researchable issues were developed: that parent-child purchase interaction is a complex, family decision making process (rather than an individual purchase process), and that the outcome of the process is effected by the situational context (which products are requested, where the request occurs), by the nature of existing patterns of parent-child interaction (not purchase related), and by the characteristics of the participants in the interaction (including demographic characteristics as well as behavioral characteristics, such as existing patterns of consumption decision making).

These issues were addressed in an experimental survey administered to 320 mothers in the Boston metropolitan area involving a scenario of a request from their child for a hypothetical product. They were asked to select a response from a closed set of nine response alternatives. The hypothetical products, scenarios, and the response set were generated from a series of focus groups followed by a series of pretests. The mothers were also given a detailed interview with regard to their patterns of interaction with their children, the way they functioned as consumers, their attitudes toward television advertising, and basic demographics.

The analyses indicated that the nature of the product had a dramatic effect on a mother's response to her child's purchase request while the location where the request occurred appeared to have little effect. Further, the presence of overt references to television advertising in the child's request had no effect on the mother's response.

Mothers who were likely to spend more time on consumption related activities themselves were shown to be likely to spend more time in responding to their children's requests (i.e., giving negotiating responses). Similarly, mothers who had developed patterns of positive interaction with their children were more likely to give negotiating responses to requests. The child's age was also significantly related to the mother's response, with mothers being more likely to give positive negotiating responses to older children.

Although the overt mention of television in the request did not effect the mother's responses, their attitudes towards television advertising did have an effect. Mothers who had strong negative feelings towards television advertising directed to children (particularly when that advertising was mentioned in a purchase request) were significantly more likely to give negative negotiating responses to the requests (regardless of whether the request contained a reference to television advertising).

290. A Study of the Reactions of Young Children to a Selected Group of Television Commercials and the Associated Products.* Folkerts, Bonnie Jean, University of Iowa, 1978. 210p (7822401; Reprint: DC).

The purpose of this study was to obtain descriptive information regarding young children's reactions to television commercials and the products associated with these commercials. The basic descriptive mechanism used was that of comparison. The comparisons were made among the following groups: (1) First and fourth grade children, (2) Boys and girls in first and fourth grade, (3) Parents and children, (4) Children and a panel of nutritional experts, and (5) Parents and a panel of nutritional experts.

The major determinants in establishing the effect of television commercials upon young children were the results obtained by administering a series of ten questionnaires. The administration of the questionnaires was accompanied by a viewing of each television commercial and a tasting experience with each advertised product.

The study was conducted in the first and fourth grades of the Iowa City Community School District. The population sample numbered 150 children. The sample was composed of 80 children in first grade, 41 girls and 39 boys. In fourth grade there were 70 children, 37 girls and 33 boys. Based on empirical judgment, it was assumed that a majority of the children came from middle-class homes.

On the basis of the analysis of the data collected, the following results are presented:

1. A change in reaction to television commercials and associated products does occur as children progress from first to fourth grade.

2. First graders want a product immediately after they have viewed the commercial. Fourth graders may or may not want the product at this time.

3. First graders do not necessarily think a product will taste good until they have actually tasted the product. Fourth graders hold generally the same opinion about the product's taste both before and after a tasting experience.

4. First graders respond strongly to a prize offered with a product.

5. Fourth graders respond strongly to the quality of a product promoted as being good for them.

6. The main character in a commercial exerts the most impact on fourth graders and girls in both the first and fourth grades in regard to their reactions to the commercials; however, boys indicate a higher consensus of agreement in their main character choices.

7. The impact of the main character does not relate to whether or not the child wants the promoted product.

8. As boys progress from first to fourth grade, they become more likely to believe that any product will be good for them.

9. As girls progress from first to fourth grade, they become less likely to believe that candy and gum will be good for them.

10. Both boys and girls in both grades prefer main characters in television commercials in the following order: animated cartoon characters, cartoon characters with more lifelike characteristics, and non-cartoon live characters.

11. Parents, children, and nutritional experts consider presweetened cereals to have a higher nutritional value than snacks, candy, or gum.

12. Children believe there is more nutritional value in snacks, candy, and gum than do parents or nutritional experts.

291. Television Advertising to Children: Exposure Effects and Parental Influence.* Wiman, Alan Russell, University of Tennessee, 1979, 204p (7918662; Reprint: DC).

This research has two major objectives. The first is to explore whether or not exposure to television advertising is related to certain cognitive, attitudinal, and behavioral variables. The second objective is to determine the importance, if any, of parental influence in mediating these effects. In this regard, parental influence through (1) parent-child interaction, and (2) structural control of the viewing environment is of special interest.

Data for this research was generated through personal interviews with children and their mothers in the subjects' homes. A procedure of dual interviewing was utilized whereby child and parent responses were recorded simultaneously by two interviewers in different rooms, eliminating any opportunity for interaction and influencing of one subject by the other. The three primary independent variables measured include the number of hours of children's programing viewed weekly by the child (exposure), the frequency of parent-child interaction on the subject of TV advertising (interaction), and the frequency of control actions by the mother (control). The dependent variables included the child's misunderstanding of the concept and purpose of commercials (cognition), recall of advertised brands (recall), attitude toward TV advertising (attitude), and frequency of purchase requests for products and services (purchase requests). The sample consisted of 222 third- and fourth- grade children and their mothers.

The findings can be summarized as follows:

1. Cognition was not found to be related to exposure or interaction. It was, however, correlated positively with the child's age, his/her attention level during the viewing of commercials (as compared with that during programing), parental control, and recall of advertised products.

2. Recall was not found to be related to exposure or control. However, it was found to correlate positively with cognition and negatively with attitude toward TV advertising.

3. Attitude was not found to be related to exposure, but correlated negatively with control. The child's attitude generally correlated with that of his mother, but the magnitude of the difference between them was positively correlated with the amount of parent-child interaction. The child's attitude correlated negatively with grade level and with recall. Finally, males' attitudes were more negative than those of females.

4. Children's purchase requests were found to be positively related to exposure, parent-child interaction, and parental exposure to television. A negative relationship was found between purchase requests and the number of older siblings present in the household. Parental control was not found to influence the frequency of purchase requests.

This study presents strong evidence to support the claims of parents and consumerists that television advertising stimulates requests by children for products and services. It also indicates that parents who create more opportunities for such requests to occur by interacting more frequently with their children do indeed receive more requests. The findings can also be interpreted to show that parents have more influence in the formation of their children's attitudes toward TV commercials than the amount of commercials to which the child is exposed.

Finally, cognition and recall appear to be a function of variables not measured in this study. A multitude of opportunities remain for the exploration of additional variables and the processes in which they operate.

292. Television and Alcohol Consumption and Abuse. Rand Paper Series No. P-5621. Comstock, George, Rand Corporation, Santa Monica, CA, Mar 1976, 12p (ED 140 163; Reprint: EDRS).

This article examines the contribution of television and other mass media to alcohol consumption and its abuse. The author notes that there is no scientific evidence available that addresses this point directly, and the importance of such an issue is not recognized in the scientific literature. The absence of this information interferes with the ability to act wisely in regard to portrayals of alcohol in entertainment and advertising on television. The author delineates four issues that are of central importance in examining the portrayals of alcohol consumption on television: (1) the pattern and character of such portrayals; (2) the contribution of such portrayals to the concepts held by young people about alcohol; (3) the contribution of portrayals to maintaining or altering patterns of alcohol consumption among adults; and (4) the potential role of television in altering patterns of alcohol consumption and abuse.

293. To the Federal Trade Commission in the Matter of a Trade Regulation Rule on Food/Nutrition Advertising. Choate, Robert B., Council on Children, Media, and Merchandising, Washington, DC, Oct 1976, 230p. Filmed from best available copy (ED 135 456; Reprint: EDRS—HC not available).

Food advertising and its effects on children are discussed in this document petitioning the Federal Trade Commission (FTC) to amend a proposed rule on food promotion for the benefit of children under 12. Extensive information is presented on television food commercials and their influence on children's nutritional beliefs and eating habits. The FTC's responsibility to protect children in commercial situations is emphasized, with suggestions given as to how the proposed amendments could be implemented within the framework of prevailing practices. It is claimed that the repeated advertising of food to children without factual nutritional information, particularly on the calorie-nutrient relationship, constitutes an unfair and deceptive act. It is proposed that, with proper research, the food industry could find the means, perhaps in graphic form, of revealing nutritional worth while promoting food products. A behavioral study on a sample graphic showed that children at various age levels were able to learn to comprehend the complex relationship of calories and nutrients and to use both these dimensions in evaluating foods. Included in the document are specific technical recommendations to the FTC for carrying out goals and views expressed. Appendices present extensive data on food advertising and children's television viewing patterns, as well as a brief description of children's cognitive development and the influence of television on it. Samples of current advertising and experimental graphics are included.

294. Young Children's Ability to Isolate Nutritional Elements in a Television Commercial, Their Knowledge of and Their Parents' Attitudes toward Nutrition, Dental Health and the Effects of Sugar Consumption.* Anderson, Joann Clark, Florida State University, 1979. 129p (7926710; Reprint: DC).

Industry guidelines require at least one audio mention and one video depiction of a breakfast food in a nutritional setting. This investigation studied the extent of recall four- and eight-year-old children had of the nutritional elements in a commercial meeting those voluntary guidelines. Further, it investigated the knowledge those children were able to orally express regarding nutritional and dental health along with their ability to express deleterious effects of sugar consumption and its relation to dental and nutritional health. Using a sample of 83 children, this study sought to determine whether the variables of age, socioeconomic status (SES), and/or race influenced the verbal expressions of children on these major topics. Because children are influenced by parental attitudes, this study further sought to determine parental attitudes regarding nutrition and dental health practices of their children and whether those parental expressions were influenced by race, age of child, or SES.

Data were collected using focus group research, a qualitative data collection technique. Eighty-three children from the Tallahassee area were grouped homogeneously into 16 groups by age, race, and SES.

Each group viewed a color video recording of a sugared cereal commercial and were then asked to recall what they had seen. During the remaining portion of the session, using primary and secondary probes, responses were elicited by the researcher and observed by four certified elementary teachers. Data on parental attitudes were collected using a questionnaire distributed to the parents of all group participants.

In this sample, one out of five nutritional elements of a sugared cereal commercial viewed once were recalled by four-year-olds and three out of five by the eight-year-olds. Four-year-olds as a whole were unable to express the deleterious effects of sugar. Eight-year-olds tended to express the negative effects while offering contradictory statements regarding their avoidance of sweets. Parents expressed both awareness and concern that their children purchased and consumed sweets but offered no solution to the problem. From a total of four food groups, four-year-olds averaged 2.6 in their responses to nutritional probes while eight-year-olds referred to an average of 3.4 food groups. In response to dental questions, from a total of five dental elements, four-year-olds referred to an average of 2.0 and eight-year-olds 3.5.

Of the variables considered—age, SES, and race—differentiation of responses appeared to be most related to age. Parental attitudes differed only slightly when compared by SES or race.

BOOKS

295. Children's Television Advertising. Barry, Thomas E. Chicago: American Marketing Association, 1977, 80p (Monograph Series No. 8).

The purpose of this monograph is to collate and review empirical research to date (both published and unpublished studies) on children's television advertising and to analyze investigation and enforcement methods in the field. The author concludes that the evidence as yet does not demonstrate that advertising harms children but that regulators are likely to respond to public perceptions that this is the case.

296. How Children Learn to Buy: The Development of Consumer Information-Processing Skills. Ward, Scott et al. Beverly Hills, CA: Sage Publications, 1977, 271p.

Using a theoretical basis in Piagetian cognitive development theory, the authors conducted a study of 615 kindergarten, third-grade, and sixth-grade children and their mothers to determine children's ability to process information from television commercials and the effects of those commercials on consumer skill development. It was concluded that cognitive development theory is highly relevant to the study of consumer socialization, although there are wide variations in learning ability within age groups. It was found that family context factors were an important mediating influence in children's response to TV commercials.

Reading and School Achievement

JOURNAL ARTICLES

297. Children, Television, and Reading. Feeley, Joan T. *NJEA Review*. v53, n9, p15, May 1980 (EJ 229 487; Reprint: UMI).

The author summarizes a research review conducted at William Paterson College. Information is presented on the amount of time spent watching television, types of programs preferred by different age groups, and the impact of television on reading habits and achievement. No consistent relationship between TV viewing and achievement was found.

298. The Classroom's No Longer Prime Time. Feinberg, Susan. *Today's Education*. v66, n3, p78–79, Sep-Oct 1977 (EJ 170 770; Reprint: UMI).

Perhaps the most disturbing aspect of television's impact lies in its creation of a generation of viewers incapable of making critical judgments about the media, their world, or themselves, and expecting to "get by" with minimal effort.

299. "Cold" Media Victims. Grant, Barbara M. *Theory into Practice*. v15, n2, p120–25, Apr 1976.

The solo activity of watching television makes children function as passive receivers of ideas rather than as creators; the teacher should counter this by encouraging team play and active involvement in group situations so that the child's ability to understand and communicate with others and to make value judgments is developed.

300. ERIC/RCS: The Impact of Television on Reading. Barth, Rodney J.; Swiss, Thom. *Reading Teacher*. v30, n2, p236–39, Nov 1976.

Reviews the literature in the Educational Resources Information Center (ERIC) on how television influences the reading behavior of children.

301. The Effect of TV Viewing on the Educational Performance of Elementary School Children. Anderson, C.C.; Maguire, T.O. *Alberta Journal of Educational Research*. v24, n3, p156–63, Sep 1978.

The number of TV shows viewed appears to have only a marginal negative relationship with educational achievement, while encouraging behavioral impulsivity. Types of programing preferred varies with age. More study in this area is urged.

302. Effects of Preschool Television Watching on First-Grade Children. Burton, Sydney G. et al. *Journal of Communication*. v29, n3, p164–70, Sum 1979 (EJ 217 489; Reprint: UMI).

Five first grade classrooms in two schools—one racially mixed, low socioeconomic, urban school; one White middle-income suburban school—were studied. Children who watched a lot of television in their preschool years earned lower grades than those who watched less. They tended to choose as friends those who did a similar amount of viewing.

303. The First Curriculum: Comparing School and Television. Postman, Neil. *Phi Delta Kappan*. v61, n3, p163–68, Nov 1979 (EJ 210 979; Reprint: UMI).

After examining the nature of the ''curriculum'' of television, the author asks to what extent the biases of television can be balanced by the biases of other information systems, particularly those of the schools.

304. Fostering Creativity in Children: Does the Medium Matter? Meline, Caroline W. *Journal of Communication.* v26, n3, p81–89, Sum 1976.

Examines written, visual and sound messages directed toward children and suggests that there is a significant difference among various mediums capacity for stimulating creative thinking: sixth- and seventh-grade children exposed to concrete video presentations gave consistently and sometimes significantly fewer original solutions than children exposed to audiotape and print problems.

305. Immediate Man: The Symbolic Environment of Fanaticism. Nystrom, Christine L. *ETC.: A Review of General Semantics.* v34, n1, p19–34, Mar 1977 (EJ 209 340; Reprint: UMI).

Points to signals that people in the West have entered into an environment hostile to rational thought and shows how the major characteristics of United States media environments contribute to this hostility. Suggests ways that teachers can assure the conservation of rational thought and restore the balance between reason and experience.

306. Influence of the Medium on Children's Apprehension. Meringoff, Laurene K. *Journal of Educational Psychology.* v72, n2, p240–49, Apr 1980.

This study compared children's apprehensions of an unfamiliar story either read to them from an illustrated book or presented as a comparable televised film. There were 48 children, ages 6–10. Children exposed to the televised story remembered more story actions, offered estimates of shorter elapsed time and distance traveled for carrying out a repeated story event, and relied more on visual content as the basis for inferences. In comparison, children who were read the story in picture book form recalled more story vocabulary, based their inferences more on textual content, general knowledge, and personal experience, and made more use of the storytelling situation as an opportunity to ask questions and make comments about the story. To the extent that children have repeated experience with specific media, such differential medium effects on apprehension suggest important implications for children's cognitive development.

307. Media Use and Academic Achievement of Mexican-American High School Students. Tan, Alexis S.: Gunter, Dell. *Journalism Quarterly.* v56, n4, p827–31, Win 1979 (EJ 219 544; Reprint: UMI).

A survey of 93 Mexican American high school seniors revealed no relationship between total use of English-language mass media and academic performance, a negative relationship between grade point average and television use for entertainment, and a positive relationship between grade point average and newspaper use for public affairs information.

308. Reading, Imagination, and Television. Singer, Dorothy G. *School Library Journal.* v26, n4, p31–34, Dec 1979 (EJ 216 468; Reprint: UMI).

Describes past television research on children related to imagination and vocabulary, visual and verbal processes, and TV exposure and reading; and recommends that television be used with discretion, with other modes of information and entertainment—especially books—becoming a habitual part of a child's life.

309. Reprogramming the Media Researchers. Gardner, Howard. *Psychology Today.* v13, n8, p6, 12, 14, Jan 1980.

Suggests that, due to differences inherent in the media, television viewing and reading are qualitatively different experiences, not ones that can be compared as ''superior'' and ''inferior.'' Encourages researchers to examine the different cognitive skills developed by reading and television and their educational implications.

310. Schools vs. Television. Fiske, Edward B. *Parents' Magazine.* v55, p54–58, Jan 1980.

This article discusses research findings that children who spend too much time watching television are fatigued and have poor social relationships at school. Several elementary school programs designed to limit TV use through parent cooperation are described.

311. The Short-Tale Life. Getlein, Frank. *Progressive.* v43, p52–53, Apr 1979.

Members of the television generation are superficially brighter, quicker, and more sophisticated than children of previous decades, but they lack the ability to sustain attention. This, not its vulgarity and cheapness, is the most frightening aspect of commercial television.

312. The State of the Nation's Literacy: A Conversation with Clifton Fadiman. Houts, Paul L. *National Elementary Principal.* v57, n1, p54–64, Oct 1977 (EJ 188 608; Reprint: UMI).

Clifton Fadiman discusses the role of television in the decline of America's literacy and social values.

313. TV and Kids: What Teachers Are Complaining About. Larrick, Nancy. *Learning.* v8, n2, p44–46, Oct 1979.

From her interviews with teachers around the nation, the author concludes that teachers believe that children today are different from children in previous years, and they lay most of the blame on too much television viewing. Specific complaints are discussed.

314. TV—How Much Is Too Much? Edwards, Virginia. *Scouting.* v66, p30,72,74, Oct 1978.

The author reviews some of the findings on the positive and negative effects television can have on the emotional and academic development of children. She considers use of commercial television by teachers to attract students to schoolwork and reading as a cop-out and urges parents to exercise control over television usage in the home.

315. Television Access and the Slowing of Cognitive Growth. Hornik, Robert C. *American Educational Research Journal.* v15, n1, p1–15, Win 1978 (EJ 187 930; Reprint: UMI).

Reading skills, general ability, and academic achievement were studied in El Salvadoran junior high school students who had recently acquired a television. There were no obvious effects on short-term achievement, but consistent negative effects on reading improvement were found. In the most disadvantaged students, general ability growth was negatively affected.

316. Television and Its Effects on Reading and School Achievement. Neuman, Susan B. *Reading Teacher.* v33, n7, p801–05, Apr 1980.

The author reviews 12 selected studies on the relationship between amount of television viewed and reading achievement in the elementary grades, concluding that the relationship is not significant. She also discusses the potential of commercial television as a tool in reading instruction, to motivate students, and to teach skills.

317. Television and Its Influence on Reading. Splaine, John E. *Educational Technology.* v18, n6, p15–19, Jun 1978 (EJ 189 087; Reprint: UMI).

Studies in Minnesota and Maryland indicate an interaction between television and reading. Previous research cited suggests that the relationship is not exclusive. Educators should make use of such findings to support the use of technology.

318. Television and Reading Achievement. Moldenhauer, Deborah L.; Miller, Wilma H. *Journal of Reading.* v23, n7, p615–19, Apr 1980.

In this study of 78 mainly middle-income seventh graders, the hypothesis that there is no significant correlation between TV viewing and reading achievement was clearly confirmed. All students averaged about four hours of television viewing per day on weekdays. Saturday and Sunday viewing data were excluded.

319. Television, Books, and Teachers. Mulholland, Robert E. *English Education.* v10, n1, p3–8, Oct 1978 (EJ 190 289; Reprint: UMI).

Encourages mutual respect between bibliophiles and electronic-media-philes and stresses the positive impact of television on book sales and circulation.

320. Television Viewing and Reading: Does More Equal Better? Morgan, Michael. *Journal of Communication.* v30, n1, p159–165, Win 1980 (EJ 221 302; Reprint: UMI).

This study examined the relationship of amount of viewing to both IQ and achievement in a cross-sectional sample of 625 students in the sixth through ninth grades in a New Jersey public school. Over 200 of these students and their parents completed questionnaires and interviews over a three-year period (1974–77). Results indicated, among other findings, that students who are heavy users of TV tend to read more but comprehend less than light viewers.

321. Television Viewing, Children's Reading, and Related Classroom Behavior. Zuckerman, Diana M. et al. *Journal of Communication.* v30, n1, p166–74, Win 1980 (EJ 221 303; Reprint: UMI).

Reported is a study of above-average third to fifth graders who were moderate television viewers (approximately two hours per day). The particular types of programs watched, not television viewing per se, predicted children's reading habits, imagination, and enthusiasm in school.

322. Television's Effects on Reading: A Case Study. Busch, Jackie S. *Phi Delta Kappan.* v59, n10, p668–71, Jun 1978 (EJ 181 498; Reprint: UMI).

Television has had a major impact on the reading habits and achievement of children. Preschool and primary students benefit the most from viewing, but after age 12 students' total knowledge declines as they increase viewing. Differences are apparent between high and low ability students.

323. The Viewing of TV, Perceptual Passivity and Reading. Fisher, Richard; Bruss, William. *Colorado Journal of Educational Research.* v15, n3, p33–37, Spr 1976.

A survey of 120 fifth- and sixth-grade children indicates that the number of hours spent viewing TV is significantly related to perceptual passivity: that a negative correlation between perceptual passivity and reading achievement is not indicated; and that a negative correlation between the number of TV viewing hours and reading achievement does exist.

MICROFICHE

324. Analysis of Supplemental Background Questions on Homework and TV. Education Commission of the States, Denver, CO, National Assessment of Educational Progress, 1977, 7p (ED 159 055; Reprint: EDRS; also available from Education Commission of the States, National Assessment of Educational Progress, 1860 Lincoln Street, Denver, CO 80295).

A National Assessment of Educational Progress (NAEP) statistical analysis deals with the amount of homework of 17-year-old students in 1976, the amount of television viewing, and presence or absence of various items in the home (e.g., a specific place for study, magazines, etc.). The data suggest that a higher performance on mathematics assessment task is associated with: (1) more reported homework; (2) less reported television viewing; and (3) more reported items in the home. The narrative is supported by tables of descriptive statistics.

325. Can TV Do It? Partridge, Susan, 1978, 9p (ED 158 247; Reprint: EDRS).

Since the average child spends an estimated 30 hours a week watching television, it is important to consider the negative and positive effects of television viewing on the development of reading attitudes and habits. Possible negative aspects of television viewing include the following: the rapid pacing of programs encourages shallow reading; the immediacy of content and setting creates impatience with lengthy prose descriptions; the emphasis on fantasy material reduces interest in written fiction; and the popularity of books based on television specials fosters a pursuit of easy reading. On the positive side, teachers and parents who recognize the unique qualities of each child can use television viewing as a motivational tool or a supplement in the development of reading interests and skills. Specific ways to use television in reading development include contrasting authoritative materials on nutrition with the misconceptions presented on commercials, encouraging critical thinking through discussions of programs based on books, and pointing out the advantages of reading over television by offering a wide variety of reading experiences and setting an example of good reading habits.

326. Children's Television Behaviour: Its Antecedents and Relationship to School Performance. A Study of the Television Viewing Behaviour of Children in Grade 6 of State Primary Schools in the Metropolitan Area of Melbourne. Occasional Paper No. 14. Sharman, Kevin James, Australian Council for Educational Research, Hawthorn, Jun 1979, 93p (ED 179 190; Reprint: EDRS—HC not available).

A study was conducted to describe the television viewing habits of children in primary schools within the metropolitan area of Melbourne, Australia; to examine the nature of the relationships between factors found to be relevant in explaining television behavior; and to examine the relationship between television behavior and school achievement. Data were collected from a two-stage cluster sample of 271 grade six children using a questionnaire; tests of intelligence, self-esteem, and comprehension in social studies; and a diary of television viewing over a period of seven days. A questionnaire was also completed by the subjects' teachers. Statistical analyses involved simple descriptive statistics, bivariate correlation and multiple regression analyses, and canonical analysis. The hypothesizing and subsequent testing of causal path models of the interrelationships between variables enabled the study to cope more efficiently with the complex interrelationships between variables. Results confirmed the important influence that television has on the lives of children and the importance of home background variables and personal characteristics in influencing television viewing patterns and school performance. On the basis of simple correlations, heavy viewers of television did less well in school.

327. A Comparative Study of Non-School Activities of the Kindergarten Child.* Corley, Gerald Bennett, Saint Louis University, 1978, (7814545; Reprint: DC).

Twenty-nine kindergarten teachers in 17 elementary schools were asked to list five pupils in their class who exhibited a high level of maturity using the criteria on a maturity ranking scale. They were also asked to list the names of five pupils in their class who exhibited a low level of maturity using the same criteria.

A random selection of 30 subjects from each of the high and low maturity categories was conducted. The mother of each subject was asked to complete information on the home environment and the daily routine activities of the subject while not at school. Four null hypotheses were defined to the effect that children ranked high and low in emotional maturity would not differ significantly in amount of time spent in solitary play, number of hours of television viewed daily, socioeconomic level, or family dwelling styles.

The level of difference in the activities between the high maturity and the low maturity subjects was statistically insignificant in all cases. The only area which proved to be significantly different was the socioeconomic level of the two groups. The conclusion was that the higher the socioeconomic level of the family, the more likely the teacher would perceive the pupil to demonstrate a high level of maturity.

328. The Dual Schooling Systems: Televiewing and Formal Schooling.* Sandberg, Barbara Reneé, Columbia University, 1976, 80p (76–29, 859; Reprint: DC).

The primary purpose of this study was to determine whether an instrument could be developed which would measure accurately time spent in televiewing. Television exposure was measured two ways: (1) VTT (verified televiewing time): number of programs each individual pupil reported televiewing on a cued-recall listing of television programs as verified by two true or false questions per program for all those programs for which program content was available; (2) recognition index: number of correct identifications of photographs of television characters either by name or by the name of their television program. This study then sought to determine the relationship of televiewing time with school achievement (reading comprehension and mathematics), IQ, SES, and out-of-school activities.

The sample consisted of 482 students, grades 6–11, who were randomly selected from a public school system in Westchester, NY.

The results indicate a strong, positive relationship between the VTT and the recognition index indicating the strength of the instruments for measuring televiewing. With these instruments, students reported a mean of 29 hours televiewing time per week. Televiewing time tended to increase from grade 6–9 (mean VTT of approximately 28–33 hours per week) and then decreased during 10th grade (mean VTT of 30 hours per week) and 11th grade (mean VTT of 22.5 hours per week). Male high school students were found to be spending significantly more time in televiewing than female high school students, though sex differences in televiewing time were not found earlier in grades 6–8. No relationship was found between televiewing time and school achievement, IQ, or SES. A moderate negative relationship was found between televiewing time and the incidence of reporting independent reading; no relationship was found between televiewing time and the incidence of reporting working on hobbies. The mean number of television sets found in each home was 2.8.

329. Entertainment Television in Rural Alaska: How Will It Affect the School? Forbes, Norma. Apr 1979, 12 p. Paper presented at the Annual Meeting of the American Educational Research Association (San Francisco, CA, April 1979) (ED 174 192; Reprint: EDRS).

The development of the Satellite Television Demonstration Project in Alaska, delivering commercial entertainment television, is briefly described and important educational issues related to the delivery and usage of commercial television via satellite in Alaska are discussed, including (1) justification for the demonstration project; (2) implementation of the project; (3) the project as an opportunity for research on the effects of commercial television on rural native populations in Alaska; and (4) possible beneficial and harmful cognitive and affective influences of commercial television in Alaska, especially when delivered to rural children in their schools. Several studies related to relevant television and minority culture research are cited.

330. The Influence of Television on the Readiness and Potential Literacy of Pre-School Children.* MacKinnon, Colin Frederick, University of Massachusetts, 1979, 164p. (7912698; Reprint: DC).

The preschool readiness scores of 200 preschool children from a rural community were compared to the number of hours of daily television viewing reported by parents during a preschool interview as one means of establishing the relationship between television viewing and its possible influence on the reading readiness of preschoolers. The areas of readiness assessed were fine-motor, gross-motor, perceptual-motor, and personal-social domains. (The language development of the preschoolers was not addressed in this study.) Anecdotal evidence from the writer's experiences, field observation in a rural school, as well as curricular guidelines were offered against a background description of an overview of literacy and growth of nonprint media.

Although no significant effect of television viewing was established as a result of this study, the depression of fine-motor, gross motor, and personal-social scores among children viewing more than two hours of television daily was noted, as was the overall effect of television experiences on the readiness of those sampled.

The study concludes that the kinds of activity choices available in the homes of preschoolers can affect the child's readiness to read if the dominant activity is television viewing. There must be a balance between television viewing and skill building activities in the psychomotor domains. Even though the study shows that television does offer a slight benefit in the perceptual-motor area, it fails to provide readiness experiences in the other psychomotor areas.

331. Influence of Visual Domain on Score Decline: Some Conjectures. Randhawa, Bikkar S., Iowa University, Iowa City, College of Education, Feb 1977, 8p (ED 135 369; Reprint: EDRS). This report is in response to invited comments for the CEEB/ETS Panel on Score Decline.

Rich visual stimuli provided by the television medium may affect youngsters' cognitive processes and strategies in academic performance. Previous studies have revealed that television viewing enhances their achievement test scores through grade four, but scores decline after grade four. This paper suggests that visuals used in instructional context are not comparable in quality to those presented in television. In addition, curriculum beyond grade four level emphasized verbal content, and some youngsters find it difficult to shift the cognitive process from random scan in the visual mode to sequential and linear scan in the verbal mode. Inadequate reading ability and comprehension of verbal materials further affect performance in other academic areas. It is suggested that systematic training may solve this difficulty: However, empirical research evidence is needed in order to determine the various factors accounting for the score decline.

332. The Relationship of Children's Television Viewing to Achievement at the Intermediate Level. Quisenberry, Nancy L.; Klasek, Charles B., 1976, 26p. Sponsoring agency: Southern Illinois University, Carbondale, Office of Research and Projects (ED 143 336; Reprint: EDRS).

This study investigated the television viewing habits of 341 intermediate grade children and examined the relationship between their viewing habits and their achievement scores on standardized tests. Weekly viewing diaries were used to record information on television viewing. The study does not support either the premise that television assists children in school or that it is detrimental. Eleven data tables are provided.

333. The Relationship of Homework and Television Viewing to Cognitive and Noncognitive Student Outcomes. Kohr, Richard L. Apr 1979, 25p. Paper presented at the Annual Meeting of the National Council for Measurement in Education (San Francisco, CA, April 1979) (ED 175 441; Reprint: EDRS).

This paper reports on secondary analyses of data collected in March 1978 by the Pennsylvania Educational Quality Assessment Program, which was designed to examine television viewing and the amount of school assigned homework in relation to student cognitive and noncognitive outcomes. Also examined were television viewing and homework patterns for groups categorized by sex, race, type of community, stability of home residence, parental educational level, size of family, and expectation level; data used were derived from 90,000 students in grades 5, 8, and 11 in 750 schools participating in a statewide assessment. Related studies from the states of Rhode Island and Texas are compared to this study. A student level analysis involving television indicates that there is little evidence of a meaningful relationship with cognitive or noncognitive achievement. In the school level analysis, where inferences defer to characteristics of schools rather than individuals, a strong negative relationship between television viewing and cognitive achievement was indicated.

334. A Study of Academic Achievement in Terms of Television Viewing Practices.* Roth, Louis Boissac, Jr., Louisiana State University and Agricultural and Mechanical College, 1979, 64 p. (7927501; Reprint: DC).

This study established that a negative correlation coefficient existed between the number of television viewing hours per day and SRA Achievement Test scores of selected fourth and seventh grade students in one southwest Louisiana parish. The general hypothesis tested was that an increased number of television viewing hours resulted in decreased achievement test scores in all components of the SRA Achievement battery.

The control group to be tested consisted of 457 fourth-grade students and 445 seventh-grade students in one parish school system. The investigator conducted the surveys of two viewing days per week for four weeks. Each subject marked the appropriate item (program viewed). Number of hours viewed and SRA Achievement Test data were then correlated by computer, and a coefficient was established by using Pearson's Product Moment procedure. A negative correlation indicated that there was an inverse relationship between the number of television hours viewed and scores on the SRA Achievement Tests. The correlation was statistically significant at the .01 level of confidence.

The investigator recommends that further study be conducted which would include use of more variables (socioeconomic background, race, reading level, sex) so that data can be used more effectively in academic counseling. The length of the data collection period should be extended to allow for varying academic maturation rates of the subjects. Finally, a comparative study among parishes would provide more data in order to establish a paradigm both for gathering such data and for evaluating its effect on the educational process.

335. Television, Imaginative Play and Cognitive Development: Some Problems and Possibilities. Singer, Jerome L. Aug 1977, 41p. Paper presented at the Annual Meeting of the American Psychological Association (85th, San Francisco, CA, August 26–30, 1977) (ED 148 460; Reprint: EDRS).

This paper compares the effects of television viewing to the effects of imaginative play on children's cognitive development. The major developmental tasks which confront the growing child are presented and the significance of imaginative play as a critical feature of the child's cognitive and affective development is discussed. The cognitive properties of the television medium as they may affect the child developing in an environment in which TV is viewed three hours or more a day are then examined. Next, the relevant research relating play or reading as an active process and television as a more passive one are discussed. Finally, approaches to training parents to control children's viewing patterns more effectively and to use TV material to stimulate children's imaginative development are described.

336. Television Viewing, Achievement, IQ, and Creativity.* Childs, John Hansen, Brigham Young University, 1978, 115p. (7911886; Reprint: DC).

It was the purpose of this study to determine if there was a relationship between commercial television viewing and the academic, IQ, and creativity scores of second- and sixth-grade students at Naples Elementary School. The findings indicate a significant negative relationship between the hours of viewing commercial television and (1) math and reading scores of

second-grade students, (2) math, reading, and language usage scores of second-grade girls, and (3) reading scores of sixth-grade girls. There was a significant positive relationship between (1) hours of viewing commercial television and the originality scores of second-grade boys, (2) number of hours viewed by second- and sixth-grade students and the number of hours viewed was perceived by their parents, (3) math scores of girls in second and sixth grade who viewed 10 hours or less than those who viewed 30 hours or more, and (4) math scores of girls in the second and sixth grades who viewed 20 to 30 hours and those who viewed over 30 hours of commercial television.

337. Television Viewing and Reading Achievement in Second Grade. List, Carol, Apr 1978, 56p. Master's thesis, Kean College of New Jersey (ED 159 617; Reprint: EDRS).

Both teachers and parents assisted in a study of the effect television viewing has on reading achievement. Second-grade teachers in the Montclair (New Jersey) school district identified students who read at least one year above grade level (high achievers) and students who read at primer level or below (low achievers). Parents of these students received letters asking them to complete and return enclosed calendars for the week of December 3, 1977, indicating what television programs their children watched at what times. Parents of five of 36 low achievers and 15 of 41 high achievers returned calendars. The data reveal that low achievers watch an average of 18.7 hours of television per week, while high achievers average 12 hours of television viewing per week, indicating a negative relationship between reading and televiewing. The data also reveal that cartoons, family comedy situations, and holiday specials were the favorite programs of both groups during the survey period. Two recommendations made as a result of the study are to continue this type of research with larger subject populations and to urge school systems to inform parents of television viewing's benefits and deficits.

338. Television Viewing and School Grades: A Cross-Lagged Longitudinal Study. Gadberry, Sharon. Mar 1977, 14p. Paper presented at the Biennial Meeting of the Society for Research in Child Development (New Orleans, LA, March 17–20, 1977) (ED 140 973; Reprint: EDRS).

This study attempted to determine whether amount of television viewing independently affects school performance. The television viewing amount and school grades of 43 male and 47 female middle class subjects from three age groups (6 to 7, 8 to 9, and 10 to 11) were measured twice, 18 months apart. Cross-lagged panels were tested using correlations between viewing amount, academic grades, and effort grades. The amount-effort panel supported the causal hypothesis that increased television viewing caused lower school grades. The difference between cross-lagged correlations for effort and academic grades of six to seven-year-olds and effort grades of low achievers provided strongest support for the prediction. For the latter groups, two specific content categories positively affected academic grades and two content types decreased grades. Effort grades were generally decreased by total viewing irrespective of content dimensions.

339. Television Viewing: Its Relationship to Early School Achievement. Perney, Jan et al. 1976, 22p (ED 153 723; Reprint: EDRS).

To examine the relationship between television viewing and early school achievement, children's quantitative and verbal test scores were correlated with parental responses to a questionnaire concerning the television viewing habits of their children. The sample consisted of 202 kindergarten children and their parents from two suburban school districts north of Chicago. It was found that the time spent watching comedy-variety-drama shows was negatively correlated with verbal and quantitative ability for girls. Time spent watching "Electric Company" was positively related to quantitative ability for boys. There was a negative correlation between the girls' verbal ability and the parents' use of television as a reward or punishment, and a positive correlation between the girls' verbal ability and the parents' conscious use of television as a teacher. The total amount of television watched correlated negatively with quantitative scores, but correlated positively with verbal scores for both girls and boys.

340. What Effect Is TV Having on the Young Learner? Mukerji, Rose. Mar 1977, 13p. Paper presented at the Annual Conference, Association for Supervision and Curriculum Development (Houston, TX, March 19–23, 1977) (ED 138 589; Reprint: EDRS).

A brief overview is presented of the effect of television viewing on the cognitive and affective learning processes of young learners and on the growth of the social interaction skills of this same viewing audience. The main conclusions of the report are that (1) the effects of television viewing are complex and are both positive and negative; (2) these effects vary from age group to age group and among the different forms of learning; and (3) the medium offers a unique, attractive opportunity for the education of young children, provided that educators, parents, and producers act in a responsible manner, not only in the viewing process and content themselves but in the development and education of the child in nonviewing time.

BOOKS

341. The Plug-In Drug. Winn, Marie. New York: Viking Press, 1977, 231p.

The author's indictment of television focuses not on television content but on the act of viewing. She considers TV a dangerous addiction, particularly for the preschool child, and presents her case through an analysis of television's negative impact of children's use of leisure time, their scholastic achievement, their creativity, and their self-sufficiency.

TELEVISION AS A TEACHING TOOL

Television as a Teaching Tool

JOURNAL ARTICLES

342. The ABC/NEA SCHOOLDISC Program is Under Way. Wilhelms, Fred T. *Today's Education.* v69, n3, p57, 62–63, Sep–Oct 1980.

Describes the development of a collaborative project between the American Broadcasting Company and the National Education Association to produce instructional programs on videodiscs, with teaching guides, for grades 4–6.

343. CBS Speaker Couples Books with Television. Jankowski, Gene F. *AV Guide.* v59, n8, p1, 4, Aug 1980.

The president of the CBS/Broadcast Group discusses the complementary nature of television and books and describes the Read More about It Project, a cooperative effort of CBS and the Library of Congress to promote reading in relation to selected television programs. This article consists of excerpts from a speech delivered at the 1980 American Library Association convention.

344. Can Television Be Used to Teach Essential Skills? Levinsohn, Florence Hamlish. *School Review.* v85, n2, p297–311, Feb 1977.

Investigates whether television should be called upon to assist in teaching young students the basic skills that they seem not to be learning very well. Discusses the introduction of television teaching in El Salvador and evaluates the work of the Agency for Instructional Television to see how it is approaching the teaching of basic skills.

345. A Child and His Television Set: What Is the Nature of the Relationship? Fowles, Barbara R. *Education and Urban Society.* v10, n1, p89–102, Nov 1977.

In this literature review, the author considers what commercial and educational television can do for the preschool child. She concludes that the impact of television on children's cognitive development can be favorable due to television's merging of fantasy and reality, which can objectify the thought processes of the preoperational child, but that this cognitive development potential is limited by the lack of linguistic interaction. Ultimately, verbal interaction with humans is necessary for intellectual growth beyond a certain point.

346. Children's Television and Modeling of Pro-Reading Behaviors. Almeida, Pamela M. *Education and Urban Society.* v10, n1, p55–60, Nov 1977.

The development and mastery of reading skills are essential to success in school and in work. Current educational children's programing (e.g., "Sesame Street" and "The Electric Company") has demonstrated that television can have a significant impact on these skills. However, television as a vehicle for developing positive attitudes toward reading has been underused. By including peer role modeling of proreading behaviors in children's television, a renewed interest in and love for reading may be sparked in the children of the electronic generation.

347. The Drive to Convince Teachers of the Educational Value of Commercial TV. Pines, Maya. *Phi Delta Kappan.* v61, n3, p168–71, Nov 1979 (EJ 210 980; Reprint: UMI).

Some of the specific reasons for using or discussing specific kinds of television programs in the classroom do make sense—in specific cases. The trick is to select such programs very carefully, without capitulating to the pressure from the networks, and to keep a firm grip on one's goals.

348. Education and the Telefuture. Bonham, George W. *Change.* v11, n8, p12–13, Nov–Dec 1979.

This editorial calls for educators to join the telecommunications revolution, stating that, with a nation facing a future of a predominantly adult population and an ever-accelerating need to cope with change, education will be damaged by the myth that television is for entertainment and the classroom is for learning.

349. Environmental Enhancement of Prosocial Television Content: Effects on Interpersonal Behavior, Imaginative Play, and Self-Regulation in a Natural Setting. Friedrich-Cofer, Lynette K. et al. *Developmental Psychology.* v15, n6, p637–46, Nov 1979.

Two questions were addressed in a field experiment: Does prosocial TV affect the behavior of urban poor children? Are environmental supports that stimulate rehearsal and labeling of TV content effective in a field setting? The social, imaginative, and self-regulatory behavior of 141 children in Head Start centers was observed before and during one of the following four experimental treatments: (a) neutral films, (b) prosocial TV only, (c) prosocial TV plus related play materials, and (d) prosocial TV plus related materials plus teacher training for rehearsal using verbal labeling and role playing. Subjects in each condition saw 20 films in 8 weeks. Prosocial TV alone produced few behavioral differences from the control group. When classrooms were otherwise comparable, children receiving TV plus related materials had high levels of positive social interaction with peers and adults, of imaginative play, and of assertiveness and aggression. Those whose teachers were trained as well showed high levels of positive social interaction with peers, imaginative play, and assertiveness, but did not increase in aggression. Self-regulatory behavior was unaffected by treatments.

350. The Evolution of Televised Reading Instruction.
Tierney, Joan D. *Journal of Communication.* v30, n1, p181–85, Win 1980 (EJ 221 305; Reprint: UMI).

Describes several studies using television and television technology to assist in teaching reading and reading skills.

351. Exit Dick and Jane? Dalzell, Bonnie. *American Education.* v12, n6, p9–13, Jul 1976.

Describes the highly successful TV Reading Program initiated in Philadelphia public schools in which utilization of actual television program scripts in combination with program viewing has improved reading skills and increased motivation among elementary and high school students.

352. First-Time Exposure to Television: Effects on Inuit Children's Cultural Images. Caron, Andre H. *Communication Research.* v6, n2, p135–54, Apr 1979.

The purpose of this research was to investigate the effects of first time exposure to television on Inuit children's (8–13-year-old) cultural "images" of their own and other cultural groups. A pretest and posttest design was used. The specific series chosen for the experiment were both prosocial in nature, with one portraying cultural groups from a number of different countries (the "Big Blue Marble" series) and the second portraying various aspects of the traditional Inuit way of life (the "Tuktu" series). Findings revealed that television may bring about some changes in children's images of familiar and unfamiliar cultural groups.

353. From the Fonz to Faulkner: TV Makes Literature Get-at-Able. Blythe, Hal; Sweet, Charlie. *Audiovisual Instruction.* v24, n7, p16–17, Oct 1979 (EJ 209 897; Reprint: UMI).

The introduction of literature through topic parallels in popular commercial television produces gratifying results,

making students feel more at ease, more confident, more able to participate, and more willing to enter the new world of watered-down literature.

354. Helping Emotionally Disturbed Children through Prosocial Television. Elias, Maurice J. *Exceptional Children.* v46, n3, p217–18, Nov 1979.

The effects of videotapes of the instructional television program "Inside/Out" depicting coping difficulties (along with group discussion) on the prosocial behavior of 109 emotionally and academically handicapped boys (ages 7 to 15) in a residential treatment center were studied. Findings showed that Ss in the treatment group improved in their abilities to exercise self-control.

355. HiHo Time. Haynes, Ralph L. III. *Audiovisual Instruction.* v23, n6, p36–39, Sep 1978 (EJ 187 113; Reprint: UMI).

In an effort to determine if television can be used to teach severely and profoundly retarded children, an interdisciplinary team began production of the "HiHo Time" series. The program's content, staff, production techniques, and indications of its success are described.

356. How TV Can Be Good for Children. Harrison, Barbara Grizzuti. *McCall's.* v105, p165,215–16,218,220,222,224, Oct 1977.

This mother believes that even the worst television programs—sometimes, especially the worst television programs—create the opportunity for older children to develop moral and aesthetic judgments and to analyze their own values in discussions with their parents. She asserts that it is preferable in many cases for children to make these value explorations in their own living rooms, rather than on the street. Finally, she refutes arguments that television alone is at fault for violence in society, lack of communication, and unrealistic views of family life.

357. TV and Secondary Schools. *NASSP Bulletin.* v64, n437, p1–59, Sep 1980.

This special theme section provides 11 articles on current problems and practices with instructional television. Included are discussions of the effectiveness of ITV; descriptions of its use in various schools for counseling, science instruction, language arts, and gifted education; an article outlining a secondary curriculum, "Inside Television: A Guide to Critical Viewing"; and a national directory of ITV personnel.

358. The Impact of School Television on Groups of Pupils Aged 9–11 Years. Oxley, D. W. *British Journal of Educational Technology.* v10, n3, p229–40, Oct 1979.

Studies the impact of school television programs on groups of 9-to 11-year-old pupils of above average, average, and below average IQs, with special reference to variance in attitudes of receiving, in responding to, and in valuing the transmissions.

359. An Interview with a Pioneer. Potter, Rosemary Lee. *Teacher*. v95, n8, p44,46,48, Apr 1978 (EJ 184 374; Reprint: UMI).

Michael McAndrew, director of educational services, Capital Cities Television Productsion in Philadelphia, is interviewed about his development of the Television Reading Program, which employs television scripts to improve student reading.

360. Introducing Children to Books via Television. Gough, Pauline B. *Reading Teacher*. v32, n4, p458–62, Jan 1979.

Discusses a number of instructional television programs which are being developed to interest children in specific books and reading in general.

361. Is Children's Programming Improving? Potter, Rosemary Lee. *Teacher*. v96, n7, p34,40–43, Mar 1979 (EJ 215 401; Reprint: UMI).

Susan Futterman, a former teacher and early childhood specialist for Action for Children's Television, comments on changing formats for children's programs, as well as on the role of educators in using television as a learning vehicle.

362. Prime Time in the Classroom. Lee, Barbara. *Journal of Communication*. v30, n1, p175–80, Win 1980 (EJ 221 304; Reprint: UMI).

A national sample of secondary students, their teachers, and their parents were interviewed about their participation in the CBS Television Reading Program, which provides scripts and learning guides in relation to selected commercial broadcasts. The majority of respondents reacted favorably to the program. Ways of increasing script use and parental involvement were also examined.

363. Prime Time School Television: Doing Something about TV. Minow, Newton N.; Mills, Lynn M. *Phi Delta Kappan*. v59, n10, p665–67, Jun 1978 (EJ 181 497; Reprint: UMI).

The Prime Time School Television Program alerts teachers about broadcast television programs that might hold special interest for them, develops instructional units, and is attempting to develop a definition of quality television.

364. Reading TV: Today's Basic. Brown, Don W. *Educational Leadership*. v36, n3, p216–18, Dec 1978 (EJ 192 422; Reprint: UMI).

Television, with its undeniable impact, is here to stay. Educators should learn to use the medium to their advantage to improve reading instead of constantly decrying its content.

365. Roots: Reflections from the Classroom. Protinsky, Ruth A.; Wildman, Terry M. *Journal of Negro Education*. v48, n2, p171–81, Spr 1979 (EJ 205 709; Reprint: UMI).

The impact of the televised version of "Roots" on the knowledge, interests, attitudes, and actions of 181 Black and White high school students is assessed in this study.

366. "Roots" Touched Children: Planned or Not. Greathouse, Betty. *Young Children*. v32, n4, p57–61, May 1977.

Explores children's reactions to the televised version of Alex Haley's "Roots" through interviews with 30 eight-year-old third graders (10 Black, 10 Mexican American, 10 White) from two classrooms in South Phoenix, Arizona.

367. Sesame Street around the World: Cognitive Skill Learning across Cultures. Salomon, Gavriel. *Journal of Communication*. v26, n2, p138–44, Spr 1976.

Cites evidence from an Israeli study which indicates that media effects on cognition interact with a child's initial level of skill mastery. While all children learned, information gain and improvement were especially pronounced among those who were already more advanced.

368. Superheroes, Antiheroes, and the Heroism Void in Children's TV. Berckman, Edward M. *Christian Century*. v96, p704–07, 4 Jul 1979.

Based on an analysis of late afternoon and Saturday morning television since 1977, the author examines television's potential for providing children with imitatable heroes who may serve as positive role models in real-life situations. He looks at successes and failures in TV's use of superheroes, its treatment of heroic characters, and its emphasis on didactic moral instruction.

369. TV and Kids: What You Can Do: More than 25 Ways for You to Sponsor Prime-Time Learning. Kahn, Linda. *Learning*. v8, n2, p47–49, Oct 1979.

Presents multidisciplinary learning activities related to three popular network television shows: "Little House on the Prairie," "Superfriends," and "Mork and Mindy."

370. TV and Reading: What Can Parents and Teachers Do? Feeley, Joan. *NJEA Review*. v51, n8, p16–19, Apr 1978 (EJ 182 896; Reprint: UMI).

Because of the great amount of time children spend watching television and the effect that this may have on their reading achievement, it behooves parents and teachers to be concerned and knowledgeable about the issue. Discusses some methods for developing children's interest in reading through properly guided television viewing and relating television to reading programs.

371. TV as a Teacher's Ally. Quisenberry, Nancy et al. *Instructor*. v87, n8, p82–84, Mar 1978 (EJ 176 170; Reprint: UMI).

A collection of brief essays on ways teachers can use commercial television to stimulate reading, science, math, social studies and language arts curriculum.

372. TV as a Tool to Improve Basic Communication Skills? Strickler, Darryl S.; Farr, Beverly. *Language Arts.* v56, n6, p634–40, Sep 1979 (EJ 209 256; Reprint: UMI).

Discusses language development in children and describes how instructional television programs can contribute to that development.

373. TV Scripts for Language Arts. Roettger, Doris et al. *Audiovisual Instruction.* v24, n1, p30–32, Jan 1979 (EJ 203 443; Reprint: UMI).

A study of the use of television scripts and viewing to involve students in reading found that both teachers and students thought the CBS Television Reading Program had a positive effect upon student reading comprehension, enjoyment of reading, listening, and class participation.

374. TV Succeeds after Traditional Methods Fail. Fowlie, George; Porteous, Jean. *Special Education in Canada.* v52, n1, p5–7, 11, Fall 1977 (available from: Special Education in Canada, Dave Muir, Subscription Manager, 12 Doucett Place, Scarborough, Ontario M1G 3Ms).

Tape recorded television programs were used to increase reading comprehension and word attack skills of special education students. Lesson development is outlined.

375. TV Talk: Instant Classroom Celebrities with TV Game Shows. Sheppard, Marti. *Teacher.* v94, n7, p34–37, Mar 1977.

Suggests some learning activities that can be used to capitalize on the popularity of TV game shows so that students can build their learning skills. These game show formats can also strengthen and reinforce many areas of the elementary curriculum.

376. TV Talk: TV and the Classroom: An Index. Potter, Rosemary Lee. *Teacher.* v97, n8, p8–9, May-Jun 1980 (EJ 229 354).

This article provides a subject index back to 1975 of the "TV Talk" and other "Teacher" magazine articles concerning television. Topics include the use of TV in elementary language arts, math, reading and social studies, as well as suggestions for parents and articles on television as a medium.

377. TV Talk: Using Commercial TV in the Classroom. O'Brien, Clare Lynch. *Teacher.* v94, n1, p45–46, 51–52, Sep 1976.

Describes a method for capitalizing on children's interest in television by developing learning activities with high classroom appeal.

378. TV: The Classroom Co-Star. Scherer, Marge. *School and Community.* v63, n9, p24–26, 41, May 1977.

Describes some of the advances made in instructional television in recent years.

379. TV: The Effective "Aide" for Affective Education. Van Hoose, John. *Phi Delta Kappan.* v59, n10, p674–75, Jun 1978 (EJ 181 500; Reprint: UMI).

The vast majority of the teachers surveyed responded positively to questions about the practical value of the ITV series, "Inside/Out," which is designed to deal openly and directly with social, emotional, and physical problems that typically confront 8- to 10-year old students.

380. Teaching Children to Read: An Argument for Television. Fowles, Barbara R. *Urban Review.* v9, n2, p114–20, Sum 1976.

Concludes that the television medium embodies a code of its own, combining auditory and visual conventions, just as print language is a conventional code. These codes enhance each other in some ways that assist the process of learning to read. Special attention is given to "Electric Company."

381. Teaching the Terminal Children. Bronson, David B. *English Journal.* v67, n3, p43–48, Mar 1978 (EJ 181 230; Reprint: UMI).

Students should become involved in the production of messages to be transmitted by both nonelectronic and electronic media.

382. Teaching Thinking by Television. Gough, Pauline B. *Education Leadership.* v36, n8, p561–65, May 1979 (EJ 203 060; Reprint: UMI).

"Thinkabout," a new series of instructional television programs designed for fifth and sixth grades, will reinforce basic skills while helping students learn to solve real-world problems.

383. Television and Reading: Industry Initiatives. LeGrand-Brodsky, Kathryn. *Journal of Reading.* v23, n1, p9–15, Oct 1979 (EJ 209 288; Reprint: UMI).

Describes script-reading projects, teachers' guides, and parent participation workshops offered by the broadcast industry to stimulate reading.

384. Television and the Development of Aesthetic Literacy in Children. Sudano, Gary R. *Contemporary Education.* v49, n4, p223–27, Sum 1978 (EJ 193 404; Reprint: UMI).

Color television and background music accompanying shows provide children with basic knowledge of emotional response to art forms and symbols. In order to increase their aesthetic literacy, however, they should be exposed to more subtle artistic experiences.

385. Television and the English Teacher. England, David A. *English Journal.* v68, n8, p99–102, Nov 1979 (EJ 214 049; Reprint: UMI).

Suggests why four-prime time television series are worthy of attention in the English classroom and suggests topics for classroom discussion and writing activities based on them.

386. Television May be Just What's Needed to Teach the "Basics." Thompson, Margery. *American School Board Journal.* v165, n1, p41–42, Jan 1978 (EJ 171 558; Reprint: UMI).

The Essential Learning Skills television project is a series of 60 quarter-hour programs for the fifth and sixth grades being produced by the Agency for Instructional Television for a consortium of Canadian and American education organizations.

387. Television Programs as Socializing Agents for Mentally Retarded Children. Baran, Stanley J. *AV Communication Review.* v25, n3, p281–89, Fall 1977 (EJ 176 011; Reprint: UMI).

Television dramas employing mentally retarded children as actors in everyday situations may facilitate socialization and development of self-esteem in mentally retarded children.

388. Television Tie-Ins in the School Library. Singer, Dorothy G. *School Library Journal.* v26, n1, p51–52, Sep 1979.

Cites a number of inexpensive methods librarians can use to promote children's interest in the library through their interest in television.

389. Television's Hidden Curriculum. Fox, Sandra; Huston-Stein, Aletha. *National Elementary Principal.* v56, n3, p62–68, Jan-Feb 1977.

Examines the goals, formats, and effectiveness of current educational programing and provides insight into some important questions, such as: What are the alternative instructional messages of television programing? How are they best communicated?

390. Tonight's Assignment, Watch Television. Hawley, Richard A. *American Film.* v5, p59–61, Apr 1980.

Examines efforts by the television networks to promote education about television and television/reading projects. Suggests that such activities may in the short run be beneficial but in the long run will only make youngsters even more dependent on television.

391. Understanding Exceptionality through TV. Potter, Rosemary Lee. *Teacher.* v96, n2, p42, 47–48, 51, Oct 1978 (EJ 195 638; Reprint: UMI).

Class discussions of television shows that portray disabled people can be used to help children correct their misconceptions about those who have handicaps.

392. Using Entertainment Television Shows on Videotape to Teach the Retarded. Solomon, Bernard. *Reading Improvement.* v13, n3, p180–81, Fall 1976.

The Television Reading Program, which uses videotapes of popular shows with scripts and related learning activities, is reported to have been successful with a class of retarded children, ages 8–12, in supplying motivation, reading activities, and values exercises.

393. Using Musical Television Commercials to Teach Reading. Hirst, Lois T.; O'Such, Twila. *Teaching Exceptional Children.* v11, n2, p80–81, Win 1979.

A program of teaching reading through the use of musical television commercials was initiated with 8- to 10-year-old disadvantaged students. Both motivation and achievement improved.

394. Using Popular Television as a Teaching Tool for the Linguistically Diverse. Wall, Muriel. *Journal of Educational Technology Systems.* v7, n2, p143-50, 1978-79.

Illustrates how media communication techniques can be adapted for curriculum development. Popular television series suggested by the students are used to provide recommendations for lessons to develop pronunciation, oral communication, plot analysis, and writing composition, as well as analysis of cultural factors concerning ethnic diversity.

395. Using Videotape to Motivate the LD Student: The Television Reading Program. Solomon, Bernard. *Academic Therapy.* v11, n3, p271–74, Spr 1976.

The Television Reading Program, as conceived by Bernard Solomon, Michael Marcuse, and Michael McAndrew, uses videotapes of popular television shows to motivate children to read. A student survey is used to determine favorite shows, then tapes and scripts are requested from television executives. Teachers analyze the scripts and create lessons around them. In Philadelphia, the program has resulted in reading gains for students of various ages and ability levels.

MICROFICHE

396. CTW Research Bibliography. Research Papers Relating to the Children's Television Workshop and Its Experimental Educational Series: "Sesame Street" and "The Electric Company"—1968–76. Children's Television Workshop, New York, NY, 1976, 23p (ED 133 079; Reprint: EDRS; also available from Children's Television Workshop Library, One Lincoln Plaza, New York, NY 10023). For a related document see citation 418.

This selected annotated bibliography of research-related papers and reports covers major research activities in connection with the development of "Sesame Street" and "The Electric Company," the two experimental educational series produced by the Children's Television Workshop. These writings date back to the origins of CTW in 1968 and have been contributed by members of the CTW research and production staffs as well as by outside experts and intitutions. References include formative and summative research studies for both series, research on the international versions of "Sesame Street," and other theoretical and scholarly discussions of research topics within the scope of media and children.

397. A Challenging Picture: The Status of ITV Utilization in Secondary Schools. Schneller, Paul, Agency for Instructional Television, Bloomington, IN, Mar 1977, 27p (ED 157 536; Reprint: EDRS; also available from Agency for Instructional Television, Box A, Bloomington, IN 47401). For related document see citation 418.

The Agency for Instructional Television (AIT) solicited information from 28 individuals having responsibilities in various local, regional, and state instructional television organizations and agencies in the United States and Canada. AIT asked each individual to respond to three sets of questions on (1) the current status of secondary school television in the respondent's area, (2) a statement of the respondent's philosophy regarding television use in the secondary schools, and (3) examples of significant successes or failures in the respondent's area. Responses of agencies indicate that secondary school television is underused, underfinanced, and unexciting. Appendices include the letter requesting responses to the survey questions, and names of the 22 agency representatives responding to the survey. While the sampling procedures are not scientific, the data seem representative, based on AIT's knowledge of the field and active agencies. This initial probe is designed as a basis for further analysis and in-depth case studies.

398. Children's Television Workshop: The Electric Company. Final Report on a Television Reading Series. Children's Television Workshop, New York, NY, Jun 1978, 83p. Sponsoring agency: Office of Education (DHEW), Washington, DC (ED 162 639; Reprint: EDRS).

The early development, prebroadcast research, early production concepts, formative research, summative research, evolution of production, and promotion and outreach activities of "The Electric Company" (TEC) are presented. Conclusions discuss (1) the uncertainty of the future of TEC despite its success and positive reception as an educational innovation; (2) some immediate questions regarding promotional activities, funding, valuable products, and teacher utilization; and (3) steps which have been taken to begin to answer these questions. A list of references is included.

399. Differential Effects of Television Programming on Preschoolers' Cognition, Imagination and Social Play. Tower, Roni Beth et al. 1977, 43p. Tables and figures have been filmed from the best available copy (ED 153 713; Reprint: EDRS).

This paper reports on an experiment to determine: (1) the effects of two different styles of television program format on the ability of preschool children to recall program content and (2) the cumulative effect of sustained viewing of particular programs upon spontaneous play behavior. Three groups of preschoolers (totaling 58) were exposed to two weeks' daily

viewing of either "Misterogers' Neighborhood," "Sesame Street," or a control series of nature and animal films. Hypotheses tested considered whether format differences designed for constructive impact actually yielded such results, and the extent to which format may have special impact due to developmental and personality differences among children. Interactions of child age, sex, IQ, and imaginativeness with the stimulus conditions were considered. Results included indications that the slower paced format and other characteristics of the "Misterogers" program yielded positive changes, especially for initially less imaginative children, in imaginativeness of play, positive affect, concentration, and social interaction with adults and peers.

400. Educational Television in the United States. Hitchens, Howard, Oct 1978, 24p. Paper presented at the 1 Convencion Internacional de TV y Educacion (Barcelona, Spain, October 11, 1978) (ED 164 011; Reprint: EDRS).

Major developments in the history of education and television centered around broadcasting in the 1950s, then closed circuit applications, the growth of video recording, and more recently the use of satellites. During its 25-year history, educational television in the U.S. has seen the growth of a television college in Chicago, a video university (the University of Mid-America) in Nebraska and the midwest, the Children's Television Workshop programs for preschool education ("Sesame Street") and for reading improvement ("The Electric Company"). The results of a major survey of instructional television uses throughout the United States by the Corporation for Public Broadcasting indicate that television is firmly established in the formal education system of the country. Television's effectiveness for many applications in the educational system in the United States has assured it a firm place in instructional programing at the elementary, secondary, and postsecondary levels. TV applications currently include several county wide systems, and a brief description of the Broward County, Florida, and Washington County, Maryland, systems concludes the presentation.

401. The Effects of Televised Skill Instruction, Instructional System Support, and Parental Intervention on the Development of Cognitive Skills. Final Report. Henderson, Ronald W.; Swanson, Rosemary, Arizona University, Tucson, Arizona Center for Educational Research and Development, 1977, 111p. Sponsoring agency: Office of Child Development (DHEW), Washington, DC (ED 148 379; Reprint: EDRS).

Research during the first two years of this project indicated that television alone can be an effective medium for teaching complex conceptual behaviors, some more than others. The major task during the third year was to develop and test the efficacy of parental intervention procedures to augment televised skill instruction. Subjects were three- to five-year-old Native American children attending Head Start Centers on the Papago Reservation in Arizona. A parental support system was implemented for the four skill areas: seriation, enumeration, conservation, and question-asking. The four experimental groups included (1) television only, (2) televised instruction with ancillary support, (3) televised instruction with parental support, and (4) television with both types of ancillary support. In the question-asking, seriation, and enumeration studies, performances of the televised instruction group was significantly superior to control groups. Only in enumeration was a condition involving ancillary instruction more effective than television alone. In general, the results of the experiments during this grant have demonstrated that televised instruction based on social learning theory and task analysis can be effective in teaching abstract rule-governed behaviors to preschool children and that, under certain conditions, simple ancillary support may enhance the effects of televised instruction alone.

402. The Effects of Sesame Street Programming on The Cooperative Behavior of Young Children.*
Silverman, Linda Theresa, Stanford University, 1977, 153p (77-25, 727; Reprint: DC).

Fifteen female and 15 male pairs of children at each of three ages watched a 15 minute television program excerpted from "Sesame Street." One-third saw a program which emphasized cognitive skills like number recognition and the other two-thirds watched programs which emphasized social skills like cooperation. For one-third, cooperation was presented as a way of resolving conflict. For the remaining third, cooperation was demonstrated in a nonconflict situation. Then the children played a simple game. By comparing the three groups, assessment was made of (1) whether televised teaching of social skills caused the children to behave more cooperatively when playing the game, and (2) which method of social teaching was more effective.

In the game, a modified "tug of war," children were instructed to obtain marbles by pulling a marble-holder to their side of a game table. When the children pulled against one another, the marble-holder broke apart and the marble rolled "to the dump." Only by taking turns could either child acquire any marbles.

The older the pair of children, the less likely they were to take turns in order to obtain marbles. On the average, pairs of three-year-olds acquired more marbles than five-year-olds who acquired more marbles than seven-year-olds. Although older children recalled more of the social information provided by the television programs and gave more complex definitions of social concepts such as cooperation and sharing, they were not likely to apply this knowledge in the marble-pull game. No children played the marble-pull game in a more prosocial way after seeing positive social behaviors demonstrated on television. However, those children who watched programs containing prosocially resolved conflict had a more uneven division of marbles than children in the other two program conditions. The responsibility for this result lies in the performance of the three-year-olds.

The results are interpreted from the perspective of the developmental changes which occur in the child's understanding of what behaviors are appropriate for playing games. While three-year-olds apparently took the initial demonstration of how to play the game as a literal model which they imitated exactly, older children seemed to assimilate it into a total system of games as tests of skill or workings of chance. Neither the demonstration nor the prosocial messages induced older children to take turns. By contrast, the younger children readily adopted the taking turns strategy modeled in the demonstration as the rule for playing the game, unless they had just watched a program containing the conflict-resolution spots. Under that condition, three-year-olds were less likely to take turns.

403. The Effects of the Television Series "Feeling Free" on Children's Attitudes toward Handicapped People.*
Storye, Kim Susan, Harvard University, 1979. 235p (8010537; Reprint: DC).

"Feeling Free," a series of six television programs designed to promote children's positive attitudes toward handicapped people, was developed to facilitate mainstreaming—the integration of handicapped children into regular schools. This thesis systematically examines the impact of the television series in mainstreamed classrooms. It attempts to determine if "Feeling Free" promotes children's awareness, understanding, and acceptance of handicapped people. The effects of previous experiences with handicapped people and of different types of classroom discussions on the impact of the series were also explored.

A total of 12 upper elementary mainstreamed classrooms, 8 experimental and 4 comparison classrooms, participated in the study. The sample contained an equal number of boys and girls and the mean age was 9.5. The classrooms were selected from four schools in four different communities in Boston.

The general design of the research was a pre/post quasi-experimental design. We presented the six 15-minute "Feeling Free" programs to handicapped and nonhandicapped children in eight classrooms scheduled once or twice per week. We observed and rated teacher-led postviewing discussions. Questionnaires were administered before and after viewing to seven of the eight experimental classrooms and to an additional four comparison classrooms who did not view. One experimental class received only the postquestionnaire to assess effects of pretesting. The Children's Attitudes toward Handicapped People questionnaire was designed to determine children's familiarity with and attitudes toward handicapped people, and to assess any changes after viewing and discussing "Feeling Free."

The main hypothesis was confirmed: Children who viewed the "Feeling Free" television series and participated in classroom discussions following viewing were more aware, more understanding, and more accepting of handicapped people than those who did not, as measured by the two attitude rating scales in the questionnaire. On one scale, viewing "Feeling Free" increased children's positive attitudes toward handicapped people in general on the dimensions: (1) capabilities, skills, and potentials of handicapped people; (2) feelings of handicapped people; (3) handicapped people as friends; and (4) general perceptions of handicapped people. On the second scale, after viewing "Feeling Free" children were able to recall the specific abilities and lifestyles of each of the handicapped cast members. Thus attitudes toward blindness, deafness, dwarfism, dyslexia, and toward people who use crutches or wheelchairs were affected.

Analyses which examined age and sex indicated that the series is equally effective for both boys and girls and for children 8-to-12-years-old.

A comparison of the experimental class which received only the posttest and the other experimental classes indicated that the posttest only class had significantly lower attitudes than the other experimental classes toward the program specific content but not toward handicapped people in general. These findings suggest that taking the pretest elevated the posttest scores, but only for the items which assessed attitudes toward program specific content.

The two subsidiary hypotheses were not confirmed: (1) although children's attitudes differed on the basis of amount and kind of experience they had had with handicapped people, these differences in experience did not affect the impact of the series; (2) different types of classroom discussions following viewing of "Feeling Free" did not affect the impact of the series. In addition, although positive attitude change was detected on the two attitude rating scales, this change was not apparent on the two descriptive instruments.

404. Evaluation of Eight "Infinity Factory" Programs: Part I: Analysis of the Eight-Show Series. Harvey, Francis A. et al., Education Development Center, Inc., Newton, MA, Jun 1976, 61p (ED 129 330; Reprint: EDRS).

The "Infinity Factory" television series was developed to help children ages 8 through 11 to understand the usefulness of some basic mathematics skills for everyday life. Aimed primary at Black and Latino children, the series concentrates on: the decimal number system; measurement, especially the metric system; estimation; mapping and scaling; and graphing. Throughout the series there is emphasis on creative problems solving techniques and on a positive student self-image. An evaluation of eight of the programs was conducted using 1,000 students and their teachers in 39 third through sixth grade classes in four cities as subjects. The evaluation measured student attention, appeal of the overall programs and major segments of each program, student comprehension of story line and gains in math skills, attitudes toward math, social attitudes, and teachers' opinions of the effectiveness and usefulness of the series. This report gives a detailed analysis of the evaluation of the series taken as a whole.

405. The Frequency of Creativity Components on Two Children's Television Programs, and Studies of the Ability of Seventeen Three-Year-Olds to Exhibit These Same Creativity Components. Dillon, Mae, Dec 1977, 84p (ED 152 409; Reprint: EDRS).

This paper reviews research on creativity, children's television-viewing habits, and television's effects on children; rates two children's programs for creativity content; and describes the results of creativity presented to three-year-olds. In section I, various definitions of creativity (as related to person, process, product and environment) are discussed. Seven possible components of creativity considered important by Torrance and Guilford are listed. Section II reviews research on the effects of television (positive and negative) on children. Section III reports the ratings of 10 one-hour "Sesame Street" and 10 half-hour "Misteroger's Neighborhood" programs for frequency of the seven creativity components. Section IV reports the results of a study in which 17 three-year-olds were presented with four creativity tasks shown on Sesame Street. Preschool teachers' independent ratings of children's flexibility were compared with task scores as were maternal estimates of how often their children viewed "Sesame Street" and "Misteroger's Neighborhood" each week. Implications for education are discussed. Appendices contain program creativity data and data from the study.

406. An Integration of the Visual Media via "Fat Albert and the Cosby Kids" into the Elementary School Curriculum as a Teaching Aid and Vehicle to Achieve Increased Learning. Costy, William Henry, Jr., University of Massachusetts, 1976, 267p (77-6369; Reprint: DC).

This study examines the failure of urban schools to meet the educational needs of minority children and explores the possibilities of using television as a tool for educational change. It discusses three television series ("Sesame Street," "The Electric Company," and "Fat Albert and the Cosby Kids") with regard to their success as teaching/learning instruments and their attempts to combat institutional racism; it then reports on an evaluation of the effectiveness of "Fat Albert and the Cosby Kids" as a teaching aid in the elementary classroom. The evaluation indicated that the series can serve as a useful addition to existing curriculum materials.

407. Is Television the New Egalitarian Educational System? A Comparison of Learner Characteristics Associated with Successful Achievement in Formal vs. Television Systems of Schooling.* Presser, Anne Susan, Columbia University, 1978, 109p (7819414; Reprint: DC).

The purpose of this experimental study was to investigate to what extent measures of achievement in the formal schooling system predict achievement in the alternate schooling system of television. The sample consisted of 568 students in grades 1–6 from three New York City parochial schools. Reading achievement was measured by SRA assessment survey, primary and multilevel edictions. A televiewing comprehension inventory (T-V-C) was designed to measure comprehension of televised material. The 45-item multiple choice instrument was presented orally and did not require reading or writing by the testee. It was based on a 30 minute segment from a popular television program. T-V-C score equalled the number of questions for which the pictorial response choice was correctly marked. Mean T-V-C performance increased by grade. Strong positive relationships were found across grades 2–6 between T-V-C scores and reading achievement scores. No sex differences were found in T-V-C performance. The data suggest that measures of achievement in formal schooling are effective predictors of performance in the television schooling system. The results of this study were discussed in terms of a set of learner characteristics required for success in either schooling system. Television seems to be niether a compensatory educational system nor one free of the SES and IQ learner advantages associated with formal schooling. Thus, television is not a new egalitarian educational system, but another educational system—pervasive, well attended and highly motivating which will teach the most to those who learn faster, just as formal schooling has done.

408. Language Learning from Television: What Is Known and What Is Needed? Epstein, Robert H., International Association of Cybernetics, Namur, Belgium: University of Southern California, Los Angeles, Annenberg School of Communications, 1976, 42p (ED 134 332; Reprint: EDRS). For related documents see citations 32, 417.

This paper, prepared as part of the Project in Television and Early Childhood Education at the University of Southern California, summarizes and examines issues found in past and current research in the area of television and children's language acquisition. It is assumed that television is an increasingly large part of children's early experience and the language to which they are exposed. Four questions are used as a framework for discussion: (1) Is the television language heard by the child relevant intake resulting in acquisition? (2) When and why does the television language heard result in acquisition? (3) How is television language acquisition different from nontelevision language acquisition? (4) Why are these differences, if any, worthy of consideration for policy regarding the development of children's television programming?

409. Motivation and Children's Learning from Television.* Lometti, Guy E., University of Wisconsin—Madison, 1979, 212p (8008826; Reprint: DC).

The purpose of this research was to replicate and extend developmental research on children's learning from the media and to validate the uses and gratifications approach to the study of media effects by manipulating motivations. Two kinds of learning were studied; central learning (plot-relevant information) and peripheral learning (plot-irrelevant information).

A field experiment was carried out. Two televised segments were shown to 343 children from the fourth, sixth, seventh, and eighth grades. The TV shows differed in their complexity (amount of information) which was varied by adding to the audio portion of the program ("Wild Kingdom") information about the show's content (porpoises). This version constituted the high-complexity program. The low-complexity program did not contain this additional information.

Two levels of motivation were manipulated (surveillance and entertainment). A third condition received no motivation. In the surveillance condition, subjects were instructed to watch the program and learn all they could because they would have a quiz immediately after the program. In the entertainment condition, subjects were instructed to sit back and relax with their friends and have a good time while they watched the program. Control condition subjects received no instructions.

Central learning increased from fourth- to both sixth- and seventh-grade children. Peripheral learning increased from fourth- to seventh-grade children while the decrease approached significance between seventh- and eighth-grade children.

When interest in the TV show, sex of the subject and their perceptions of reality (for the program) were controlled, older children (sixth and seven graders) learned more than younger children (fourth graders). Similarly, eighth graders learned more than fourth graders. Controlling interest, sex and perceived reality revealed that peripheral learning increased from fourth to seventh graders while it decreased from seventh to eighth graders.

Children's perceptions of central and peripheral material were consistent across grade levels. However, children and adult judges differed in their perceptions of these materials.

Control-group children learned more central material than either the surveillance- or entertainment-group children. While this study manipulated motivations, children's self-report measures of why they watched the programs were also assessed. the high-measured-surveillance-motivated children learned significantly more central and peripheral material than the low-measured-surveillance-motivated children. Both of the measured motivations (surveillance and entertainment) were positively related to both forms of learning. Only the relationship between entertainment and central learning remained significant after interest and sex were controlled statistically.

410. New Avenues of Special Education Resources: "Sesame Street" Programming for the Exceptional Child. Kolucki, Barbara. Apr 1977, 10p. Paper presented at the Annual International Convention, The Council for Exceptional Children (55th, Atlanta, GA, April 11–15, 1977) (ED 139 199; Reprint: EDRS).

Described are activities of Community Education Services (CES) in providing "Sesame Street" programing designed for and featuring children with mental retardation and other developmental special needs. Supplementary materials provided by CES are noted to include training films for teachers and parents, an activity book, and special activity suggestions for reinforcing the segments designed for children with mental retardation.

411. New Avenues of Teaching Resources—"Sesame Street" Programs for the Mentally Retarded Child. Ardi, Dana B. Apr 1977, 13p. Paper presented at the Annual International Convention, The Council for Exceptional Children (55th, Atlanta, GA, April 11–15, 1977) (ED 139 197; Reprint: EDRS).

Evaluated with 173 mentally retarded (MR) children (4 to 12 years old), 45 day care program children (mean age 4.3 years), and 45 second graders were the "Sesame Street" "Play to Grow" materials designed to foster positive self-image of retarded children. During sample tape presentations, children's visual attention, verbal comments, and motor behavior were recorded. Among findings were that attention of both MR and normal samples averaged from "high moderate" to "very attentive"; that MR children were more involved with their viewing; that children's comprehension of "Play to Grow" segments was excellent; and that although normal second graders were very aware of the differences in the way the MR children went about performing "Play to Grow" activities, bias and prejudice could not be detected. (A list of the program's values and a sample segment outline are provided.)

412. Nonprint Media and Reading: An Annotated Bibliography. Dillingofski, Mary Sue. International Reading Association, Newark, DE, 1979, 36p (ED 174 946; Reprint: EDRS; also available from International Reading Association, 800 Barksdale Road, Newark, DE 19711; Order no. 334).

The 72 items in this bibliography concern the use of nonprint media in reading instruction. A section on audio and visual channels concerns the use of audiovisual materials, tape recordings, and filmstrips as instructional aids. The section on television and film includes items on film, learning from television, commercial television, public television, and locally produced television. The final section concerns computer assisted instruction in reading. A list of recommended readings is included at the end of this bibliography for those who would like practical suggestions for applying educational technology in the reading curriculum.

413. Parenting Education through Television: An Evaluation of the Middle Road Traveler Series for Adolescents. Will, Edward E.; Hotvedt, Martyn O., Baylor College of Medicine, Houston, TX, Mar 1977, 290p. Parts marginally legible due to small type. Sponsoring agencies: Texas Education Agency; Texas State Dept. of Community Affairs; Office of Early Childhood Development, Texas State Dept. of Public Welfare, Austin (ED 161 436; Reprint: EDRS).

Formative and summative evaluations are presented for the "Middle Road Traveler," a televised in-school parenting education series intended for junior high school students who are neither current nor expectant parents. Data collected contributed to the development of the pilot test—the principal evaluation activity. A total of 280 students were both pre- and posttested during the 12-week pilot test in the Fall of 1976. Measures of knowledge and attitude change directly referred to the curriculum objectives, were supplemented by measures of program appeal and viewer rapport. Results revealed that "Middle Road Traveler" viewers made numerous significant gains over pretest in the various parenting curriculum areas. Affective learning gains were more numerous and more substantial than cognitive gains. Differences between various sample subgroups in both curriculum-referenced learning and viewer rapport were also examined. Data from relevant federal parenting education projects were compared and sex- and race-related differences in learning discussed. Program development, pilot testing, and analysis are detailed.

414. Patterns of Performance: Public Broadcasting and Education 1974–1976. Carlisle, Robert D. B., Comp., Corporation for Public Broadcasting, Washington, DC, 1978, 147p. Small print may be marginally legible (ED 166 763; Reprint: EDRS).

Intended as a practical inventory of ways public broadcasting has been used for education, this volume is divided into three sections dealing with television, radio, and research articles. The section on television discusses the method, material, and changing context of educational broadcasting; analyzes the programing and funding of preschool television; compares different approaches to programing for the school age child; and describes a number of approaches for teaching the adult learner. The section on radio presents a status report on education through radio including special programs for professionals, the young, and the blind; distinguishes the role of radio at various educational levels; and summarizes the needs of the radio industry if it is to expand. The final section contains research articles on satellite technology and public service telecommunication, open learning and postsecondary education, the effectiveness of "The Electric Company," and the role of instructional television in the educational community.

415. "Plaza Sesamo" and Spanish Language Learning. Pearson, Sulamita R. 1978, 44p. Best copy available (ED 155 890; Reprint: EDRS).

The Spanish version of "Sesame Street" was used in a project in a class of 12 students in the second semester of first-year Spanish at Phillips Exeter Academy, and an attempt was made to evaluate the usefulness of the series in second-language acquisition. This account of the project has five parts: (1) a history of the production of "Plaza Sesamo" in Latin America; (2) a description of Exeter Academy—its history, curriculum, and student population; (3) an analysis of the data derived from questionnaires on the students' motivation, needs and interests in their study of Spanish; (4) a description of "Plaza Sesamo" films, indicating similarities to and differences from the English- language version; and (5) some preliminary conclusions. The students believed that the greatest benefits of the films were improvement in vocabulary, especially through visual representation of words, and improvement in listening comprehension skills. Association with visual images occurred within the students' own cultural concepts and role models; they reacted more favorably to dubbed segments taken directly from "Sesame Street" than to segments produced live in Mexico. It is hypothesized that cognitive concepts must be taught, on the introductory level, in terms and images that are culturally recognizable to the audience.

416. Project "Freestyle": Baseline Studies. LaRose, Robert. Apr 1978, 18p. Paper presented at the Annual Meeting of the International Communication Association (Chicago, IL, April 25–29, 1978) (ED 157 107; Reprint: EDRS).

Project "Freestyle" involved the development of prototypical television materials and a comic book intended to combat sex-role stereotyping in the career-related attitudes of 9- to 12-year-old children. This paper reports the results of four types of research conducted during the early development of the television series to determine the degree to which the thinking of children in the target audience is affected by sex-role stereotypes, important influences on children's sex-typed behavior, children's liking and comprehension of prototypical "Freestyle" materials, and audience reaction to the entire first pilot program and to the characters in it. The paper discusses highlights of the research results, measures used to determine audience response and to ascertain differences among different segments of the target audience, and implications of the research for development of "Freestyle" materials. Analysis of the results indicated that sex-role stereotypes are still in effect in the target audience and are supported by people designated as "significant others" in children's lives, and that the "Freestyle" message must be slanted to the needs of quite diverse audience segments.

417. Rationale and Activities of Project on Television in Early Education: Progress Report, July-December 1975. Smart, Margaret E.; Williams, Frederick, International Association of Cybernetics, Namur, Belgium; University of Southern California, Los Angeles, Annenberg School of Communications. Jan 1976, 38p (ED 134 330; Reprint: EDRS). For related documents see citations 32, 408.

This progress report discusses the rationale and activities of the Project on Television in Early Childhood Education at the University of Southern California. Since January 1975, the Annenberg School and the School for Early Childhood Education have cooperated in a program of faculty and student interaction and informal research projects aimed at investigating the role of television in children's cognitive and linguistic development (infancy through 60 months). Described are plans to develop and evaluate prototype materials and procedures for parent and child interaction. Recent activities of project staff members are reviewed, and the following points are elaborated on: (1) preschool children watch substantial amounts of commercial television; (2) strategies should be developed by which this time spent with television can contribute to cognitive, social, and linguistic development; (3) a developmental perspective is necessary to interpret the impact of television (the theoretical position of Jean Piaget has been adopted); (4) Parent-Child-Television Interaction Kits (PCTI) are a hypothesized method for stimulating certain aspects of learning from commercial television experiences; and (5) plans for the preparation and use of kits should be derived from significant findings of parent-child interaction research.

418. Research on the Use of Television in Secondary Schools. Research Report 48. Dignam, Monica, Agency for Instructional Television, Bloomington, IN, Jun 1977, 26p (ED 156 166; Reprint: EDRS; also available from Agency for Instructional Television, Box A, Bloomington, IN 47401). For related documents see citation 396.

Problems associated with the use of television in secondary schools which are examined in the context of current research include equipment, scheduling, availability of television programs, and teacher resistance. To overcome these problems, many researchers believe that more attention should be given to improving teacher training, while others call for more systematic evaluation of television use before problem solving is attempted. However, the future of television use in secondary education is not as bleak as the studies reported here indicate: recent technological advances and a relaxation of off-air taping regulations granted by some software distributors may ease the scheduling and equipment difficulties. Probably the most significant breakthrough is the development and expansion of the videocassette and videodisc consumer markets.

419. Sesame Street: 1,000 Hours of a Perpetual Television Experiment. Cooney, Joan Ganz, Children's Television Workshop, New York, NY, Sep 1976, 28p. Editorial Backgrounder (ED 130 634; Reprint: EDRS).

During its seven-year history, "Sesame Street" has maintained high popularity while introducing such innovations as new cognitive curricula, new characters, bilingual elements, and effective and social education. Early goals emphasized 40 predominantly cognitive objectives aimed at helping the disadvantaged child. Additions have included location-based programs, specially designed segments for the mentally retarded, the Muppets, original music, and guest stars. Both formative and summative research have been conducted. Though attracting an audience was initially a problem, the program now has an extensive global audience. A chart of curriculum innovations is included.

420. Since They Are Going to Watch TV Anyway, Why Not Connect It to Reading. Hutchison, Laveria F. 1978, 8p. Study prepared at University of Houston (ED 155 606; Reprint: EDRS).

In view of the great amount of television viewing among poor readers, the learning model for watching television was developed to capitalize on students' television watching proclivities. The model encompasses three major overlapping component skill areas to reinforce classroom learning: active listening skills, auditory word recognition skills, and comprehension skills. A task sheet is distributed to each student on which to record his or her name, television program watched, the time of broadcast, and responses to tasks. Tasks range from auditory word recognition, such as listening for words beginning with certain consonants or for the number of times a character uses two syllable words, to comprehension skill tasks requiring students to note words that express certain emotions. Students should be encouraged to develop their own guides based on classroom learning, but the guides should always require active listening and should include either isolated word attack and comprehension skills or an integration of those skills. (A sample task sheet is appended.)

421. Students' Recall of Short Story Content Following Presentation in Print and Television Media.* Parsons, Rolf William, University of Minnesota, 1978, 183p (7912063; Reprint: DC).

This investigation attempted to illuminate the interaction of print and television media as it may affect students' recall of essential elements of short story literature. It explored two areas of interaction: the enhancement of story recall due to redundancy of information conveyed in the two versions; and media dominance when discrepancies exist in the two versions.

In order to measure these effects, two types of multiple choice test items were written. The first (used to measure recall) had a stem with five responses, only one of which was correct for both versions. The second (used to measure preference) also had a stem with five responses, but one was correct for the television version while another was correct for the print version. Students were randomly selected from 10th grade communications classes at White Bear Lake, MN, and grouped by sex, and two types of class, one for average students, the other for students requiring structure and treatment. Four treatments were employed: print only, television only, print followed by television and television followed by print.

It was concluded that (1) Dual media (television and print) presentations together result in better student recall of short story content than single media presentations. (2) When students only read a story, reading comprehension is moderately correlated to recall of story content, but when students view a television version and read the story, the correlation is less. (3) When presented with two media versions of a story and media keyed test items, students most commonly choose the item response keyed to the medium providing the most specific and concrete information. This usually results in the television medium dominating the print medium. (4) Students most frequently choose test item responses which are keyed to the last medium presented.

422. A Study of the Origin, Development, and Impact of the Davey and Goliath Television Series, 1959–1977 and its Present Effectiveness in Teaching Religious Values to Children.* Klos, Frank William, Jr., Temple University, 1979, 265p (7910008; Reprint: DC).

The "Davey and Goliath" television programs produced by the Lutheran Church in America's Department of Press, Radio and Television have been the longest running and most successful series ever developed by a church group for child viewers. Distributed free of charge to commercial television stations in the United States and Canada through the auspices of the National Council of Churches, the series has also been shown in seven languages in 19 other countries. In addition, the programs were used in nine Roman Catholic metropolitan area parochial school districts via closed circuit classroom television and were adapted as special film programs for use in congregational Christian education curricula.

This study traced the history of the "Davey and Goliath" series, analysed the many facets of producing and using the programs, and evaluated the impact of the episodes by documenting the size of the audiences reached and ascertaining whether or not representative episodes actually teach religious values to children.

The study dealt with questions related to: perceived needs that led to the origin and development of the programs; the selection of themes, objectives, and storylines; the annual number of commercial stations in North America carrying the programs; the introduction of the series in other countries; the educational usage of episodes in classroom situations; the estimated viewing audiences; and possible changes in children's religious values as a result of seeing the programs.

It is concluded that the programs do teach religious values to third-, fourth-, and fifth-grade children; since new children audiences emerge annually, the series with its timeless appeal should be a useful educational medium for the church for years to come.

423. A Study of the Relationship between Television Exposure and Language Acquisition of Pre-school Children.* Selnow, Gary W., Michigan State University, 1978, 143p (7917784; Reprint: DC).

This research focused on the relationship between television viewing and language development of preschool children. It also considered relationships between language development and maternal factors, then language development and sibling variables.

In the first series of analyses, child language ability was correlated with total television viewing time and then with five subcategories of program types. The next series considered language ability in terms of a composite exposure-language level index which represented program exposure weighted by language sophistication modeled by television programs. Language ability, total television viewing and viewing of programs by category were then considered in terms of the mother's education level. Finally, there was an analysis of two elements of Zajonc's Confluence Model which predicted relationships between (1) sibling number and language ability and (2) birth order and language ability.

Language samples were collected according to clinical procedures outlined by the developmental sentence scoring analysis for 93 children. In addition to language samples, data on television viewing patterns of subjects were collected from logbooks maintained for a one-week period by parents. Demographic information was also obtained. Scripts of frequently viewed programs were then analyzed according to developmental sentence scoring procedures.

The analysis revealed a relationship between television viewing and language development for this sample. Viewing time across all program types was negatively related with language ability and this negative relationship was strongest for cartoons and family drama programs. Using the exposure-language level index, it was discovered that children who viewed a greater number of hours of language-sophisticated shows tended to score higher on the language assessment instrument. Those who viewed a greater number of language-poor shows tended to score lower on language measures.

Mother's education level was positively related to the child's language ability, as sociolinguistic theory predicts. Mother's education level was also positively related to the language sophistication of programs viewed by children. Partialling out mother's education reduces, but does not eliminate, the correlation between language ability and television viewing.

424. Teaching Reading with Commercial Television Viewed at Home: An Evaluation. Mason, George E., 1976, 69p. Report prepared at University of Georgia (ED 141 764; Reprint: EDRS).

This report reviews research and opinion concerning the teaching of reading with in-school television and describes a commercially televised reading program for sixth- and seventh-grade Duval County (Jacksonville, Florida) schoolchildren, who watched television at home but who received correlated instruction in school classes. Pretest and posttest data were taken from a stratified sampling of approximately 1870 students. Analyses of the data indicate that the three-week, 12-episode program increased vocabulary and words-in-contest scores but did not increase comprehension or reading-attitude scores. Opinions of a sample of the participating teachers were obtained by structured interviews and are reported in the study. The report concludes that televised instruction of this sort could both motivate and teach, especially when accompanied by in-classroom instruction, and that television program scripts, such as ones used in the featured study, are a valuable tool for the reading teacher.

425. Telecourse Students: How Well Do They Learn? Purdy, Leslie. Apr 1978, 16p. Paper presented at the Annual Convention of the American Association of Community and Junior Colleges (58th, Atlanta, GA, April 9–12, 1978) (ED 154 851; Reprint: EDRS).

One question has dominated the research on televised instruction for many years: How well does it compare to on-campus, face-to-face instruction? The overall results of such studies show that broadcast instruction works: either no difference is found in comparative studies or televised course students are found to have a higher achievement rate than campus-based students. What is important now is for researchers to begin to distinguish among types of TV courses, factors that increase achievement and completion, and types of students most likely to succeed in TV courses. Two generalizations seem to hold true at present. First, coordinated instructional systems are more effective than simple broadcast courses using uncoordinated components. TV programs, textbooks, study guides, and exams must all be designed to serve the same instructional objectives. Second, the amount and type of support services offered with the course are vital to achievement and completion as the course design. The degree of student involvement and the frequency and type of feedback are particularly crucial. Future research should look at the effect of different video treatments, the attention span and concentration ability of adult viewers, and the content of TV courses. (A 28-item bibliography is appended.)

426. Televised versus In-Class Instruction—What the Literature Implies. Segalla, Angelo, Golden West College, Huntington Beach, CA, n.d., 25p (ED 125 695; Reprint: EDRS).

This paper presents a review of research on the effectiveness of educational television compared to traditional face-to-face instruction. The studies reviewed are presented under seven rubrics: TV as a catalyst for learning; two-way TV; use of commercial TV shows; simulation of a real situation; TV integrated as part of the classroom lecture; TV courses instead of lecture in the classroom; and TV courses in the home. The author concludes that while TV has proved effective for teaching basic knowledge, it is deficient for teaching cognitive skills requiring more than "level I" knowledge. A bibliography is appended (the latest reference is to a 1975 publication).

427. Television and Oracy: A Psychological Viewpoint. Noble, Grant. Jul 1979, 9p. Paper presented at the Conference on Developing Oral Communication Competence in Children (Armidale, Australia, July 12–18, 1979) (ED 180 030; Reprint: EDRS).

Australian studies show that television assists in the socialization of immigrants, changing and shaping their self-images and perceptions of reality and fostering their interpersonal communication skills. Studies conducted to evaluate the introduction of television have found that television helps in the vocabulary development of young children. Comparisons of "Sesame Street" with the Australian program "Playschool" suggest, among other findings, that "Playschool" is more appropriately designed for four-year-olds than is "Sesame Street" and increases oral competence in a much more generalized way than does "Sesame Street," that "Playschool" encourages oral responses from children, and that the success of "Playschool" may stem from its promotion of associative learning of word meanings. Other studies suggest that television can provide children with a shared symbolic structure, thus facilitating interpersonal communication. A study of the uses and gratifications provided by the television program "Happy Days" suggests a number of conclusions, among them that adolescents watch the show so they can talk about it with others; that younger adolescents interact with the characters, making use of inner speech processes; that younger adolescents learn social skills and assertiveness from the program; and that the majority of adolescents respond to—rather than identify with—the program's characters.

428. Television: Images and Meaning. Mays, Luberta. Mar 1979, 9p. Paper presented at the Annual Meeting of the National Conference on Language Arts in the Elementary School (11th, Hartford, CT, March 23–25, 1979) (ED 177 604; Reprint: EDRS).

Knowledge of how children "read" television pictures can provide understanding of how powerful a tool television is for teaching and learning. Turning off television is not only turning off experiences but also turning off opportunities for learning and preventing youngsters from looking through that window on the world. Television provides visual images that enable people to see beyond the screen.

429. Television Script Intervention as a Prescriptive Program for Adolescent Sub-Literacy.* Nadeau, Oneta Dorris, United States International University, 1977, 83p. (7909594; Reprint: DC).

The objective of the study was to answer four questions: (1) What is the relationship between amount of time adolescents spend watching television, and time spent in extracurricular reading? (2) Will high-interest television scripts motivate adolescents to increase the amount of their reading? (3) To what extent will the subjects' word literacy increase after sixteen weeks' television script intervention? (4) What is the relationship between word literacy improvement and time spent watching television, time spent in extracurricular reading, and broadened scope of reading? The importance of the study derives from the need expressed in the literature for instructional alternatives to methods thus far unsuccessful in eliminating the subliteracy problem of adolescents. Since adolescents evaluate television programs as highly interesting in visual form; then perhaps television scripts might show great potential as a national resource for literacy material.

The method included a quasi-experimental design. Two standardized tests—the Wide Range Achievement Test and the Gates-MacGinitie Reading Test—along with subjects' self-reporting and investigator's observations provided data for determining the relationships between the variables and the overall evaluation of the research. Hypotheses were: (1) There will be no significant difference between the amount of time the subjects spend watching television and the time the subjects spend reading outside their formal learning environment. (2) There will be no significant increase in the number of books and magazines read. (3) There will be no significant difference between the television script internvention program and improved word literacy-reading growth. (4) There will be no significant relationship among the following variables and word literacy improvement: (A) the amount of time subjects spend watching television; (B) the amount of time subjects spend in extracurricular reading; and (C) broadened selection of reading materials on a voluntary basis by the subjects. The 54 subjects were selected on the basis of having serious persistent reading problems, a willingness to participate voluntarily, and no evidence of learning incapacity.

The subjects' television viewing time exceeded their extracurricular reading, statistically significant at the .01 level. Increased reading of books and magazines was observed by the investigator, self-reported by the subjects, and in statistical measurement was significant at the .01 level. Therefore, null-hypotheses 1, 2, and 3 were rejected. Findings on null-hypothesis 4, parts A and B, were significant at the .05 and .01 level. Part C was insignificant; therefore, parts A and B were rejected and C was accepted. It was concluded that television scripts show significantly high potential as literacy resource material.

BOOKS

430. Me and My TV. Heintz, Ann C. et al. Shabbona, IL: Journalism Education Association, 1976, 72p.

This research report documents how three high school English teachers made use of popular prime time television in the classroom to increase students' verbal and reasoning skills and to improve cross-cultural and parent-teenager communication. Included are teaching ideas related to specific television programs and a how-to manual, "Adapting Television to Your Home or Classroom."

431. Television and the Preschool Child: A Psychological Theory of Instruction and Curriculum Development. Lesser, Harvey. New York: Academic Press, 1977, 261 p (Educational Psychology Series).

The central tenet of the book is that the educational potential of television for preschoolers is largely untapped. It criticizes research purporting to show that violence on television engenders violent behavior; uses data from the ETS evaluation of "Sesame Street" to show that the program is least effective among the very preschoolers who—because the rest of their environment does little to prepare them for school—need its help most; reviews American, Soviet, and Swiss (Piagetian) research on the development of cognition, language, perception, and memory in children; and presents a proposal, grounded in this research, for improving television instruction of preschoolers. The book also features a general introduction to the history and economics of children's television, discussion of the limits imposed on instruction by the passive qualities of viewing, and an examination of such new developments as computer-assisted instruction in their relation to television.

432. Television and the Teacher: A Handbook for Classroom Use. Hilliard, Robert L.; Field, Hyman H. New York: Hastings House, 1976, 94p.

This practical handbook is designed to help the teacher use instructional television (ITV) productively. It provides background information on ITV and guidelines on selecting programs, preparing students, conducting TV lessons, and providing follow-up. A resource list is appended.

IMPROVING THE SITUATION

Teaching Television Viewing Skills

JOURNAL ARTICLES

433. An Activist Approach to Critical TV Viewing.
Steenland, Sally. *Media and Methods.* v15, n2,
p22,25,63–64, Oct 1978 (EJ 190 383; Reprint:
UMI).

Outlines classroom activities whereby high school
students learn to monitor and evaluate their own television
viewing.

434. Adolescents' TV Relations: Three Scales.
Rosengren, Karl Erik et al. *Communication
Research—An International Quartelry.* v3, n4,
p347–66, Oct 1976.

Presents three scales for measuring relationships between
adolescent television viewers and the television content
consumed by them.

435. Basic Skills of TV Viewing. Shorr, Jon. *Today's
Education.* v67, n2, p72–75, Apr-May 1978 (EJ
186 159; Reprint: UMI).

Given that, in the last quarter of the 20th century, most
people aren't reading very much but are watching a great deal
of television, schools must begin to teach television viewing
skills to every student. Activities of the Milford, OH school
system suggest ways that television education goals might be
met.

**436. Cross-Examining the Commercial: The
Language of TV Advertising.** McGarvey, Jack.
Media and Methods. v16, n5, p47–49, Jan 1980
(EJ 215 865; Reprint: UMI).

Argues that television advertising is now the most
powerful language in existence. Provides a TV advertising test
to prove the point and outlines a unit designed to make secondary students aware of the language of television commercials
while improving their writing and thinking skills.

437. Developing a Curriculum for Teenagers.
Lloyd-Kolkin, Donna et al. *Journal of
Communication.* v30, n3, p119–25, Sum 1980.

This article describes the development of a critical TV
viewing curriculum for high school students, based on four
critical viewing skills: being able to evaluate and to manage
one's own TV viewing behavior; to question the reality of
television programs; to recognize and be able to counter argue
the persuasive arguments and messages on TV; and to recognize
the effects of television on one's own daily life.

438. Developing Discriminating Consumers. Roberts,
Donald F. et al. *Journal of Communication.* v30,
n3, p94–105, Sum 1980.

In this two-part study with children in grades two through
eight, those who watched the most television and those who
were the most susceptible to commercial appeals learned the
most from instructional films about how television advertising
works. The smaller gains made by older children were attrib-
uted to the fact that they had already developed considerable
skepticism about TV commercials.

**439. Helping Elementary School Children Learn
about TV.** Singer, Dorothy G. et al. *Journal of
Communication.* v30, n3, p84–93, Sum 1980.

This study was designed to develop, implement, and
evaluate a series of eight lesson plans that would teach third-,
fourth-, and fifth-grade children to understand television and to
use their interest in it in conjunction with reading, writing, and
discussion skills. Students made a number of significant gains
in knowing how television "works," and the lessons proved
useful in teaching academic skills, but parental viewing habits
and attitudes toward TV remained a strong influence on
behavior.

**440. Hey, Mom, Who Put the Television in the
Closet?** Larrick, Nancy. *English Education.* v8, n1,
p3–11, Fall 1976.

A discussion of television advertising's impact on
children and what teachers can do to guide children in their
viewing of television.

441. Looking at Mass Media. Sive, Mary Robinson. *Curriculum Review.* v18, n4, p270–72, Oct 1979.

This article offers a bibliography of recent inexpensive filmstrips, slide sets, and study prints that can expand students' awareness of such issues as psychic manipulation in TV commercials, the intrusion of show biz into news reporting, and the role of the advertiser in determining media content.

442. New Literacy. Foster, Harold. *Early Years.* v10, n6, p25–27, Feb 1980.

The author advocates media education that begins as soon as the child enters school. He suggests a visual literacy approach which familiarizes children with technical television devices, such as editing, sound, and lighting, and their effects.

443. A Practical Guide to Critical TV Viewing Skills. Kahn, Linda. *Media and Methods.* v16, n2, p32–34,90–92, Oct 1979 (EJ 209 309; Reprint: UMI).

Offers guidelines, sample approaches, and lists of resources for use by educators in developing student television viewing skills.

444. Prime Time Television in the Classroom. Hendrick, Larry. *Community and Junior College Journal.* v48, n6, p16–18, Mar 1978 (EJ 179 611; Reprint: UMI).

Discusses the instructional strategies used in a junior college course on television as a popular art form, in which students use their regular television viewing to develop a critical awareness, learning tools and techniques for analyzing dramatic form and content.

445. The Second Teacher: Recent Research on Television. Comstock, George. *National Elementary Principal.* v56, n3, p16–21, Jan-Feb 1977.

The evidence in behalf of the power of parents and others to modify TV's impact is, in fact, evidence that educators have an equally great—or even greater—role to perform.

446. Students as Active Viewers of Television. Wimmer, Roger D. *Communication Education.* v28, n2, p147–50, May 1979 (EJ 213 978; Reprint: UMI).

Describes a 10-category evaluation list designed to allow students to make an educated guess on whether a new television program or series will be successful or why a program has become popular. Student predictions are compared with what actually happens at the three television networks. This is seen as a useful technique for encouraging high school and college students to be more critical viewers of television.

447. TV Talk: Critical Viewing Projects: A Second Look. Potter, Rosemary Lee. *Teacher.* v97, n6, p32–33, Mar 1980 (EJ 226 959; Reprint: UMI).

Presented is an update of the special Critical Viewing Skills curriculum projects (reviewed in "Teacher," April 1979) sponsored by the U.S. Office of Education. The update provides feedback on the projects.

448. Teacher vs. Program. Corder-Bolz, Charles R.; O'Bryant, Shirley. *Journal of Communication.* v28, n1, p97–103, Win 1978 (EJ 184 686; Reprint: UMI).

Outlines a study designed to determine if adult interpretive comments significantly influence children's attitudes toward television entertainment programs and the amount of information learned. These hypotheses were confirmed.

449. Teachers' Guide to TV Know-How. McCorkle, Jeanne. *School and Community.* v65, n1, p14–16, 54, Sep 1978.

Described are class activities designed to teach sixth graders' television viewing skills. A short bibliography of books about television for elementary students is included.

450. Television and the English Teacher. England, David A. *English Journal.* v68, n7, p95-96, Oct 1979 (EJ 212 149; Reprint: UMI).

Discusses how to help students prepare for, evaluate, and understand the "new" television season.

451. Television Literacy for Young Children. Dorr, Aimee et al. *Journal of Communication.* v30, n3, p71–83, Sum 1980.

The authors developed three different curriculums to teach critical television viewing skills to kindergarten and primary grade children. The children were able to learn the contents of all three curricula and to apply them in discussions about television reality, but such learning did not seem to mediate television's impact on social attitudes.

452. Television: The Anonymous Teacher. *EPIEgram Materials.* v6m, n13, p1–4, 1 Apr 1978.

This article questions the assertion by the national PTA that, since curriculum materials for critical television viewing skills does not exist, the PTA should develop them. Existing materials and sources for teachers are cited.

MICROFICHE

453. Children and Film/Television. Factfile No. 6. Elsas, Diana, Comp., et al., American Film Institute, Washington, DC, Apr 1977, 10p (ED 153 653; Reprint: EDRS—HC not available; also available from American Film Institute, National Education Services, John F. Kennedy Center, Washington, DC 20566).

This is a guide to organizations and publications relevant to children and film/television aimed at elementary through high school levels. It lists key organizations with addresses, telephone numbers, and brief descriptions; and literature and films, including books and pamphlets, selected periodicals, and filmographies.

454. A Comparison of Four Different Instructional Approaches Designed to Teach 6–11-Year-Old Children about Television Commercials as Persuasive Messages.* Triplett, Jan Frances, University of Texas at Austin, 1979, 325p (8009942; Reprint: DC).

In the spring of 1979, 133 ethnically and socio-economically mixed children, ages 6–11, in the preoperational, concrete, or transitional stages, from three private schools in Austin participated in a curriculum intervention project to teach them consumer skills related to television advertising. These skills consisted of (1) the ability to recognize and distinguish between programs and commercials of all types (product oriented, service oriented, public service announcements, program promotions, teasers, etc.) and the ability to identify purposes of specific commercials and (2) the ability to verbalize an accurate concept of commercials by recalling pertinent characteristics.

Four instructional methods (traditional, creative dramatics, video, and a combination of these methods) were used in an attempt to discover the best way to teach children of various ages and backgrounds about commercials. The information presented in each of the four half-hour lessons presented to all the groups except the video group, did not vary. The curriculum was designed to fit into an already existing curriculum in English, math, history, geography, social studies, etc. The aim of the study was to suggest that commercials were a form of persuasion, one derived from earlier forms or persuasion, in order to suggest to children that persuasion, in any form, was not necessarily good or bad, but something that human beings had used from the dawn of time in order to get other people to do what they might not ordinarily do.

Results of statistical analyses indicated that all of the methods improved learning gain of "commercial literacy" but that some methods worked better than others depending upon the sex and ethnic group (Anglo, Black, or Chicano) of the child. Only the combination method worked well for both sexes and all three ethnic groups, although it did *not* produce the highest learning gain. The creative dramatics method produced the highest gain for measures of recognition and identification. The video method produced the highest gain for measures of verbal ability. However, because of its less than successful effects on one of the sexes and ethnic groups it is *not* recommended unless used in combination with other methods.

455. Mediating Effects of Television Violence through Curriculum Intervention.* Buerkel-Rothfuss, Nancy Louise, Michigan State University, 1978, 206p (7917680; Reprint: DC).

This study presented an experimental test of two instructional modules designed to teach children to be more critical consumers of television violence. Two global objectives provided the groundwork for development of the curriculum modules: (1) to decrease students' liking for television violence; and (2) to decrease students' exposure to television violence.

The rationale for this research study was essentially a pragmatic one. Given, on one hand, data indicating a positive relationship between amount of exposure to television violence

and personal aggression and, on the other hand, the paucity of parental mediation routinely practiced, an alternative mediation strategy seemed necessary. At the time of this writing, several similar intervention curricula were in the development stage, but virtually no research evidence existed which either confirmed or denied the efficacy of such an approach. This study was an exploratory step in the direction of formulating and evaluating such a curriculum intervention strategy.

Module I, content realism, attempted to demonstrate that dramatic television does not portray a realistic image of the world. The ultimate intent of this module was to devalue television as a viable source of "real world" information for the student. Module II, decision-making, attempted to guide students toward making conscious, criteria-based decisions regarding television viewing. The central focus of this module was on development of personal awareness and control of behavior regarding television.

One hundred thirty-six fourth- and sixth-grade-students in Haslett, Michigan, comparised the sample for the experimental study. Intact classrooms were assigned by principals to three experimental conditions: (1) module I instruction plus module II instruction; (2) module II instruction only; and (3) control (no instruction). Each module required five, 45-minute sessions of regular class time to complete. All material was presented by an elementary teacher hired and trained for the study.

All hypothesis testing took the form of analyses of covariance using a two-group (one experimental and one control) by two-grade (fourth and sixth) factorial design. In all, 21 research hypotheses were tested.

Findings suggested that neither module alone had dramatic impact on students' attitudes and behaviors regarding television violence, although 28 out of 35 changes examined were in the posited directions. Grade level was found to be an important consideration for many variables of interest.

456. Sex Stereotyping in Instructional Materials and Television: Awareness Kit. Butler, Matilda, Women's Educational Equity Communications Network, San Francisco, CA, 1978, 51p. Best copy available. Sponsoring agency: Office of Education (DHEW), Washington, DC Women's Program Staff (ED 168 548; Reprint: EDRS).

This awareness kit provides information on the portrayals of women and men in two media—instructional materials and television; discusses how to evaluate and choose the best media materials from those that exist; recommends actions that will help to eliminate sex stereotyping in instructional materials and television; and suggests an approach to teaching children how to be aware of sex stereotyping in the media so they can better counter it themselves. In recognition that sex is only one basis for stereotyping, ways of developing an awareness of other stereotypes in media messages are suggested whenever possible. References and a selected bibliography are included, as well as sample checklists and examples of guidelines.

457. Teaching Children to Become More Critical Consumers of Television. Lemon, Judith. Sep 1976, 9p. Paper presented at the American Psychological Association (Washington, DC, September 5, 1976). Sponsoring agency: Office of Child Development (DHEW), Washington, DC (ED 135 333; Reprint: EDRS). For related documents see citation 70.

With television operating as an important socializing influence, children need to become critical consumers and they can be taught the necessary evaluative skills. Explicit discussion is seen as a means of developing awareness of various facets of TV programing, e.g., the relationship of reality to content, stereotyped images presented, any bias which may be introduced by the commercial basis of much TV production. Games are suggested as a method to be used by parents and children, and the TV industry is asked to provide more examples of how programs are produced as well as more explicit labeling for programs based on true incidents. The most important means of transmitting these skills are coviewing and discussion with parents.

458. Technological Culture and Human Communication. Carney, John J., Jr. Jul 1979, 15p. Paper presented at the Conference on Developing Oral Communication Competence in Children (Armidale, Australia, July 12–18, 1979) (ED 180 024; Reprint: EDRS).

Children need to develop skills enabling them to respond to television efficiently, analytically, and discriminately. Removing children's advertising from television will not help them to understand the nature of the appeals used by the advertiser, who will find other means of reaching children; and advocating no violence on television brings children no closer to understanding human aggression. Education is the way to guard human communication from the liabilities of technological culture. Broadening perspectives about mass culture should help to decrease anxieties about the mass media. The next step is to recognize that technology does not introduce a new problem nearly so much as it aggravates very old ones; this means that the basic problem is one of human interaction and communication. Instead of worrying about the child's interaction with television, teachers should concentrate on how television affects other forms of human interaction, for the communication revolution has brought people together while estranging them at the same time. By teaching fundamentals, developing the critical thinking skills that enable more complex decisions about television viewing and media usage, and teaching the maxims of mass communication, teachers can show their students how to understand and thereby control the mass media.

459. Television Receivership Skills: The New Social Literacy. Anderson, James A.; Ploghoft, Milton E. 1977, 25p. Paper presented at the Annual Meeting of the International Communication Association (Berlin, Germany, May 29–June 4, 1977) (ED 140 364; Reprint: EDRS).

The literature relating television viewing to the cognitive, social, moral, and behavioral development of children can be divided into three general areas: investigations of the relationship between televised violence and aggressive behavior, studies of television as an agent of consumer socialization, and examinations of the role of television as a behavioral model. This paper provides a review of research in each of these areas and suggests that the development of children's critical awareness of the dynamics of television programing is essential. Goals for analyzing the nature and uses of television in the United States, for evaluating entertainment programing, commercials, and news, and for establishing awareness of personal uses of television and awareness of value conflicts

implicit in the medium are summarized. The five curricular modules which have been extrapolated from these goals suggest, among other techniques, keeping a personal diary of viewing habits, investigating the role of news and documentary programing, and analyzing the values presented in entertainment programing.

460. Television Watching as an Information Processing Task: Programming and Advertising. Wartella, Ellen. Sep 1979, 16p. Paper presented at the Annual Meeting of the American Psychological Association (87th, New York, NY September 1–5, 1979). Sponsoring agency: National Science Foundation, Washington, DC (ED 180 607; Reprint: EDRS).

A two-week consumer training program was designed to teach kindergarten children about advertising claims on commercial television programs. One objective of the program was to teach kindergarteners that commercials are designed to persuade people to buy products. Kindergartners were taught to recognize the difference between commercials and other classes of television content. A second objective was to teach kindergartners to look for information about products when they watched commercials. Children were taught to recognize four types of appeals made by commercials: product information appeals, fun and entertainment appeals, premium offers, and social acceptability appeals. These concepts were taught through a variety of physical activities (for example, having children raise their hands when a break occurred between a program and a commercial) and having children discuss their own experiences. The total time spent on training was about three and one-half hours over the two-week program. Performance was generally high by the end of the program. In addition, children who had participated in training performed better than a control group after an eight-month time delay. Following the delay, there was some decline in children's ability to identify commercials and understand persuasive intent, though performance level was still above that of the pre-training performance level.

BOOKS

461. The Incredible Television Machine. Polk, Lee; LeShan, Eda. New York: Macmillan Publishing, 1977, 148p.

Designed for secondary students, this illustrated volume outlines the workings of television—how shows are put together and how commercials get their messages across. It is intended to help students take a critical look at the role television plays in their lives.

462. Television Awareness Training: The Viewer's Guide for Family and Community. Logan, Ben, ed.; Moody, Kate, ed. New York: Media Action Research Center Publications, 1979, 280p.

This text provides articles and worksheets to help people examine television programs and their own viewing habits. Topics include violence, sexuality, stereotypes, sports, and children.

The Parents' Role: Monitoring Television Use in the Home

JOURNAL ARTICLES

463. Children and Television: Tackling "The Tube" with Family Teamwork. O'Bryant, Shirley L.; Corder-Bolz, Charles R. *Children Today.* v7, n3, p21–24, May-Jun 1978 (EJ 182 021; Reprint: UMI).

Reports on studies of television viewing patterns of four- and five-year-olds suggesting that teamwork may be the most effective method of control for families to cope with television in their homes. Discusses some mediation techniques.

464. Do You Have TV Interference? Larrick, Nancy. *Today's Education.* v67, n4, p39–40, 86, Nov-Dec 1978 (EJ 202 444; Reprint: UMI).

The effect of television viewing on children and their reading ability is discussed with emphasis on encouraging both parents and children to be more discriminating viewers. Several parent-teacher cooperative projects for controlling television use are cited.

465. Families, Mass Communications and the Marketplace. Jenkins, Gladys Gardner. *Childhood Education.* v54, n2, p67–70, Nov-Dec 1977 (EJ 172 370; Reprint: UMI).

Discusses ways to deal with children's desires for consumer goods advertised on television and touted by peer groups. Considers needs, wants, and wishes of children and how each can influence purchase decisions.

466. Help the Kids Get Some Good out of TV. *Changing Times.* v34, p29–31, Aug 1980.

This article provides parents with a general overview of research on TV's effects on young children as well as advice on how they can educate their children to use television wisely. Sources of information and parent education guides are listed.

467. The Parent Participation TV Workshop. Kirshner, Gloria. *Audiovisual Instruction.* v22, n5, p28–31, May 1977 (EJ 168 187; Reprint: UMI).

This pilot project, using television as a catalyst for parent child communication, was conducted in three school systems: (1) Americus, GA, (2) Charlottesville, VA, and (3) New York City.

468. Parents' TV Guide. Adler, Richard P. *Learning.* v7, n4, Supplement 1–8, Dec 1978.

This guidebook for parents presents useful tips about rewarding ways to watch and discuss television with children. For those who wish to speak out about children's television, a directory of government, network, and citizen action organizations is provided.

469. School/Parent Participation through TV Workshops. Potter, Rosemary Lee. *Media and Methods.* v16, n2, p70–72, 74, Oct 1979 (EJ 209 311; Reprint: UMI).

Contends that television workshops are an opportunity to foster open and dynamic communication across generations. Reports on several successful programs using this approach.

470. Summer TV: It's "All in the Family." Potter, Rosemary Lee. *Teacher.* v96, n9, p28,30,32, May-Jun 1979 (EJ 218 942; Reprint: UMI).

A dozen TV-related activities are suggested for parents for use with their children during summer vacation to reinforce skills in reading, writing, listening, planning, and following directions.

471. TV Talk: Gloria Kirshner Talks about Parent Participation. Potter, Rosemary Lee; Kirshner, Gloria. *Teacher.* v97, n7, p12, 14, 16, Apr 1980 (EJ 229 277; Reprint: UMI).

One successful program which is receiving nationwide attention as a key to TV use and family communication is the "Parent Participation TV workshops." Gloria Kirshner talked to the author about these workshops.

472. Television, Families, and Schools. Gilbert, Steven W. *Independent School.* v37, n3, p29–35, Feb 1978 (EJ 180 814; Reprint: UMI).

Suggests that independent school teachers and administrators need to know as much as possible about television and that they can and should influence the role television plays in their students' lives. Critically evaluates television programing and its impact upon parents and students. Also gives some TV guidelines for parents concerned about their children's television viewing.

473. Television Viewing Guides and Parental Recommendations. Heald, Gary R. *Journalism Quarterly.* v57, n1, p141–44, Spr 1980.

Parents of elementary and middle-school students, initially contacted through voluntary interviews, were mailed free weekly television guides which highlighted shows as either appropriate or inappropriate for children. Regardless of format, the guides were effective in causing parents to restrict their children's viewing of antisocial programs.

474. Use of Commercial Television in Parent and Child Interaction. Williams, Frederick et al. *Journal of Broadcasting.* v23, n2, p229–35, Spr 1979 (EJ 205 232; Reprint: UMI).

Reviews a project to promote the incorporation of commercial television viewing experiences as a topic of parent and child interaction, examining specifically how to promote joint viewing of programs by parents and children for conversational purposes and whether changes in the nature of interaction would result.

475. Watching Television with Your Children. LeShan, Eda J. *CMLEA Journal.* v1, n2, p4–7, Win 1978.

Noting that television can enrich childrens' lives as well as harm them, the author asserts that it is the parents' responsibility to select and control children's TV viewing. She describes how shared television viewing can be a valuable family experience.

MICROFICHE

476. The Home, The School, The Child: The TV Connection. Gray, Sandra T. Mar 1979, 11p. Paper presented at the Regional Conference on Parent Participation TV Workshops for Civic, Religious, Educational and Parent Leaders and Their Families (Princeton, NJ, March 17, 1979) (ED 178 055; Reprint: EDRS).

This paper discusses effective parenting and how television can be used to stimulate communication between parent and child. Research on viewing habits and social statistics on teenage pregnancy and drug and alcohol use provide a background for examining parent-child communication and lead into a discussion of Kohlberg's theories of moral development and Bloom's patterns of parental behavior.

477. Who Is Sylvia? Children and TV: Watch It Student Guide—Footsteps. Report No. 5. Barry, Sharon et al., Applied Management Sciences, Inc., Silver Spring, MD: Educational Film Center,

Springfield, VA; Maryland University; College Park, Institute for Child Study, 1979, 17p. Best copy available. Sponsoring agency: Bureau of School Systems (DHEW/OE), Washington, DC (ED 169 931; Reprint: EDRS—HC not available; also available from University Park Press, 233 East Redwood Street, Baltimore, MD 21202; and films and tapes only from Reference Section, National Audiovisual Center, General Services Administration, Washington, DC 20409).

This student guide for a program exploring both the harmful and helpful aspects of television viewing for children is designed around a magazine format to allow maximum flexibility to different groups using the materials. The guide is divided into: (1) an overview of the theme and contents; (2) a summary of the major learnings of the theme; (3) feature articles containing the major content and including practical suggestions for parents; (4) a film review section which includes a synopsis of the accompanying film program and a related discussion question; (5) three activities aimed at both individual and group participation; (6) a selection of field activities, discussion questions, and research topics designed to reinforce the ideas presented in the articles and meet the needs of a wide variety of classroom groups; and (7) a bibliography for further reading on the theme.

BOOKS

478. The ACT Guide to Children's Television: or How to Treat TV with T.L.C. Kaye, Evelyn. Boston, MA: Beacon Press, 1979, 226p (Revised Edition).

This new edition of the Action for Children's Television basic handbook, prepared with the cooperation of the American Academy of Pediatrics, provides an overview of broadcasting, advertising, and children's programing; practical advice on how to make television a rewarding part of children's lives; and a comprehensive resource directory of government agencies, broadcast stations, organizations, and publications concerned with children's television.

Changing Television: Regulation and Consumer Action

JOURNAL ARTICLES

479. The Big Picture: NEA Involvement in TV. Kahn, Linda. *Today's Education.* v69, n3, p64–65, Sep-Oct 1980.

Describes current projects of the National Education Association to improve television and make it useful as an instructional tool. Included are TV reading projects, critical TV viewing skills curriculum projects, and parent/teacher workshops.

480. The Broadcast Reform Movement: At the Crossroads. Branscomb, Anne W.; Savage, Maria. *Journal of Communication.* v28, n4, p25–34, Fall 1978 (EJ 204 401; Reprint: UMI).

Presents a study comparing the goals, resources, activities, and operating procedures of a sample of media reform groups. Assesses how the changing environment for reform will affect groups in the future.

481. Children's TV: Growing up? Waters, Harry F. *Newsweek.* v95, p62,65, Mar 31 1980.

The author looks at some of the networks' recent attempts to improve the quality of children's programing by providing information spots with educational value interspersed in regular programing and some full-length shows. He also notes new competition for the networks by cable channels which specialize in commercial-free children's programing.

482. Compromise in Commercials for Children. Ward, Scott. *Harvard Business Review.* v56, n6, p128–36, Nov-Dec 1978.

The Federal Trade Commission's "kidvid rule" is the heaviest attack to date on children's television advertising. However in the recent war between consumer activists and regulatory agencies, on the one hand, and the TV advertisers, on the other, the real issues underlying the various charges against TV advertising for children are far from clear-cut, says this author. He points out that both sides of the controversy are adopting a political-legal approach that involves a costly and protracted battle, and he suggests a more rational alternative using research-based educational methods.

483. Family Viewing: A Balancing of Interests. Wiley, Richard E. *Journal of Communication.* v27, n2, p188–92, Spr 1977.

Traces the conception, development and formulation of the "family viewing" plan and contends that family viewing represents an important step in the evolution of industrial self-regulation in the public interest.

484. Family Viewing: An FCC Tumble from The Tightrope? Geller, Henry; Young, Gregg. *Journal of Communication.* v27, n2,193–201p, Spr 1977.

Investigates the legal issue of whether the FCC has authority to adopt a rule or policy embodying the family viewing concept.

485. The Future of Television in the Lives of Children. Goodman, Frederick L.; To, Cho-Lee. *Viewpoints in Teaching and Learning.* v55, n4, p36–40, Fall 1979.

Using the International Year of the Child as a rallying point, this article is a plea for educators to involve themselves in an attempt to make television viewing less passive, especially in an era when more and more countries throughout the world are "importing" American-style television. Various levels of "acTiVision" are sketched in an effort to alert educators to the potential of existing technological possibilities.

486. Influence of Mass Media on Today's Young People. Srygley, Sara Krentzman. *Educational Leadership.* v35, n7, p526–29, Apr 1978 (EJ 179 211; Reprint: UMI).

This article discusses the growing concern over the impact of television on children, as viewing time and access to television increase. Efforts by citizens' groups to control violence and the television industry's attempt at self-regulation, the "family viewing" plan, are considered.

487. Networks Hold the Line. Schneider, John A. *Society.* v14, n6, p9,14-17, Sep-Oct 1977.

The author, president of the CBS/Broadcasting Group, critiques George Gerbner's "Violence Profile No. 8" and discusses the approach CBS takes toward programing of televised violence.

488. Potential Secondary Effects of Regulating Children's Television Advertising. Rotfeld, Herbert J.; Reid, Leonard N. *Journal of Advertising.* v8, n1, p9–14, Win 1979 (EJ 214 153; Reprint: UMI).

Notes that the proposed regulation of children's television advertising may eliminate competition, increase consumer costs, and result in poorer programing.

489. Public Policy toward Television: Mass Media and Education in America Society. Hirsch, Paul M. *School Review.* v85, n4, p481–512, Aug 1977 (EJ 169 044; Reprint: UMI).

Focuses on some of the larger social issues involved in the structure and function of television, with how our society sets up, regulates, and finances the institution of television and how it, in turn, reflects and impacts on American culture.

490. The Regulation of Televised Violence. Baran, Stanley J.; Henke, Lucy L. *Communication Quarterly.* v24, n4, p24–30, Fall 1976.

A comparison of government action in the areas of broadcast violence and sexually offensive materials can provide the basis for stricter control of that televised violence. The Federal Communications Commission has been reluctant to deal with violence, citing First Amendment considerations, but historically has shown little such concern in the regulation of "sexually offensive" materials. Precedents and arguments are offered and examined and the stricter control of violent and aggressive program content is urged.

491. Rhetoric of the Kidvid Movement: Ideology, Strategies and Tactics. Duncan, Rodger Dean. *Central States Speech Journal.* v27, n2, p129–35, Sum 1976.

With particular attention to its most prominent organization, Action for Children's Television (A.C.T.), this article explores the ideology of the Kidvid movement and the rhetorical strategies and tactics it employs to reach its goals.

492. Schools and the Power of Television. Herndon, Terry; Robbins, Maria. *Today's Education*. v69, n3, p49–52, Sep-Oct 1980.

In this interview, Terry Herndon, chairman of the National Council for Children and Television, talks about television's effects on student achievement, the use of commercial and instructional television in the schools, and efforts by the National Education Association and other groups to improve television.

493. Self Regulation of Broadcasting—Does It Exist? Persky, Joel. *Journal of Communication*. v27, n2, p202–10, Spr 1977.

Analyzes the National Association of Broadcasters' Code Authority and changes in the Television Code since 1952 and suggests that the enforcement of these codes and the penalties for violating these codes are such that there is no real self-regulation of broadcasting by the NAB.

494. Sex on Television, More or Less: The Most Conservative of the Media. Rubens, William S. *Vital Speeches of the Day*. v44, n6, p171–74, 1 Jan 1978. Available from Vital Speeches of the Day, City News Publishing Company, Box 606, Southold, New York 11971).

Recounts a speech in which William S. Rubens, vice-president of National Broadcasting Company, covers some current issues, focusing on television sex and violence and network policy.

495. Should Advertising Be Banned from Children's Television? Charren, Peggy; Keeshan, Bob. *Instructor*. v89, n2, p34, Sep 1979 (EJ 213 020; Reprint: UMI).

Peggy Charren, president of Action for Children's Television (A.C.T.), insists that children's television advertising is deceptive and should be banned. Bob Keeshan, the actor who has portrayed Captain Kangaroo for 30 years, asserts that parents, not the federal government, should control what children watch and teach them to be intelligent consumers.

496. TV: A Look at What Might Have Been. Carr, William G. *National Elementary Principal*. v56, n6, p52–54, Jul-Aug 1977.

Reports on attempts that representatives of the educational community made to influence commercial television programing over 20 years ago.

497. Television and Children—Issues Involved in Corrective Action. Somers, Anne R. *American Journal of Orthopsychiatry*. v48, n2, p205–213, Apr 1978.

Economic, legal, and political/moral factors affecting the state of children's programing on television are reviewed, and their effects on the effort to encourage "prosocial" programing are considered. It is suggested that the leadership of child-care

professionals is essential in the battle to reduce gratuitous violence, limit questionable advertising, and increase positive programing for children.

498. Television Programing: An Image in a Looking Glass. Morlan, Don B. *Intellect*. v106, n2391, p234–36, Dec 1977 (EJ 176 955; Reprint: UMI).

The American public enjoys a greater degree of control over media content than any other national media system. Discusses four principles that support the American system of network television programing and six forces that show that the American system of broadcasting is unique in the world. The intent is to illustrate that criticism leveled at television content has been consistently misplaced.

499. Violence, the Media, and the School. Wiley, Richard E. *NASSP Bulletin*. v60, n400, p19–25, May 1976.

The author, chairman of the Federal Communications Commission, states that the role of the FCC should be to provide direction and encouragement for the television networks to adopt self-regulatory reforms, rather than to provide strict regulation itself. The "family viewing" plan is a result of the networks' attempts at self-regulation.

500. What Should Be the Federal Role in Children's Television? Mielke, Keith W. *National Elementary Principal*. v56, n3, p44-48, Jan-Feb 1977.

Considers the issues involved when the federal government gets involved in funding children's educational television.

501. What You Can Do About TV Violence. Dommers, John. *Early Years*. v8, n5, p28–30, Jan 1978.

After briefly reviewing the effects of TV violence on children and the relationship of television viewing to school performance, the author describes actions being taken by the national PTA and other groups to improve television. TV violence resources are also listed and ways are suggested to teachers for improving children's TV habits.

502. Who Controls Children's TV? Groller, Ingrid. *Parents' Magazine*. v53, p58–60, Oct 1978.

This article presents portraits of the directors of children's programing on CBS, NBC, ABC, and PBS.

MICROFICHE

503. Audience Influence on the Programming of "Sesame Street" from 1969 through 1975. Poggi, Patricia May. 1978, 335p. Ed.D. dissertation, Teachers College, Columbia University (ED 162 627; Reprint: EDRS).

The quarter annual reports about "Sesame Street" from the Children's Television Workshop (CTW) from 1969 through 1975 were analyzed for evidence that criticism in the periodical literature had influenced the programing and decision making policies of CTW during that time, as well as the audiences involved. Significant evidence that audiences other than children affected changes in programing was not found; the quarter annual reports failed to identify such critical reactions for correlation with programing and policy decisions. Appendices include the citations of the reports and the 187 books and articles analyzed in this study.

504. Children's Advertising Guidelines. Council of Better Business Bureaus, Inc., New York, NY, 1976, 7p (ED 140 325; Reprint: EDRS).

These guidelines have been developed for the use of advertisers and advertising agencies and for the self-regulatory mechanism which these groups have established, the National Advertising Division, to help ensure that advertising directed to children is truthful, accurate, and fair to children's perceptions. Preliminary sections set forth basic principles which underlie the guidelines and discuss interpretation of the guidelines and their scope. The guidelines deal with eight aspects of advertising: social and moral values portrayed; type of presentation; promotion by program character, editorial character, or personal endorsement; comparative product claims; pressure to purchase; ways in which products are shown being used; claim substantiation; and the use of premiums in advertising.

505. Children's Television Advertising: An Ethical Morass for Business and Government. Turk, Peter B. Aug 1978, 17p. Paper presented at the Annual Meeting of the Association for Education in Journalism (61st, Seattle, WA, August 13–16, 1978) (ED 163 475; Reprint: EDRS—HC not available).

Differing ethical approaches increase the confusion of the controversy over children's television advertising between the Federal Trade Commission (FTC) and representatives of marketing and broadcasting. Marketers and broadcasters base the argument for the status quo on teleologic (situational accommodation) grounds: namely, the competitive nature of the marketplace makes it unthinkable for individual companies to institute any unilateral reforms in children's advertising practices. The ''FTC Staff Report on Television Advertising to Children'' is based on a deontologic (sense of moral right) ethical stance based on idealism and professional training to protect the underdog. Each side overplays threats and harms, knowing that compromise is the inevitable result of differing opinions. However, the stances of the adversaries leave little room to consider such alternatives as reducing commercials permitted during children's television, expanding the definition of children's programing, increasing the authority of the Federal Communications Commission to institute sanctions for code offenders, and taxing station promotions in order to subsidize children's information spots to fill the time left by reducing the number of commercials.

506. FTC Staff Report on Television Advertising to Children. Federal Trade Commission, New York, NY Bureau of Consumer Protection, Feb 1978, 397p (ED 178 083; Reprint: EDRS; also available from Superintendent of Documents, US Government Printing Office, Washington, DC 20402; stock no. 620-944/108 1–3).

This report addresses the problems created by the large volume of current television advertising being directed to children, many of whom naively accept the messages and cannot perceive the selling purpose of television advertising or otherwise comprehend or evaluate it; and recommends that lawmaking proceedings begin to (1) ban all television advertising for any product which is directed to very young children, (2) ban advertising directed to older children for sugared products which pose serious dental health risks, and (3) require that advertisements directed to older children for other sugared products be balanced by nutritional and/or health disclosures funded by advertisers. Various sections of the report deal with the factual background of televised advertising to children, including children's exposure to television commercials concerned with sugared foods and commercial impact; legal implications of advertising to children in light of the Federal Trades Commission Act; the absence of jurisdictional or constitutional impediments to the regulation of advertising to children; and remedies available to cure the deceptiveness and unfairness of current advertising to children.

507. The Pacifica Case: The Supreme Court's New Regulatory Rationale for Broadcasting. Trauth, Denise M.; Huffman, John L. Nov 1979, 13p. Paper presented at the Annual Meeting of the Speech Communication Association (65th, San Antonio, TX, November 10–13, 1979) (ED 184 149; Reprint: EDRS).

The rationale for broadcast regulation has undergone some changes over the years. At first, the rationale for such regulation was based on the concept that the airwaves are owned by the public and that the regulatory bodies act as agents for the public in controlling what is transmitted. In 1943, the United States Supreme Court built a rationale for regulation based on the limited radio frequency spectrum. This scarcity rationale later evolved into a preferred position rationale, which said that once the scarcity rationale was applied existing broadcasters are in a preferred position over others who might wish to enter the field, and that this alone could become the basis for regulation. In the *FCC* v *Pacifica Foundation* case, the Supreme Court articulated a new rationale: the pervasiveness of the broadcast media. This was taken to mean that the broadcast media have established a uniquely pervasive presence in the lives of all Americans and that broadcasting is uniquely accessible to children. The implications of this rationale allow the Federal Communications Commission to assume a protectionist stance toward regulation that is consistent with trends occurring in other regulatory bodies.

508. The Political and Symbolic Uses of Effects: A Social History of Inquiries into Violence on Television and the Political Legitimation of Mass Communications Research.* Rowland, Willard Daniel, Jr., University of Illinois at Urbana-Champaign, 1978, 303p (7913597; Reprint: DC).

This dissertation examines the political uses of the debate about the effects of violence on television. It analyzes the interaction of three communities that have shaped the terms of the debate in public policymaking for broadcasting—the Congress and related national-level commissions, the broadcasting industry, and the communications research academy.

The discussion begins with a brief review of the Payne Fund studies on violence in film (1928–1933). It then deals with the reviews of violence in television associated with the Harris congressional hearings (1952), the juvenile delinquency investigations (Hendrickson-Kefauver, 1954–1955; Dodd, 1961–1964), the inquiries of the National Commission on Violence (1968–1969), and the research of the Surgeon General's Committee on Television and Social Behavior, guided by the Pastore hearings (1969–1972).

This analysis traces the rise of broadcasting through the history of the conflict between popular, liberal expectations for it and the realities dictated by economic imperatives. It sketches the history of social science and the development of applied broadcasting audience research, demonstrating how important aspects of American science have been influenced by the needs of government and industry. These needs and related popular attitudes are found to have established a set of relationships with social science that have had important impact on the forms and findings of television effects research.

Within this context the dissertation analyzes the practical consequences for the chief parties at interest in the television violence debate. The broadcasting industry is found to have guided the applied and academic realms of communications research, using its investment in the scientific tool as a symbol of social responsibility while subtly influencing the academic models and findings to exonerate television.

The dominant direct and limited effects models are found to be closely tied to the respective agendas of progressivist reform causes and the terms established by the industry. The social science study of media impact rises in part on the strength of its apparent ability to deliver a means for critically appraising television. For its efforts, and for willingly avoiding uncomfortable questions about epistemology, techniques and findings, communications research is promoted by both industry and government. In the end confusion about its findings prevails, and, while being widely invoked, its work can usually be refuted.

As social science has ascended in government, competing with law and engineering as another major universe of discourse about broadcasting, the political community relies increasingly on the scientific tool. Yet it too finds in effects research the vehicle for projecting an image of concerned inquiry while insuring that, due to fundamental constitutional and political economic considerations, that inquiry does not force any significant legislative action. The popular veneration of scientific method is celebrated, but the research findings tend to be inconclusive.

The dissertation finds in the ascension of violence effects research the processes of political avoidance, industrial rationalization, and intellectual compromise that are attendant upon the arrival of the social and behavioral sciences to a place of influence and authority in contemporary American public affairs.

509. Religious Groups v. TV's Sex, Violence. Schicht, Jack, Freedom of Information Center, Columbia, MO, Jan 1980, 9p (ED 182 783; Reprint: EDRS).

Religious organizations have played an important part in the national movement to combat sex and violence in television programing. Attempts by religious organizations to exercise some control of the visual media began in 1907 with a concern for movies and has continued to the present. Although many churches and church organizations have expressed concern about the amount of sex and violence on television, fewer have organized particular movements to bring about change. Campaigns have included organized letter writing to broadcasters, advertisers, and regulatory commissions; boycotts of sponsors of programs found to be objectionable; and boycotts of television programs and stations. Some denominations and special interest groups provide packets of material to those interested in bringing about changes. Television networks report that some of these tactics have been effective and will continue to be so long as those asking for change can demonstrate economic power.

510. The Role of Social and Behavioral Science in Policymaking for Television. Rand Corporation, Santa Monica, CA, Jan 1977, 30p. Sponsoring agency: John and Mary R. Markle Foundation, New York, NY (ED 135 403; Reprint: EDRS).

An analysis of the present system of American television broadcasting reveals that social and behavioral science has had very limited influence on its regulatory policymaking. The television advertisement and its potential adverse effect on children have come to the attention of federal regulatory bodies as well as to consumer and children advocacy groups. However, the effectiveness of present and alternative regulatory stipulations has not been evaluated. In the nonregulatory sphere social and behavioral science have a major influence which could guide television self-regulation and improve TV service to the public. One such example is the family viewing code accepted by the industry, which has curtailed the amount of violence and sex in prime-time programs. It is suggested that empirical evidence generated from social and behavioral science research could further influence industry action, and validate the rulings made by the broadcast standards departments, thus enhancing the public welfare.

511. Schooling and Leisure Time Uses of Television. A Proposed Research Agenda Submitted to the National Institute of Education. Clark, Richard E. et al. Mar 1978, 79p. Agenda prepared at the San Diego Conference on Television and Learning (California, January 23–24, 1978) (ED 152 317; Reprint: EDRS).

Seven researchers met with three representatives from the National Institute of Education (N.I.E.) in January 1978 to draft a research and demonstration agenda for N.I.E. on the relationship between leisure time uses of television and school performance. Of particular concern to N.I.E. is the role of federal policy and programs in addressing the concerns raised by parents, the general public, the mass media, and consumer action groups. Project areas proposed by participants are outlined and listed in order of priority ranking: (1) the development of mental skills with television, (2) television literacy, (3) home environment, (4) children's use of time, (5) the acquisition of knowledge from television, and (6) television research bibliographies. Since the proposed research topics differ significantly from the original proposals, preconference papers submitted by participants R. E. Clark, G. Salomon, G. Comstock, R. Hornik, E. A. Medrich, H. Levie, and A. Dorr are appended.

512. Television Programming for Children: A Report of the Children's Television Task Force. Greene, Susan C. et al., Federal Communications Commission, Washington, DC, Oct 1979, 194p (ED 183 133; Reprint: EDRS).

These two volumes of a 5-volume report on commercial broadcaster compliance with the Federal Communications Commission (FCC) 1974 policies on programing and advertising to children provide an overall analysis of children's television, as well as a detailed analysis of broadcast industry compliance. The first volume reviews the social, cognitive, and economic factors that affect the amount, types, and scheduling of children's programs, and discusses policy options open to the FCC with staff recommendations. The analysis of broadcaster compliance in the second volume is based on a series of studies examining the policy impact on the overall amount of programing designed for children 12 years and under, the amount of educational programing, program scheduling, and overcommercialization on children's television and related advertising issues. The effectiveness of the present license renewal form as a method of assessing compliance is also examined.

513. To the Federal Trade Commission in the Matter of a Trade Regulation Rule on Over-the-Counter Drug Advertising. Council on Children, Media, and Merchandising; Washington, DC; Feb 1977, 75p. Some pages may be marginally legible due to small print of the original document; photographs may reproduce poorly (ED 138 277; Reprint: EDRS).

This report supports amending the proposed Federal Trade Commission (FTC) rule on over the counter (OTC) drug advertising to insure better protection for children, illiterate populations, the deaf, and the blind from advertising on the air-waves. Several points are addressed: (1) the difficulties of combining the rule making schedules of the Food and Drug Administration (FDA) and the FTC; (2) the nature of OTC advertising and labeling, particularly for large child audiences; (3) behavioral studies on techniques of television commercials; (4) ambiguous interpretations of FDA language on the part of those regulated; and (5) the vulnerabilities of the functionally illiterate, the deaf, and the blind.

514. Toward a National Endowment for Children's Broadcasting. Report on the Project to Ascertain the Feasibility of a National Endowment for Children's Broadcasting. Center for Action Research, Princeton, NJ, 1977, 58p. Lignt print and colored background may reproduce faintly. Sponsoring agency: John and Mary R. Markle Foundation, New York, NY (ED 165 785; Reprint: EDRS).

A project examining the need for change in children's television environment and for the establishment of a grant-making organization designed to address the needs of the children's broadcasting environment consulted a variety of interests, insights, and divergent viewpoints. Research studies, government documents, books, professional journals, and popular magazine articles were consulted and over 200 people were contacted, including commercial and public broadcasters, artists, distributors, advertisers, child psychologists, educators, federal agency spokespeople, legislators, and consumer advocates. Results indicate that change in the children's television environment is desired, as is a new grant-making service organization. It also noted that although models presented for a national grant-making entity appear adequate, none are presently deemed feasible. Three recommendations call for (1) high priority of legislative activity related to children's television, (2) the establishment of a national council on children and television, and (3) the development of alternative distribution systems for children's programing, with special reference to cable channels. Appendices include project advisory board and team members, participants, Project Overview Conference participants, project method and description, footnotes, and a bibliography of works consulted.

BOOKS

515. See No Evil: The Backstage Battle Over Sex and Violence in Television. Cowan, Geoffrey. New York: Simon and Schuster, 1979, 323p.

The author documents the attempts to control "offensive" television content which led to the imposition of the "family viewing hour" concept in 1975. As the attorney for the Writers Guild, which challenged the "family hour" in court, the author presents an analysis of this policy and its failure, citing the new sexually suggestive comedies which have begun to fill this time slot.

Subject Index

Subject Index

INVENTORY 1983